ZORINA

ZORINA

ZORINA

VERA ZORINA

FARRAR STRAUS GIROUX · NEW YORK

Library of Congress Cataloging-in-Publication Data
Zorina, Vera.
Zorina.
Includes index.
1. Zorina, Vera. 2. Dancers—Biography. I. Title.
GV1785.Z67A3 1986 792.8'2'0924 [B] 86-12055

To my mother
Du og jeg

I wish to express my gratitude to Paul Wolfe, who first urged me to write and who gave me his unfailing support and love. My affectionate thanks to Paul Horgan, a rare and beautiful friend, and to Shirley Hazzard and Francis Steegmuller for their generosity of spirit toward a neophyte. It has been a particular blessing to work with Robert Giroux, whose firmness in editorial matters was always exercised with the utmost kindness. I am indebted to him for his patience, humor, and wisdom.

My admiration and thanks to Cynthia Krupat for her creativity both in her design of the dust jacket and in the book's typography; to Lynn Warshow for her helpful and sensitive copy editing; and to Dorris Janowitz for excellent production work in seeing the book through the press. I wish to thank Barbara Shalvey and Christine Bronder for typing the manuscript with expertise and devotion, and Mrs. Theodore McClintock for the index. To Barbara Horgan and the Estate of George Balanchine I am grateful for permission to quote from his letters, and to W. W. Norton & Co., Inc., for the use of M. D. Herter Norton's translation of Rainer Maria Rilke's poem.

Above all, my devoted thanks to Peter and Jonathan Lieberson for loving their mother as she is.

ZORINA

ONE

*To remember my childhood I had to re-enter its land-
scape, its meadows and flowers, its scents and sounds,
its tastes, delights, and fears. I had to enter its streets,
houses, and rooms to refeel, to relive. My language
changed and I heard the echoes of childhood.*

My mother was pretty rather than beautiful. She had the fair,
blue-eyed look and vitality of her Norwegian ancestors. Peering at
her with the scrutiny of a child, I remember the fine, delicate
texture of her skin and her beautiful, long, red-gold hair, which
she always kept in the latest style. Unfortunately, that meant
cutting it all off in the twenties. The heavy, silky hair, coiled and
recoiled, tied with a ribbon at each end, lay like a fat, sleeping cat
in a drawer. Sometimes I opened it and gently stroked its glossy
texture, which never seemed inanimate but alive and vibrant under
my touch.

She was proud of her body, which was not lithe but femininely
compact and rounded, and very pleased with her breasts, which
she exhibited rather more than I would have liked. I was always

trying to cover her up as a child, particularly in the morning before she was dressed and wandered around unconcernedly in her transparent crepe de chine nightgown. Or at night when she went out and put on an evening dress with a deep, deep décolleté.

One night I awakened to loud screeching and laughter. I think my mother must have been dressing. Light was shining through an open door and people were coming in, trying to pull her away with them while I attempted to hide and protect her. It was frightening, and I recall my helplessness as a small child (how old was I—four?) trying to put myself like a shield between her and the people who were "threatening" her. *That* terror was probably nothing more than a boisterous party, but it illustrates how deeply attached I was to my mother—an attachment which became even fiercer as I grew older.

It was part of her daily toilette to rub her body from head to toe with a brush made of soft bristles and moistened with eau de cologne. No wonder her clothes smelled so beautifully. When I was lonely, as a child, I opened the armoire which held her dresses and poked my nose into them in order to be closer to her. Her hands and feet were beautiful and she took great care to keep them that way. I don't think she ever washed her hands without immediately applying glycerine and rosewater, afterward kneading her cuticles with a towel in a characteristic manner. The gestures were totally automatic and part of her daily beauty routine. It was a familiar sight to see her seated at the dressing table buffing her nails to a shiny pink. How exciting it was to be allowed to sprinkle a few granules from the bottle-shaped container into my palm, rub each nail in it, and then buff them like a grown-up. She also took particular care of her face and throat. Not only did she apply cold cream, but she massaged them in a rotating manner, followed by strategic patting to bring color and circulation to her cheeks. As she grew older, she looked best without a shred of makeup.

In her vanity she imagined the visual aspect of her appearance, so that when the telephone rang she patted her hair into place and composed her features before answering in a sweet "Hello." The more important the caller, the more coquettish she became, and I, without knowing who was on the other end, felt jealous. She must have been very appealing to men and had many flourishing love affairs right into her sixties—perhaps even later; it would not surprise me.

It was a definite choice on my mother's part that a little fluffing, omission, or embroidery was more agreeable than the bare truth. She relied on fate and circumstances not to expose her, but should anything so unlucky happen, she rarely faltered and, like all good embroiderers, went right on embroidering. My mother did not take the serious things in life too seriously. She rebelled against authority and I often wondered that she didn't land in jail in Berlin. If there was a *verboten* sign somewhere, she did exactly the opposite, such as deliberately walking her dog on the green *verboten* grass.

When I was a baby, she decided not to have me vaccinated. She considered it nonsense and dangerous. By the time I was six, my German uncle, a surgeon and the director of a hospital, threatened dire results if she did not comply. My mother finally agreed.

I remember the scene well. I sat on my mother's lap. Uncle Paul began making tiny incisions in my left arm, but after the second stroke kept on going until I had six vaccination punctures. My mother screamed in futility after the third stroke, but my uncle was swift. The following day my arm blew up, the six incisions began oozing, the dressings had to be changed twice a day by a professional nurse, my arm was in a sling for weeks, and after healing, there were six large, ugly, permanent scars. My mother was enraged and triumphantly confirmed her original suspicion; my uncle was equally triumphant, declaring that it just showed how urgently I had needed vaccination, and I spent a lot of time in bed being coddled, getting presents, blissfully happy.

I enjoyed being ill because then I had the full attention of my mother. I could stay in her bed and had the feeling that she really cared about me. She became concerned, loving, hovered over me, prepared special things for me to eat, all of which made up a thousand times for whatever ailed me. I had her to myself and became once more the center of her life.

Sometimes she could be very brusque. When I felt a cold approaching, with its anticipatory delight of pleasures, and said, "Mama, when I bend my head back, it hurts here," pointing to the base of my throat, she snapped back unsympathetically, "Then don't do it!" It was different when *she* was ill. I immediately became terrified that she would die and leave me, and could not believe that one could be ill for a day or a week and still recover.

Another thing that frightened me was hearing adults talk of war—the First World War and a possible future war. I remember seeing gruesome illustrations on the covers of magazines describing what it would be like—people dying in agony from gas attacks. I sat crying on my mother's lap, begging her to promise me that if war came we would leave for Norway. She always hugged and kissed me, saying that of course we would go home to Besta right away. Besta was my maternal grandmother and Norway was paradise to me.

Kristiansund North, where my mother was born, was then a small coastal town between Trondheim and Bergen. It was built on three islands, and when I was a child small ferryboats shuttled back and forth between Hovedness, Kirkegård, and the third island. Most people imagine that Norway in winter is full of snow, ice, and polar bears, but to me it meant warmth and coziness. It may have been cold outside, but it was always warm inside, with stoves glowing day and night. I was never lonely or afraid. I adored my Grandmother Besta, and respectfully loved my Grandfather Bestefar. (It's a nice Norwegian tradition that children call their grandparents "Best Mother" and "Best Father.")

My grandparents Hans Christian and Elise Wimpelmann were considered a distinguished and respectable couple who came from good families. In so small a town, where everyone knew everything about everybody else, it seemed to matter a great deal *where* you were born and *who* your family was. My mother drilled into me: "Now, Brigitta, remember your grandmother is a Synnestvet from Molde—that's very fine—and your grandfather from Surnadal— that's good, too . . ." I remember as a child listening to the endless conversations that began with our family, went on to acquaintances —such as discussions about maiden names, "Whom did she marry?" and so forth—and then radiated out to the various royal houses of Europe. I thought that my grandmother's, aunt's, and mother's knowledge of European royalty was amazing. They knew exactly what princess married what prince, all the way down the line to the third and fourth sons and daughters.

Family life at the turn of the century in a small Norwegian town was certainly a combination of strict Victoriana coupled with Ibsenism. That is what makes it all the more astonishing that my mother broke away and practically turned into a bohemian. But, then, she had always been the baby of the family, protected and spoiled by her mother. Abigael Johanne Wimpelmann, nicknamed Bille, very early on began to shock people in Kristiansund, whose culture, code of behavior, and stifling atmosphere then and now were narrow-minded and hypocritical—in short, provincial. She had loved horses ever since she was a child and was seen more than once, to the scandal of her mother, proudly sitting next to the driver of the carriage carrying the coffin in a funeral procession. I believe she had a happy childhood, but maybe her inordinate love of clothes stemmed from the fact that, with two older sisters, Hannah and Fanny, she never had a single new dress for herself but had to make do with hand-me-downs.

There also seems to have been a family tradition of teasing, and my mother was the biggest teaser of them all, particularly of her brother, Christian. He had red, wiry, unruly hair, and would spend hours slicking it down; when he had finally succeeded, my mother would sneak up in back of him, run her hand through his hair like a garden rake, and make it stand up like a fright wig. But when he began chasing her, she would set up a tremendous howl and rush for her mother, who invariably shielded her.

One of the great topics of conversation in Kristiansund was food, particularly after a dinner party, which was the main form of social life. The grown-ups would sit around the next day and discuss the entire menu from beginning to end. The opening remarks were always very cautious. After all, no one wished to be bad-mannered or impolite. Someone would begin by saying carefully, "What did you think of the soup?" This was said with the hope of receiving an agreeably negative answer: "Don't you think it was a tiny bit thin?"

"Well, perhaps. Personally, I prefer it with a little more cream. But then of course the meat could have been better. It was such a pity that the roast was overcooked, because the butcher always gives her the best cuts."

"Of course, the caramel pudding was excellent. How lucky she is to have such a good cook in Gerda."

In the era before radio, television, and movies, social life centered around good food and conversation, although Kristiansund had quite an active cultural life. The Festivitetshalle [Festival Hall] had a very nice theater where visiting acting companies performed plays and where concerts and recitals were given by touring musicians. Kristiansund also had an active opera group, which produced two operas a year, which may have given my mother the idea of becoming an opera singer. She had a high, sweet coloratura voice and was determined to have a career.

When her sister Hannah, after the death of her husband in 1916, decided to devote herself to nursing and was accepted for training in a German hospital, my mother seized the opportunity to beg her parents to let her accompany Hannah so that she could pursue her singing studies in Berlin. They finally agreed to let her leave for a few months, but she had to give her solemn promise to return by summer. At twenty-five, my mother was not all that young, but she had lived a very protected life and it *was* at the height of World War I. Undaunted, the two sisters set off on their journey.

My mother claimed that she met my father in the subway. That might have been a romantic notion in 1916—a meeting in the wicked city of Berlin brought about by a bizarre new method of transportation—but I think this story was one of her embroideries. They really met at their singing teacher's, where they studied hard but also managed to fall in love. My father had come to Berlin for the same reason as my mother. He had a beautiful light tenor voice, and he too wanted to become an opera singer. They found they had a great deal more in common—both had lively temperaments, good looks, and, in spite of considerable geographical distance, backgrounds which were remarkably similar. Both came from "good" and well-to-do families and each was the youngest of four children. Both rebelled against their conservative backgrounds and left the security of their homes in the midst of war to seek artistic careers.

How my father escaped serving in the army, I do not know, but I believe he had a knee injury which he actively encouraged rather than attempted to cure. There was a story that my father, forewarned of an inspector coming to check up on him, applied wet, boiling-hot towels, so that the inspector was confronted with a swollen, beet-red knee so hot he could barely touch it. My father was by this time in genuine agony from the continuous hot poultices and, needless to say, was promptly and permanently excused from service. (It sounds like something out of *The Confessions of Felix Krull* by Thomas Mann.)

There was one decisive difference between my parents. My father was born in Düsseldorf in the Rhineland, which is predominantly Catholic, whereas Norway in the early part of this century was staunchly Lutheran and anti-Catholic. I don't think this troubled the young people very much, and I doubt whether they actually discussed marriage. Besides, summer was approaching and my mother had to return to Norway, where she joined the whole family for a vacation.

Norwegians are very fond of the "simple" life spent in the mountains, usually in a *hytte*. Anyone who can possibly afford one has a *hytte*—the equivalent of a log cabin, which is preferably situated in an isolated and remote spot and where you lead a very quiet life, devoted to fishing, hunting, hiking, eating good simple food, and practicing their Golden Rule—early to bed and early to rise. Nature is the thing and amenities are not expected—in fact, they are shunned.

In this idyllic, rugged, and isolated place, my mother realized that she was pregnant. One can only imagine how she felt, unable even to give a hint of her condition. She had to use all her powers of persuasion to convince her parents *why* she should return once more to war-torn Germany. It must have seemed like absolute insanity to them, but she managed, as she was to manage to overcome so many difficulties in her life. She arrived in Berlin in early October and married my father in a civil ceremony in November. A postcard from him to his sister Elizabeth after their marriage sounds exultant—"I am the happiest of men"—so I presume that at that time his Catholicism presented no problems, though he writes elsewhere that he had "left" the Church. I was born on January 2, 1917, the daughter of Fritz Hartwig and Abigael Johanne Wimpelmann, and baptized Eva Brigitta Hartwig in the Catholic faith.

——

A very hard life began for my mother, coming from a sheltered existence to life in chaotic Berlin. Germany was losing the war and there was a constant struggle for food, forcing her to take me frequently home to her family. My parents' life was a hand-to-mouth existence, and my father became a charming *Hochstapler*. One way to illustrate that word is to give the example of a man who dresses in evening clothes for a concert to which he has no ticket. Not only does he manage to get in, but he winds up in the best seat. That's *hochstapling*, and that is precisely what my father did. My mother told me she would join him at the concert during intermission, splendidly dressed, and they would both sweep down the aisles to seats my father had spotted as being empty.

Part of the *Hochstaplerei* was that he gave himself the title *Opernsänger* [opera singer], but this was wishful thinking. Although they both studied assiduously, neither ever achieved a professional career. One of their friends who did was the tenor Richard Tauber. He was to become a legendary opera singer, especially as an interpreter of Mozart roles. Later in his career, he became a roaring matinee idol as the star of Franz Lehár's operettas, many of which were especially written for him, and played to packed houses in the huge Deutsche Schauspielhaus in Berlin. His co-star in several productions was Gitta Alpar, a brilliant Hungarian coloratura, who transformed herself from a rather dumpy, darkhaired, uninteresting-looking woman into a blond, sylphlike movie star. It was an absolutely astonishing transformation and much discussed by her adoring public. It was rumored that she had had plastic surgery not only on her face but also on her body. It all seemed very daring. When I heard it discussed, I had a horrible vision of fat being sliced off, much as I had seen butchers prepare meat. *The Land of Smiles* was one of Lehár's greatest successes, and the song *"Dein ist mein ganzes Herz"* became a great hit. Tauber had to repeat it at each performance as many as seven or eight times, always finishing in a different way with vocal fireworks which drove the audience into a frenzy of screams and applause. But all this was still far in the future. Meanwhile, much to the despair of my mother, Tauber would invariably show up when there was a little meat in the house, tickle me under the chin, tell her what a pretty baby I was, and then eat up everything available with gusto. But my parents were young and they were gay, and I am sure that in spite of the tremendous hardships of living in postwar Germany, they managed to have a very good time.

My mother's claim that they had met in the subway was a mere triviality compared to my father's claim that he was descended from the Romans, who, centuries ago, had come as far north as the Rhineland. When he was teased about his claim, he stoutly defended it historically. Perhaps it explains his efforts to be tan all year round, because in summer he was a passionate sunbather, and in winter he regularly went to get his *Höhensonne* [ultraviolet sunlamp]. As a child, I was sometimes allowed to accompany him, and still remember the dark, ghostly room illuminated by the ultraviolet lamp, with its peculiar smell, shining down on my father, who was lying motionless and naked on the table, with only his eyes and pelvis covered. Was it to achieve the golden skin of his supposed Mediterranean ancestors? Or just plain narcissism? For he was handsome, very handsome. I have many photos of the period and invariably they show my father elegantly dressed in tweeds, beautiful overcoat, bowler hat, spats, holding pale chamois gloves, with a superb walking stick—the last no doubt for show. I also have snapshots of him at costume balls, dressed—or, rather, *undressed*—as a maharajah, complete with turban, showing off his beautiful torso; or skiing, again with the upper part of his body naked to the alpine sun; or laughing at the beach, with a girl on each arm. I remember I carefully cut those girls out, leaving only my father to smile at me. There is no arrogance in his face, only an innocent exuberance at the pleasures of life—the sun, the girls, and his own good looks. I wish that the photographer who took a formal picture of the young family had let my father cradle his baby in the same way he cradled a bunch of puppies in his arms, showing his warmth, tenderness, and acceptance of young life, instead of posing him seated, looking "appreciatively" at his wife, who is standing, holding me, while I look at the camera with big, frightened eyes.

I really only remember isolated instances of being with my father, not a continuous life together; and why should it be otherwise? There were too many disruptions and separations; not just short vacations, but being away for months with my mother in Norway. There was more of a sense of family in Kristiansund and Molde than when we came "home" to Berlin. It's curious, but I don't remember an ordinary "family rhythm"—of meals taken together, of my father reading to me at night or taking care of me, or even reprimanding me—a father's role in the life of a small child. But I *do* remember vividly that he took me away on outings and vacations. The first time I went to Misdroy, a summer resort on the Baltic Sea which was to play a significant part in my life, he and I went together alone. We did not have our own house yet and rented a room. I was bitten terribly by mosquitoes, especially behind my ears, which my father treated with cool compresses. He took me to church in Misdroy, to a small Catholic chapel, my hand in his as we walked to Mass and back. I didn't understand the Mass, but I understood that it was *feierlich* [solemn] and that I had to be quiet. I felt that people were engaged in something awesome: when a little bell sounded, all the people went down on their knees, heads deeply bowed, made fists with their right hands, moved them away from the body, and returned them to the body three times. What were they doing? And what were they thinking? Of course, it was the *"Mea Culpa"* before receiving the Host, but I don't remember my father explaining it to me. I was too shy to ask, and maybe he thought I was too young. I loved God from that time and even earlier, and I knew that He was someone one couldn't lie to because He saw everything and knew everything. *He* was my father and He loved me and He would always take care of me. It was as simple as that.

I remember my father's presence very strongly, but no words—only images; no conversations—only his face and the touch of his hand. I remember sitting on the handlebar of his bicycle, returning from a day spent in the forest, where he sunbathed and I played. It was hot and there was a strong smell of pine needles. On the way home, my right foot touched the wheel, which seared off the flesh on my instep. It hurt, but I was proud of the scar because it had to do with my father and with the day I sat on the handlebar of his bicycle. He took me to Thonon on Lac Léman, near Geneva. We stayed in a monastery high above the lake, and every day we walked down the winding road with stone walls on either side to go swimming. He taught me by simply "throwing" me in the lake while he stood guard next to me. He taught me the way a puppy swims instinctively the minute it hits the water. I remembered the walk up the hill to the monastery so well that I found it fifty years later. I walked in the gate and explained to an elderly nun that I had stayed there as a child. "Ah well," she said, "that must have been the time when the Jesuits were here," and, "*Yes*, they took in some guests."

There was a flight of stairs leading to the second floor, where our rooms overlooked the lake, and I remember how afraid I was to be alone through terrifying thunderstorms which reverberated through the surrounding Alps with lightning and crashing thunder. And I remember crying bitterly into a bowl of cocoa, which was so big I had to hold it with both hands, because my father told me he had received a letter from my mother *that* morning saying that she was ill in Berlin. I'm sure he regretted telling me, because no amount of reassurance could stop my crying inconsolably as I pictured her alone, with no one to take care of her, while I had Papa and was having a wonderful time.

By the time we returned, Mama had fully recovered, and our life continued to be haphazard, bohemian, artistic, struggling, and against convention. There never seemed to be any money, but we

managed. We lived on a little bit here and a little bit there. The
bills we owed were stuffed into drawers and thereby disposed of.
My grandmother sent food from Norway, and if there was a real
crisis, someone came to the rescue. That someone was usually
Uncle Gui, who after my parents was the most important person in
my life.

In his youth, Gustav Friederick von Schwieger, nicknamed
"Onkel Gui," had formed a close friendship with my father, and
when my parents married, he became a family member. With hind-
sight, I suspected he was too close a family member to make for
a tranquil marriage. There were many loud rows between my
mother and Uncle Gui, but no permanent rift ever occurred. Uncle
Gui continued to play a large part in my life, encouraged and
stimulated my aspirations to become a dancer, and generally helped
our little, and at times chaotic, family.

When I had an occasional engagement as a child, it was Uncle
Gui who took me to the theater and who invariably picked me up
and brought me home. He was intensely proud of me and watched
over my budding career like a mother hen and behaved more like
a stage mother than my mother did. Uncle Gui was an antique
dealer and had a prestigious shop on the Kurfürstendamm, half a
block from where we lived. Sofas, tables, or chairs would disappear
from our house, either because they were impounded for non-
payment of bills or because a potential buyer had appeared in his
shop. Later, another piece might replace it, or the original reappear.
As a result, my mother learned a great deal about the antique business and we always had excellent furniture.

We lived in an elegant part of Berlin, at Bleibtreustrasse 25. One
had to pass through the imposing red-carpeted first lobby, be scrutinized by an invariably bad-tempered *portier*, walk through a
courtyard, then through another red-carpeted lobby, and finally
arrive in a small, euphemistically named garden, which was surrounded by high walls on all sides, creating a gloomy atmosphere.

In summer it was a bit more cheerful, because one of the walls was solidly covered with ivy cascading down like a green blanket, and a lone, sad tree in the courtyard at least had some delicate leaves on it. Our tiny house, which clung to the wall, appeared like a surprise, almost an afterthought, at the end of the solid bourgeois apartment building. It must have been built by an artist, and had a large skylight on top; it was as eccentric inside as outside.

The house had only two large rooms, one above the other, connected by a staircase, but each room was high and had an upper and lower level. The upstairs room was very light and airy because of its skylight. I always liked it best, for it exuded my mother's presence, her perfume and her gift for making a room cozy. On its upper level, presiding over the room and placed lengthwise against the wall, stood my mother's big antique four-poster bed. It had heavy curtains, which could be drawn, making it an ideal hiding place for me. When I "disappeared," my mother was endlessly patient, plaintively calling, "But where has she gone? I can't find her. Maybe she has gone to the elephants?" I can't remember *why* I might have gone to the elephants; perhaps it was considered the remotest place imaginable. Hiding was my passion and the house was full of marvelous places for it: crouching in a tiny place under the steps, or flattening myself next to the armoire on the landing, or sitting on the radiator behind the huge curtains downstairs, or even, when I was brave enough, in the dark cellar. I never tired of the game, nor did my mother ever get impatient. Apart from hiding, my greatest treat was to be allowed to sleep in my mother's bed. She would cradle me, I would be nice and warm, and she would tell me stories about the adventures of "Bukken Brusc," a bear who lived in the woods of Norway, or she would softly sing to me songs from her childhood, in her high, sweet voice. When I was little my bed was next to hers in an alcove, but it might as well have been a mile away, I was always so fearful and lonely at night unless I could hear my mother's voice. Even then I was afraid that if I went to sleep she would go out and I would wake up and be alone. So I was quiet as a mouse and pretended to sleep, but stayed awake until she went to bed.

I loved sitting at her dressing table and looking at all the things on top of it and all the things in the drawers. The surface of the wood gleamed. The monogrammed brush, comb, and silver hand mirror were polished, and there were lots of little jars, with ivory and silver tops, full of different creams. Crystal bowls held powder and big fluffy powder puffs in pink and white, each topped with tiny bows. Other crystal dishes were neatly filled with hairpins and her manicure tools.

Best of all to look at and smell were the many beautiful crystal bottles containing perfumes by Coty and Chanel, which were an indefinable mystery in themselves. Among these, to me, utterly romantic objects sat the prosaic curling iron. Before using it, my mother would heat the tongs and, when she thought they were hot enough, wet her finger and lightly touch them. If they gave off a hissing spit sound, they were ready. Holding the tongs by the wooden handle, she would release a catch, open them, and put a strand of hair between, then close them and swiftly curl her hair up to the scalp, hold the tongs there for a few seconds, and release the hair. After she had curled her whole head she looked like Mary Pickford, with heavy golden spirals bobbing around her face. Although Mary Pickford was very famous at the time, that was not how my mother wanted to look. Instead, she brushed all those curls back from her forehead, did a lot of patting and smoothing, and finally achieved a very sleek, short, and wavy coiffure.

The lower level on the top floor was arranged as her living room, where she often entertained. I don't remember dinners or parties, but I do remember the ritual of afternoon teas. The table shone with highly polished silver. On a tray stood the teapot, pitcher of cream, sugar bowl, and tongs. Pink teacups with matching plates were side by side, and delicate cakes and cookies had been carefully arranged on platters by my mother beforehand. The ladies would arrive and I marveled that they were satisfied to do nothing but sit and talk.

One afternoon my mother expected a friend from America. I was very excited, because I had heard how beautiful American ladies were and had seen pictures of a "Miss America" who was a queen and wore a sash across her body which said "USA." I was always making childish drawings of them in bathing suits, in which they invariably had big blue eyes and black hair, or blond hair and brown eyes, combinations I thought the epitome of beauty. When a cuddly, white-haired woman arrived, I could not believe that this was the "lady from America." I stared at her in total disbelief and vast disappointment, since I was absolutely unprepared for any concept other than beautiful young ladies walking around in bathing suits.

There were two objects in the upstairs room which I remember well. One was a fierce-looking carved Chinese dragon, which was impaled on the wall but looked as if it wanted to spew the red wooden flames which came out of its nostrils into the room. The other was totally serene. It was a copy of the Egyptian head of Amenophis and stood on a ledge before a window. It became a symbol of my childhood. My mother was mysterious about it and told me that it had been a gift from my father while she was expecting me. She had looked at it so much that she insisted I resembled it in profile. Whenever we moved, the head of Amenophis moved with us, and today it gazes serenely into the room from a glass shelf in my New York apartment.

As a child, I was exposed to and absorbed a great deal of music. I was literally surrounded by it. We had a piano and gramophone upstairs, and music was constantly played in one form or another. Either my mother or father took singing lessons, or practiced scales, or sang arias from operas. In the evening, when they thought I was asleep, they played records. How many arias I heard by Caruso without knowing the name of the opera! I can still sing them note for note. Music played the single most influential part in my childhood—I responded to it, soaked it up, and it became part of my being.

I had piano lessons but found them boring. I much preferred to use the gramophone. It was a square wooden box which had to be wound up. Often, especially when I was alone, I cleared a little space and danced. I danced and danced without ever getting tired, stopping only to wind up the gramophone. It didn't matter that no one was there to watch me—I danced for myself and felt incredible exhilaration. I imagine that I must have looked like a young foal which bucks and does funny jumps, and suddenly runs off, discovering its own body and strength and experiencing the sheer joy *that* surprise gives it. I think that, like a young horse, I had extra energy and needed to let it out and find an expression for it. It was that need which propelled me toward ballet, toward formal training. But I still had a long time to wait.

In contrast to the upstairs room, the downstairs room in Bleibtreustrasse seemed to me gloomy. The courtyard surrounded by its three high walls was never cheerful, even on sunny days, but you didn't realize it upstairs because the skylight flooded the room with light and sunshine. The room was peculiarly shaped and had a very large window almost the length of the wall facing the courtyard. The radiator in front of it was covered with a wide ledge, so wide that I could comfortably sit on it. At night, when the curtains were drawn, it made a perfect hiding place for me. This ledge also held my collection of scrawny cacti, which never grew taller or produced any offshoots. A red lacquered ladder led to an upper level, which served as my father's bedroom. When he was out, I used to climb up the ladder to his "room" and look around as if I were going on a visit. It had a carved wooden railing around it and was always extremely orderly. Everything was meticulously arranged. His dumbbells, with which he exercised every day, were side by side on the floor, his slippers, also side by side, just peeping out from their place at the foot of the bed, his books immaculately arranged on a table, some toilet articles in perfect symmetry; and when I dared to open a drawer, it was the same inside. I never saw an unmade bed or clothes lying about. I was awestruck by the incredible neatness, and it filled me with shy respect, as if I were in a museum.

Underneath this "bedroom" was the kitchen, making it all look like a cube within a cube. In the middle of the room in front of the large window stood a table, where we ate our meals and where I did my homework in the afternoons. The room became friendly only at night, when the lamp, hanging low over the table, was lit, creating a cozy atmosphere. Mama was a very good cook, natural-born in her mother's kitchen, and never followed a recipe. She had a fondness for rice, boiled chicken, and Brussels sprouts, which I now shun, having had quite enough in my childhood. Even our dogs got rice, and since we were all very healthy, it must have been good for us.

Animals were loved by my mother as much as people, perhaps more in some instances. We always had cats and dogs living together in perfect harmony. She was never without one or the other throughout her life. Of all the dogs we had, Wolf was the best and the dearest companion of my childhood. He had adopted my father one night when Papa had gone to a party in a suburb of Berlin. As he got off the bus, a large dog came up and began to follow him. When my father went into the building, he told him to go home. Many hours later, when he came out, the dog was still there, sitting at the door waiting for him. He followed him to the bus stop, and when my father boarded the bus the dog began to run alongside. At the next stop my father took pity on him, put him on the bus, and brought him home. He had no collar but was clearly a pure-bred Alsatian and highly trained in obedience. We called the police and advertised, but no one claimed him.

I was overjoyed and we became inseparable. Wolf understood and could do everything. When the postman pushed the mail through the slit in the door, Wolf scraped the letters together with his paws and brought them proudly to my mother, sitting down politely and smiling through the mail in his mouth. If we forgot our house key, he would jump up and climb through a kitchen window, then, by putting his front paws on the handle of the door, walk backwards on his hind legs and so open the front door for us.

If my mother was upstairs, she could tell him to fetch me. This he did by running down and sitting next to me. I pretended not to know what he wanted. First, he smiled with that wonderful look of happy excitement that dogs have when they are performing a task. Next, he would nudge me by putting his muzzle under my wrist and flipping it up. If that still drew no response, he would open his formidable jaws and take my wrist in his mouth and then gently but firmly begin to tug, until I had to get up and follow him. In this position, we climbed two flights of stairs, and he would not release me until he sat down in front of my mother, still holding my wrist in his jaws.

He used to become very agitated when we went swimming in the ocean. He would pace back and forth on the beach, whining and barking, until he finally entered the water and swam out to us. This was sometimes quite far. When he reached us he circled around and then turned his back on us. What he wanted us to do was grab his tail and he would then literally pull us back to the beach. He was my most beloved friend.

There was something almost ominous about the separateness and isolation of our house. I often found its lonely existence scary. I used to play in and around an ugly grotto, an example of the whimsicality of a former owner. It was made of very sharp stones which jutted out and had deep, dank recesses where I imagined frogs lived—and maybe even snakes. I clambered around it one day and fell, cutting myself at the wrist. It did not hurt much and did not send me screaming to my mother, but a day or so later she noticed a blue line under the skin ascending from the wrist to the inside of my elbow and rushed me to a doctor. My mother told me dramatically, begging me never to play in that grotto again, that I had been saved from a possibly dangerous case of blood poisoning.

We had another drama. Coco, our white, long-haired Angora cat, who had China-blue eyes and was deaf, always wanted to jump through a ground-floor window into the cellar, where coal was kept, invariably re-emerging covered with black soot and sometimes triumphantly carrying a dead mouse in her jaws. This was a tremendous nuisance, because she had to be washed, scratching and yowling. One day, just as I saw her ready to jump, I caught her by the tail—but the window banged shut on it, leaving me with a cat hanging halfway down. We both struggled, while I yelled for my mother. Poor Coco! It was *her* time to be rushed to the doctor, swathed in a big towel, with a bad cut on her tail, growling as loud as a lion. After a few stitches were taken, she came home, but wouldn't accept my apologies or endearments. From then on, she shunned me.

––––

My mother did not acknowledge failure, even if it was obvious and irrefutable. I believe it stemmed from her upbringing and the fierce importance people attached to their position in a small town. Failures, money problems, sexual irregularities leading to scandal were of course avidly discussed in Kristiansund, but only in whispers and behind the back of the person involved. Appearances had to be kept up without fail.

Should a failure prove to be a fact, my mother would simply dismiss it with a contemptuous shrug accompanied by a characteristic sound combining a snort and a hiss. I think her attitude toward failure was the reason why she rarely spoke of my paternal grandparents except for a few facts. When I asked her questions about them, she would become vague and distant and answer me in a perfunctory manner. During the few conversations we had on the subject, my mother grudgingly gave me the barest details, such as that my grandmother had come for a visit to Berlin when I was a baby but had criticized everything, from the way she took care of me to the way she cooked. Hardly a way to endear herself to a young wife and mother! I can imagine that my grandmother, who was a very devout Catholic, was particularly displeased that her youngest son had married a Lutheran and left the Church. Knowing my mother's temperament, I can well understand that they did not get along. I do remember that my grandmother wrote me long and serious letters, and that I wrote back; but my mother did not encourage me, and although my grandmother lived to an old age, contact between us ceased during my childhood.

My mother was also incensed that my father's brother, Wolf, who was a prosperous rancher in Africa, had had the audacity to propose that, since he was childless, he wished to adopt me and give me a "good, normal" upbringing. To her, that was an insult, a stinging condemnation of the way she and my father lived. I suppose that their haphazard existence periodically wore my mother down; then she would pack up and return to Norway. Those visits were the happiest times of my childhood.

My grandparents' apartment in Kristiansund was small and crowded with Victorian furniture. I shared a room with my mother, which in itself made me happy. Early in the morning, pitch-dark in winter, a maid would creep into the room to light the wood stove. The rustling sound of paper and wood as she prepared it, followed by the crackling of the fire, was comforting while I lay in bed deep under my *dyne*.

Breakfast was as much a formal meal as dinner. The table was laden with bread, butter, jam, and a large square of *gjetost*, a pale-brown Norwegian goat cheese which is eaten at every meal except dinner. In those days, it came in a large square covered by heavy silver paper, which was peeled off and put back after each meal to

keep it moist. The cheese had to be sliced off evenly so as to create
no noticeable dips or grooves in the surface, and very thinly, so
thin that it curled up like flower petals when placed on the bread.
Coffee and cocoa aroma filled the air, and sometimes I was allowed
to mix the two and make mocha.

The table was presided over by my grandfather at one end and
my grandmother at the other. I remember his face as kindly, with
an undulating white mustache. However, he was strict and expected
good manners and, above all, quiet. This sometimes got to be too
much. Glances flew around the table, suppressed giggles would
begin, and I once sprayed cocoa all over the white tablecloth in
no-longer-controllable laughter. I don't remember any punishment.

My grandmother was tiny, with snow-white hair parted in the
middle. She was always dressed in black, even her long woolen
underwear, which she called her "*Fascist-buksene.*" (I suppose the
black Fascist uniforms must have become known in the twenties.)
I was spoiled by everybody, especially my mother, by Tante Fanny,
and my Grandmother Besta. Even having a cold was fun. I would
stay in bed and a playmate would visit me and we would eat
delicious Napoleon *kake*, which was a triple *mille-feuilles* with
vanilla-flavored icing.

In order to continue my pampered life, I exaggerated my illnesses
almost as much as my mother had when she was a child. She told
me she had observed the enormous attention her father was getting
when he was confined to bed with bleeding ulcers—so she bit her
tongue hard and ran screaming to her mother, spitting blood, and
was promptly put to bed, where she flourished for weeks.

The only thing I was denied was a birthday party like all the
other children had, which I considered a terrible injustice. When
I first began to jabber in Norwegian, to the delight of my grandmother and assorted relatives, I remember how puzzled and be-
wildered I was that my mother could never remember my birthday
and constantly made me younger than I was. She tried to hush me

up when I told everyone that my birthday was in January, when it properly could not, *should* not, have been until August. Age is so important to a little girl, and when I attempted to correct my mother, in that terrible, insisting, piping voice of a small, self-righteous child, I was sharply told to be quiet. The result was that I never had a birthday party—at least not in Kristiansund.

Although I loved my dolls, I was very energetic and enjoyed playing with boys much more. Kristiansund was such a small town that we played on the streets in winter, sledding up and down the various hills, or skiing and building mini ski jumps. I had a fierce battle with some boys because they destroyed a big snowman a few girls and I had built. When I found out, I tore down to the spot in the park and charged at one particular boy so hard that he fell face down in the snow. I then sat on him and pummeled him in total fury. After that, I trudged home and told my grandmother about the *frekke guttene*—a story she liked so much that she kept provoking me to tell it over and over again.

Tante Fanny was my favorite aunt. She was slender and pale blond, with beautiful hair parted in the middle and framing her gentle face like two gold satin curtains. But underneath that gentleness was a wicked tease and a woman of strong character. She loved to tickle me, and I began to dread it as my laughter approached hysteria. Ten days before Christmas, she would dress up as St. Lucy* and appear at night in my dark bedroom as a radiant, unearthly creature holding a candle. She would loosen her golden hair, which fell down to her waist, wear a crown on her head, and envelop her body from head to toe in a long white nightgown. Seeing her stand in the doorway, I always knew that it was Tante Fanny, but there was a magical solemnity about her apparition which stopped me from spoiling the illusion by divulging my secret.

Christmas in Kristiansund was unforgettable. Around the first

---

* The Scandinavians celebrate the Feast of Santa Lucia, an Italian saint, on December 13, as the beginning of the return of light at the darkest time of the year.

of December, baking began in every household. All kinds of different cookies, cakes, and breads were prepared and stored in tins. An aroma emanated from a thousand chimneys and hung over Kristiansund like a fragrant blanket. It mingled with the sharp cold sea air, and the smell of the fir trees which were being brought in from the country. There was also an intensified aroma in the small shops which sold chocolates, nuts, candies, and fruit—a mixture of scents which commingled tantalizingly. Christmas dinner seemed to me indescribably good and meant *ryper* [small snowbirds] with sour-cream sauce and *tyttebaer* [lingonberries], a combination of wild game, sweet berries, and sour cream which sent me into ecstasy. Best of all was the warm family atmosphere which created a cushion of love against the outside world, where nothing would intrude or hurt, where time stood still in happiness.

Tante Fanny was married to a wealthy and portly Norwegian named Harald Johnson, who was in the import/export business. They lived in one of the finest houses at the end of the harbor in Kristiansund. It was painted white, with a roof of dark-blue ceramic tile, and had a garden surrounded by a low picket fence. Going there with my mother for a visit was always a more formal occasion in the way I had to be dressed and behave. I rarely saw my cousin Beth because we were nine years apart and she was already a young lady, while I was still playing with dolls or beating up boys in the park.

Uncle Harald had also inherited a lovely country estate in Molde called Retiro. Molde is a special place, romantically called the City of Roses. Sixty years ago, when I spent many summer vacations there, it was not a city but a tranquil little town set in one of the most spectacularly beautiful landscapes in Norway. It lies inland, away from the rough North Sea, on a large fjord dotted with small islands, through which boats and ferries zigzag slowly but expertly. Molde is ringed by gently undulating hills of green fields and forests, and facing it across the fjord in the far distance is the extraordinary outline of the Romsdal mountain range, with its snow-covered peaks. On a clear, sunny day, when the sky and the fjord mirror each other in intense blue, Molde, and its surroundings, is one of God's loveliest creations.

The roses are a surprise—one hardly expects them to flourish so far north. They can be seen everywhere, tall and sturdy, with multipetaled heads as large as small cabbages, exuding their delicious scent even along the streets where they are planted around the houses like fragrant picket fences.

Retiro was situated a little outside Molde. It was a beautiful, pastoral place with farm buildings painted red and barns with roofs of turf and grass and an occasional small birch tree growing straight up in the air. Beyond lay a spacious park with a small lake, where I loved to play. The main house was Victorian, painted white, with gingerbread decorations. A few steps led up to the front door and onto the porch, and on the second floor were all the bedrooms with their gabled windows. It wasn't so bad having to go to bed early, because through the open window, I could always hear the grown-ups below talking and laughing, which was comforting and lulled me to sleep.

I loved the summers which my mother and I spent in Molde, where I was surrounded by my grandparents, uncles, aunts, and cousins, and was free to run around the farm to look and observe. Some things are indelibly marked in my memory—such as when I saw a chicken beheaded on a block with an ax, and the body got free and ran down the hill without its head! Or when my mother tried to save a rosy little piglet who had been born without an opening in its rear end. She bravely tried to make a cut where it should have been, but I don't think she saved it. She was more successful with a seemingly stillborn puppy, when she instinctively blew air into its tiny mouth and started it breathing. She taught me to love animals to such an extent that I tried to chase a rooster off a hen because I thought he was hurting her. I saw many other things which I did not understand until years later, since nobody explained anything and questions went unanswered.

Was I ever again as happy as in those days in Molde and Kristiansund? I don't think so. I remember the lakelike stillness of the fjord on a hot summer's day, when we rowed and drifted lazily or sat on the sun-warmed rocks along the edge of the water, watching the dark-green seaweed bumping gently against the shore, or following with our eyes the boats and big ships as they became smaller and smaller and finally disappeared in the distance on their journey toward the North Sea.

I remember a rush of almost unreasonable happiness when I first returned to Norway in 1955 and walked along the quay of the harbor in Kristiansund. I inhaled deeply and smelled the typical mixture of sea air, boats, tar, engine oil, and fish—not exactly Chanel No. 5, but it brought back memories of childhood, and I realized that those were the only truly carefree days of my youth.

After the warmth and security of family life in Norway, our return to Berlin must have been a shock to my mother. My father had not bettered his situation, and added to their own financial stress, the galloping inflation of the postwar years in Germany made a chaos of their lives.

It was at this point that she met Dr. Hans Thomsen, who was the antithesis of my father: well-established, a diplomat, formal, and of substantial means. He fell in love with her and urged her to leave my father. He was married, but promised to divorce his wife and marry her. As it turned out, he never did, and his oft-repeated statement "A man in my position . . ." etc. became his overriding concern and my mother's fate.

From the moment of my parents' separation, I was deprived of a vital balance in life. My mother became the half trying to be a whole, an attempt which bound me to her inextricably and left me overdependent, fearful, and rebellious. I was six years old when this happened, and I have a very clear memory of the moment when my mother told me that my father would no longer live with us. I was stunned and hurt, standing in our garden next to the little scrawny tree in the Bleibtreustrasse, trying to comprehend what I could not understand. I had a sense of abandonment and helpless frustration, and did not know whom to be angrier with— my father or my mother.

All I remember is the terrible feeling of being left alone and the certain knowledge, even at age six, that it was useless to rage or plead or cry in the face of the finality of their decision. Though my parents remained friends and were never divorced, and though I saw my father quite often, life was never again the same.

As he moved away and out of my life, he became the classic longed-for father, and when I visited him (he had moved in with Uncle Gui), I always felt the excitement of doing something naughty, something forbidden.

Tommy (Dr. Hans Thomsen) became a punctual visitor two or three times a week. He had a similar background to my mother's: Norwegian parents who had emigrated to Germany. He was nice, tall, blond, and good-looking. I alternated between liking and hating him, and flared up when he attempted to correct me by furiously telling him that he was not my father. It was an uneasy relationship, and I was jealous when my mother behaved coquettishly. Still, our existence was somewhat stabilized, and as I began school, and particularly ballet school two years later, I became totally absorbed in my passion to become a dancer and less concerned about Tommy.

What I found out years later through documents in my mother's possession was that my father was readmitted into the Catholic Church on April 8, 1924. What is far more remarkable is that on the following day, April 9, 1924, my mother and father were married once more, this time according to the rites of the Catholic Church—a year after they had separated! They did not live together again, but what this proved to me was my father's strong Catholic commitment and my mother's willingness to help him regularize his position in the Church. Their marriage appears to be a mystery, but it is a comfort to me to know that they loved each other enough so that, at first, he relinquished his faith for *her*, and that later my mother helped him to re-enter the Church, which meant so much to him. In my eyes, they are beautiful people.

TWO

I t amuses me to think that possibly only Mickey Rooney made his theatrical debut at an earlier age than I did. As I am writing this, I am amazed to realize that it was sixty years ago that I first set foot on the stage—innocent, ignorant, and unafraid.

One winter, when I was six years old, there was to be a theatrical gala evening at the Festival Hall of Kristiansund. I assume that the gala was a benefit to raise money for a new opera production. Since only local talent was to be used for the program, someone had the idea of a children's ballet. All the little girls were to be flowers, and I was chosen to be a butterfly who flitted back and forth among them. It was certainly a great opportunity for "dancing," since all the other girls had to remain still. In those days I never had any trouble improvising—just let me hear music, tell me that I was a butterfly, and I was off, dancing and performing to my heart's content.

Great plans were made. One of my aunts donated an evening dress of pale-blue silk, which was cut up and sewn together again to make a costume for me. (Did they attempt to give me wings? I don't remember.) The great evening arrived and turned into my "triumphant stage debut." I was later told that I certainly made the most of it.

When I was seven years old, my greatest wish was to become the pupil of Eugenia Eduardova. She was a distinguished Russian dancer who had opened her own school of ballet in Berlin. My mother had a Russian friend who offered to go with us for an interview. It must have been in the winter, because it was darkening when we arrived at the school.

The afternoon class had started and piano music came from inside. After our knocking, the door was flung open with great irritation. My mother's friend said something in Russian, Eduardova shouted back above the din of the piano, I was pushed forward into the light, Eduardova looked at me briefly, asked another question—which our friend answered—then another Russian shout from Eduardova and the door was slammed in our faces! Understanding nothing but slamming doors, I knew something was wrong.

This first encounter, which had started with such high hopes, turned into a "tragedy" for me. It appeared that I was too young, because Eduardova accepted no one under the age of nine. Two whole years of waiting! I was inconsolable.

That Christmas I received my first pair of ballet shoes. Real, honest-to-goodness satin toe shoes with long satin ribbons. No doll, no toy, no present could have meant more to me than those two satin slippers—but there was one *terrible* thing wrong with them: they were *pale blue* instead of *pale pink*! I turned to my mother in agony. "But, Mama—they are pale blue!! *That's* wrong!! They must be *pink*!!" My voice was rising, my eyes brimming. I loved them so, but it was almost sacrilegious—they *could* not be blue: they had to be pink. I was finally calmed down. Everyone assured me that no one would tell anyone else that I had blue ballet shoes —and by the time I could finally go to ballet school, they promised

I would get a new pink pair. At last I could hug my shoes and kiss them on top where the toes are meant to be—that's how much I loved that pair. I even liked the faint smell of glue which came from the linen sole which was glued inside, on top of the leather sole. The pale-blue satin was so soft and shiny, and the ribbons were narrow but felt like heavy cream and had a tiny pattern along the edge. I took my shoes to bed with me, and for a long, long time we three slept together every night after I had hugged and kissed them good night.

In the autumn of 1925 we presented ourselves again at Madame Eduardova's. I was very frightened. This time I was accepted, but only for a six-week trial period. (Thank God, my age was not discussed, since I was only eight and a half.) I immediately began taking class every day, Monday through Saturday, and lived in constant fear that she would not keep me. I worked very hard to be a good pupil. After the six weeks' probation, nothing was said. That week and the next I was more frightened than ever and began pestering my mother to come to school and ask Mme Eduardova whether she intended to keep me. My mother never took rules seriously and perhaps did not relish another encounter with the severe lady, but finally she came to class and asked Mme Eduardova whether I was permanently accepted. "Of course I keep her!" was the irritable answer, as if she had been insulted. Finally I could relax a little after those fearful weeks.

Mme Eduardova was an excellent teacher and gave us the best possible, pure ballet training. She was very beautiful, or so she seemed to me as a young child. She was dark-haired with green eyes, and always smelled delicious. She was also very strict and ruled her school with an iron hand and a wooden stick, which she used quite often on our legs!

Once accepted as a pupil, you had not only to conform to the severe discipline of daily class but to dress in a specifically prescribed manner. Part of your acceptance as a pupil meant that you were sent to a dressmaker (another severe Russian lady), who measured you exhaustively and then made a white linen dress to be worn for class. It had lots of little tucks and pleats (eventually to be let out for budding bosoms and growing legs), a tight waist with buttons down the back, and a wide undulating skirt—again with lots of extra seams. The dress had to be freshly washed and stiffly starched every Monday.

My mother, who was neither strict nor disciplined, could never understand my anxiety each Saturday when my dress had to be washed—invariably an inconvenience for her, especially the starching and ironing. On Mondays I would agonize over fitting those billowy waves into my small suitcase without wrinkling the skirt.

In addition, you wore white knickers held up by an elastic band around the waist and upper thighs; white socks neatly stretched up to above the calf and held there by a fine, white elastic; and, of course, pink ballet shoes with pink ribbons, which had to be crossed and recrossed around the ankle, with the bow tucked in and out of sight. Your hair had to be combed, and in order to hold it in place, you wore a white satin ribbon across your forehead. If there was the slightest variation in the uniform or anything missing, you would be sent out of class, which was a disgrace.

I remember once during class a moment of horror when the elastic waistband of my knickers suddenly broke and the top descended slowly down my thighs! Although I had to leave the room, it was understood to be an accident. Still, accidents were not supposed to happen, you were expected to check every item beforehand—a lesson well learned for the rest of my professional life.

Mme Eduardova could not abide the smell of sweating young bodies, so she wandered around the classroom liberally using a perfume spray, aromatizing the air. If, in spite of that, she detected an offender, she gave a sharp command, told the unhappy one to leave and never enter the class without thoroughly washing beforehand.

We were a very competitive group of little girls in Berlin. It mattered a lot whether you stood in the first, second, or third row after you finished the barre exercises and moved into the middle of the room in front of the mirror. It was an obvious mark of achievement to be told to move forward, the pinnacle being the middle of the first row, or to be told to be the first to begin an exercise which each girl, one after another, was to perform.

My toughest competitors were Sonja, Tamara, Lulu, and Gitta. We were very jealous of each other, though polite on the surface. I suffered over every little sign in the daily process of learning, watching whether they were ahead of me or not, and trying to master the technique step by step. It remained an endless process which never stopped as long as I danced, but I didn't know that then.

When I was old enough I went to ballet school alone in the afternoon. I took the bus and always stood in my favorite place in a corner under the stairs of the double-decker. I left shortly after four so that I would have plenty of time to get dressed for class, which began at five. The school was over a notorious nightclub called Eldorado, and we heard about strange men who performed there who had long hair and wore women's clothes. In the afternoon it was quiet and shut when we trooped up the stairs, and the only sound heard on the second floor was our excited jabbering in the dressing room as we got ready.

After class we all went to a small shop right across from the school. We bought a large chocolate cookie in the shape of a heart and a big glass of milk. It always tasted delicious. In the winter it was dark when I went home, but the trip was more fun. All the stores were lit up, and it got especially exciting as we drove around the Gedächtnis Kirche (now a landmark in West Berlin) and up the Kurfürstendamm, past the UFA Kino, where the latest movies were shown. Sometimes they played songs from the films over loudspeakers, and I remember the excitement of the first "talkie,"

The Jazz Singer, with Al Jolson, and hearing snatches of "Mammy." There were very strict laws regarding permission for children to see movies. It seems they were all *verboten,* except cowboy movies from America. These were silent and accompanied by dreadful piano music.

Going to a matinee performance for children and seeing all those horses, with cowboys wearing strange hats and Indians chasing them, or vice versa, was a special occasion. Afterward, we bought ice from a street vendor and watched with awe as he dug around in his cart and came up with pink ice, which he put on a waffle, then topped with another waffle, making a pink sandwich. It was watery but very sweet and cold.

There were peculiar sights in Berlin which no one ever explained to me. Women who stood on street corners. They looked completely different from other women and had angry expressions on their faces. Some of them looked like clowns, because they had a lot of paint on their faces and strange hair and hats. But what fascinated me most were their boots. They were laced up in front to their knees and had high heels. The women just stood there; sometimes they had a cigarette in their mouth. No one ever explained who they were, but I gathered it was something bad.

When I got off the bus, I ran home, and then often my mother and I would go out again to shop for something special for supper. I loved to go with her, watching her pick out plump red tomatoes, sausages, or cheese, and especially a big pickle for our evening meal, which I always looked forward to. It was the happiest time of the day, because it meant that Mama and I were together.

Sometimes she made me rather eccentric lunches. She put chocolate between sliced buttered rolls and told me *that* was very special. Typical of children, I found it *too* special and much preferred the rather proletarian lunch of a girlfriend who lived in the same building. They had much more money than we had and lived in the front of the building, but my mother looked down on them and the sandwich swapped with my girlfriend only confirmed her suspicion: coarse bread spread with goose fat with salt sprinkled on it.

Since I usually ate lunch alone, I began to hide the rolls under a cupboard. My mother was delighted when she saw my empty plate, but she became suspicious when our dog scratched to get underneath the cupboard. When my mother finally moved it, there were neat rows of moldy rolls side by side! Luckily, her sense of humor saved me from punishment. Only once did she attempt it, in a manner of performing a ceremony which was expected of her. She told me to lie across her lap. I dutifully trotted over and did so. She then began to spank me, but I thought it was so funny that I began to laugh. So did *she*—and that was the end of that.

I do not mean to imply that she was a totally permissive mother —far from it. She brought me up with a very strict eye for good manners, particularly table manners. For instance: (1) Eating fish with a regular knife was unforgivable. If I wasn't given a fish knife, I was to use a second fork or manage with one fork only. (2) Between bites of food, nothing was worse than placing knife and fork by their tips on each side of the plate, or putting my elbows on the table. (3) I was to stand up immediately when a woman or a man entered a room, and remain standing until they sat down. One did the same in a bus and always offered a seat to an older person. One always politely let everyone pass first through a door, and so on.

Once, my mother eyed me critically during a meal and said sharply, "Brigitta, why do you speak so uncharmingly?" I immediately began gesturing delicately and fluting my words, then innocently struck a pose and asked, "You mean like this?" We both burst out laughing, but I had learned my lesson.

In clothes, she taught me individuality. It was the custom then to have one's clothes made and Mama had to go about it prudently since we had very little money. She spent hours choosing material. I accompanied her and watched while she tried to make up her mind. The saleslady would patiently pull a bolt of cloth from the stacks, then lift it and drop it down with a soft thud onto the table. They would both unroll it and my mother would murmur approval, such as *"Schöner Stoff"* [beautiful fabric], while she carefully fingered the material to divine its quality and texture. Sometimes the table would be heaped high with bolts before the ultimate decision was made. When that point was reached, the saleslady would spread out the material and begin measuring the yardage. Then—at last—the irrevocable moment had arrived when she took a large pair of scissors and cut across the bolt, severing my mother's purchase from the rest, while reassuring her that she had made the right choice.

Next came endless hours with the dressmaker. After the design had been settled on, the fittings observed were a lesson for life. The seams of the sleeves at the shoulders or the length at the wrists were carefully scrutinized; the proper waistline, the becoming hemline, or a flattering neckline were much discussed and often altered and realtered. It proved to be irresistible information for a small child. At one of my mother's teas, I went up to a lady, took part of her skirt in my hand, fingered it knowingly, and then announced importantly, *"Schöner Stoff."*

Mama taught me that it was fun to wear clothes different from those of other little girls. Probably a bit of one-upmanship, since I wore special handknit Norwegian sweaters or fur caps or knee socks with woolen tassels all sent by my Besta from Norway. The uniforms of childhood and adolescence were not for me.

———

The observer might think I was spoiled. Spoiled for a particular kind of love, yes; but not in the ordinary sense. I once said, "Mama, why is it that to outside persons I am polite and never say the things that I say to you? I should be nicer to you than anyone on earth, and with you I am angry and nasty." Her answer was, "Well, you must let it out somewhere. That is what I am here for. And

I know how good you are . . ." And more of the same. I guess I didn't trust anyone but her to see the less attractive side of myself, and I knew she would understand and forgive me, and she always did. When someone or something made me unhappy, she always supported me without question. The unspoken possibility of fault on my part was never even hinted at; the perfect balm for a wound and the best way to heal it.

It seems to me that that kind of love comes only once: a totally accepting and unconditional love. Other people may love you, but there is always a reserve, a slightly detached attitude which registers flaws and faults with the threat of ceasing to love, and with its even greater threat of separation and being left alone. With my mother there would never be a withdrawal of love or a threat of abandonment.

Other people might discover all the things that she knew, but she considered them unimportant in the light of the child she had borne. The love we exchanged throughout my childhood—yes, and the dependence it created in me on her—obliterated her critical faculties. The streak in me which baffled and sometimes irritated my mother was a serious and puritanical one. Early on, I disciplined myself severely, set up rules and goals for achievements, and drove myself at a hard pace. In games I set myself impossible tasks: things I had to win, obstacles I had to overcome. And I never gave up. It was self-imposed. No one made me do anything. I did it myself without coercion.

I loved to play with a ball outside in the garden and evolved elaborate games rivaling those of Sparta. It began simply enough by my throwing the ball against the wall and then continuing to hit it back, first with my right palm, then my left, then both palms. After that, the same with my right fist, left fist, both fists—then fingertips, right, left, both—then doubling and tripling the same pattern until I had reached my goal, which was to complete the whole, more and more difficult series, without making a mistake or dropping the ball. If I *did* drop the ball, dire happenings would result, which could then be ameliorated only by starting again from the beginning; if I then succeeded, all was well—my wish would come true. The wish for all my obsessive games was always the same. Would I become a great (or was it famous) dancer? I raced and jumped and played almost impossible-to-win games, always with the same object in mind—trying to win and win and win.

This tenacity finally served me well when I began formal ballet training. I would not give up, and persisted and practiced until I had mastered a particular step or movement. If not today, then tomorrow; if not tomorrow, then again and again until I could do what I wanted. That is how an obsessive streak can be useful; perhaps more than useful—necessary, and certainly essential for the mastery of ballet technique. How else can one learn to stand on one toe with the other leg high up in the air?

Going to regular school every morning and ballet school in the afternoon meant that I had no time for recreation. My school friends met and played together in the afternoon while I went to ballet school. Still, I never missed it. Not for an instant did I wish for a different life or more time for play. I had no thoughts for anything but ballet. Every small achievement which my body mastered was more precious to me than diversions, parties, or whatever else life had to offer a little girl. Learning was pleasure. It filled my life completely. Coming home at night, I would hang on to a piece of furniture and show my mother what I had learned or what I was able to do at that point. While making supper, my mother had to listen to a great deal as I demonstrated, expounded, and theorized. She did her best to be interested.

Once a year Eduardova gave a recital or *Balletabend* to show off her pupils, her school, and her achievements. This was invariably topped by the highlight of the evening, when she herself performed *Le Matelot* as a solo. Dressed in a sailor suit, she danced it full of dash and naval wit, and invariably brought down the house.

In 1926, at the age of nine, I made my first appearance during the annual Ballet Evening given customarily in a concert hall such as the Blütner or Bechsteinsahl.

We had rehearsed for weeks. Too much, I thought. It was rather dull. We, the youngest pupils, were meant to be flowers and I was chosen to be a *Schneeglöckchen*, or lily of the valley. Since a *Schneeglöckchen* is such a delicate flower, consisting mostly of a long green stem topped by some tiny white flowers, my costume was an attempt to resemble it. But being very, very thin, my body totally enclosed in green tights, my head covered by a drooping white organdy cap, I looked more like a gangling frog.

The dressing room was full of noisy little girls, but I remember Eduardova taking one look at me, grabbing a big pair of scissors, and cutting off my green sleeves and green tights. There I stood in a scrawny green bathing suit, not really caring a hoot, just dying to get on the stage. That seems to have remained my pattern. I can't stand all the fussing beforehand. I just like to get on with it.

———

Mama and I became like two Chaplinesque characters. Two lonely vagabonds. We clung to each other and defied the world. We made fun of it.

She taught me her rebellion, all the rebellion she had learned as a child. She drew me into her grown-up world and spared me very little. What she did not tell me, I guessed. I tried to branch away from her and became studious, punctual, and punctilious— all the things she was not. She remained a child, irresponsible and charming, and I grew too early into an adult.

We lived alone, now, Mama and I. After my father left, I was given his room, and I tried to keep it as neat and tidy as he had. Although I was proud of having my own room, there was a price to pay. I lay awake at night, afraid of the dark and the strange noises coming from the courtyard. I tried instead to listen to the comforting footsteps of my mother in the room above me and imagined what she was doing as she moved about. But sometimes I had terrible nightmares, dreaming that a man two stories high was standing outside the window looking at me menacingly.

We could never afford a maid, and as I grew up I became more and more dependent on Mama. No wonder I enjoyed the weekends spent with the Rahmer family. They entered our life through Uncle Gui, who was devoted to Alice Rahmer. She was a round lady, fat, short, and very warm. She was married to Erwin Rahmer, a successful lawyer; but he seemed to be so busy that I rarely saw him, and when I *did*, I was scared of him. Alice was the daughter of Herr Professor Kuttner, an esteemed nose-and-throat physician. He had the lightest touch when he examined me—his hands and fingers were like feathers—and I always remembered how gentle he had been.

Alice had two daughters, Hilde and Elsbeth (nicknamed Dicke), who were my best friends. We went to the same school and spent weekends and holidays together *en famille*. Though it did not diminish the love I had for my parents, Uncle Gui and Tante Alice added a normality to my childhood which was lacking at home. Tante Alice kept an eye on my education and got me into the prestigious and expensive school her daughters attended. She paid for my education—if not all, certainly a considerable part of it.

I enjoyed regular school, especially the trolley ride in the morning. Many pupils took the same Number 176, getting on at various stops. I looked forward to that squealing camaraderie. Fräulein Lessler's Privatschule was in the Grünewald section, a beautiful suburb of Berlin between the trolley stops of Hundekehle and Rosenstock. The school was housed in a large villa surrounded by a big garden, and only a few minutes from the forest where all our sports events and most of my little triumphs took place.

I seemed to be able to run faster than anyone and was much sought after for relay races, which I always saved for my team. Needless to say, I excelled in gymnastic classes but found them boring and childish! In singing classes I often became convulsed with laughter when a girl sang off pitch. I suppose since both my parents were singers, singing off pitch, flat, or sharp—including *knödling*—was cause for hilarity.

I don't think anyone but Tante Alice was very concerned about my scholastic achievements—still, something must have sunk in, because I am quite good in mathematics, multiplying, adding, and subtracting in my head while others fiddle with their calculators.

The Rahmer household was solidly bourgeois and well ordered. They had a maid and sometimes a governess. Although I felt content there, I injected my rebelliousness and tried to make Hilde and Dicke act independently from their silly governess. I was contemptuous of their being bossed around and tried to make them more courageous. I think I mixed up courage with defiance. Since I didn't have a "proper" family of father, mother, brothers, and sisters, with a maid who cleaned and cooked meals, I turned against conventions—not like my mother, who had had too much of them in her youth, but because I had none at home and lived alone with my mother in circumstances which I sensed were open to criticism. I have never lost that streak of wanting to upset the applecart and have often astonished friends by some bizarre behavior. But what I do now is tame compared to what I was capable of as a child, when I dared a small group of children in my building—girls I didn't even like—to go up the service stairs (which only servants and delivery people used) and pee on the landing. They were flabbergasted and scared to death by the suggestion, so I did it and showed them what courage was all about, earning their horrified admiration. It was the same during summer vacations. I bossed Hilde and Dicke around and dictated all the rules of fun and games. I was the organizer and, in my opinion, clearly superior. I imagine I had that attitude because I was a serious ballet student, learning a craft which gave me, as I progressed, a certain amount of power and the absolute conviction that I was going to succeed in anything I put my mind to.

Being intimate with the Rahmer family from early childhood

made me identify Jews with the warmth I received from Tante Alice. Although I adored my mother, Tante Alice was more like the proper mother my childish mind envisaged: content with her maternal role (even her rotundity seemed evidence of that) and concerned with her children and household. My own mother was everything Tante Alice was not: young, good-looking, chic, charmingly flighty, bored by my schooling, even easily "fatigued" hearing too detailed a description of my ballet classes. It was Tante Alice who occupied herself with mundane matters and was the steadying influence during our early struggles. It makes me sad that I could not tell her how much she meant to me and how much I loved her.

During World War II, my anger toward Hitler and his atrocities became extreme. I saw only Tante Alice and the girls, not knowing what had happened to them, multiplying their faces into millions. For years, it felt as if someone were trying to drill a complicated mathematical problem into my head which I could not, could not comprehend. Something that was irrefutable but made no sense. They survived. Tante Alice was hidden in a monastery, protected by the community of nuns. She became a convert and continued to live there until her death. Both girls escaped to England and survived the war.

———

Uncle Gui had found a large corner property in Misdroy which had two small houses on it. He named it Brigitteneck, or "corner of Brigitta." Misdroy was a small resort, the smallest in a crescent-shaped bay on the Baltic Sea. It was situated more or less in a plumb line from the coast to the city of Stettin, and surrounded by bigger resorts such as Swinemünde and Warnemünde, but in all the years I summered there as a child, we never visited them. We thought Misdroy small but perfect.

The beach was miles and miles long, and you could walk on it until all the dunes stopped and the narrow wooden boardwalk came to an end. The beach was pure white, or rather light beige, fine and silky as satin, with gentle dunes and tufts of grass waving like long, delicate green flags. You could hide in the various hollows the wind and sea had created, lie cozily in the warm sand and dream. Farther away, the dunes rose into a hill and finally formed a high, steep wall of sand, joining a pine forest edging toward the sea. (I've only seen something similar near Biarritz, but not as beautiful.)

Very, very far away from our part of the beach, someone had built a steep, shallow, zigzagging staircase. We used to climb to the very top, hugging the sand-dune wall, and then jump and tumble down in the soft sand parallel to the steps. Sometimes I dream about it, but in my dream I fall and fall out of control, and it is frightening.

It was the custom on German beaches to construct a *Burg* or fortress. The idea was to create a circular enclosure out of the sand, which a family would claim as their own for the duration of their stay. The more affluent *Burgs* had a tall wicker beach chair which was curved at the top for protection against the sun or rain. Some of these enclosures were decorated with flags, and the outside sand wall with designs made of seashells spelling the owner's name, or *kitsch* names, such as *Sonnentag* or *Seeglück*. At the height of the season the beach looked like the army encampment of Henry V before the Battle of Agincourt on St. Crispin's Day.

On a rainy day, when the beach was deserted, it was extremely tempting to come down and mess up all that order and jealously guarded ownership. Woe to the family who made enemies of children like us! We couldn't wait for a rainy day to take full advantage. Naturally, there was no way the perpetrators could be discovered unless they were caught on the spot. But we were too cunning for that. Our least mischief was to overturn the beach chair and crawl underneath, hiding and shivering on the cold wet sand.

After a storm, we went to the beach very early to gather what the sea had cast up during the night. We might be lucky to find amber, perhaps even bits of fossilized amber with an insect inside. We collected seashells and made hideous objects with glue, which we then presented to our mothers.

One of the two houses on Brigitteneck was painted blue, the other yellow. The blue house stood above the garden at an L-shaped angle and had Uncle Gui's bedroom, Tante Alice's, and our bedroom—Hilde's, Dicke's, and mine. At one end was an enclosed veranda; at the other, the one and only toilet. The yellow house adjoined the garden and had several rooms and a kitchen, all opening onto a terrace. It probably had been a stable before. A grape arbor ran above the length of the terrace, shielding us from the sun. It became our outside dining room, where we ate all our meals.

The garden was large, or so it seemed to me as a child, and had a variety of berry bushes. We waited impatiently for them to ripen: the soft, slightly hairy, golden gooseberries, which exuded their sweet, sticky liquid when you bit them; or a twig of *Johannisbeeren*, which you could slowly pull out of your mouth, neatly tearing the berries off the stem with your teeth. They always tasted slightly sour.

We played a lot of hide-and-seek; in fact, I was absolutely indefatigable and wanted to play it all the time. In one part of the garden there were high fern-like leaves. I crawled under and into them. It was slightly damp and fusty there, with softly whirring noises made by tiny insects. Actually, it was slightly disgusting but a good hiding place.

After the midday meal, all the adults went to sleep and we were supposed to be quiet. We got through that boring period by anticipating wonderful afternoon events. The greatest of these was an outing in a rented horse carriage to a café in the woods about an hour's drive away. The horse and carriage would arrive at Brigitteneck, and we would all pile in, accompanied by a lot of arguing about who was to sit next to the driver on the way *to* the café and on the way home. The driver clip-clopped through the streets of Misdroy, then out of the small town and into the wooded hills.

When we arrived at the café, we had cakes and chocolate and a sip of coffee with whipped cream. Later, we rowed on the deep, inky-green lake, where lilies floated, but we didn't forget a terrible warning: "Don't touch the lilies! If you do, they will pull you into the lake and you will drown!" It was very frightening, but exciting. On the way home we were more subdued, full of cake and comfort.

Almost every afternoon we took a walk along the promenade running next to the beach. Everybody was nicely dressed and you strolled leisurely. Most afternoons an orchestra played and you circled clock- and counterclockwise in front of the bandstand, meeting the same people or bowing to friends and, later on, getting hysterical over good-looking boys. But that was much, much later.

Since Misdroy was on the sea, we ate a great deal of fish. What paradise to be given a smoked flounder and slowly dissect it! First you separated the thick, black, glistening skin from the fish, then expertly (you either were expert or could choke to death on fishbones) lifted the white, juicy meat off the skeletal bones down the spine, then separated the very fine outer fishbones, putting them aside. With it we ate black bread and sweet butter and drank milk. Or sometimes we had a special treat of raspberry syrup and soda.

At least once a day we ate a *Satte*. The *Satte* was made from fresh, rich, unpasteurized milk which had been poured into a soup bowl and left standing for twenty-four hours. During the night, the rich part of the milk rose to the top and formed a thick creamy layer, while the bottom part turned into a kind of sour yogurt. Before eating, we sprinkled the top layer liberally with sugar and black-bread crumbs. I suppose an American reading this will say "Ugh," but I salivate like a Pavlov dog at the mere thought of it!

Smoked eel was a Sunday dish compared to flounder and *Bückling* [whitefish], which required even more skill in dissecting. When we shopped for *Bückling*, we pressed the fish a great deal in order to determine whether it had plenty of roe. It was terribly disappointing if, in spite of all the touching, you discovered that you had a male fish on your hands and, with it, only some beige gook instead of the delicious pink roe—caviar, in fact!

We picked our own blueberries in the woods, carried them home in buckets, washed them—not too much—heaped big mounds into soup plates, and covered them with sugar and cream. We devoured them until our teeth and tongues were blue-black like chow dogs'. How good it tasted and what fun we had! Why does food eaten in our childhood seem so delicious in retrospect? It can't have been all that good.

My mother was not always in Misdroy during the summer, but I was, after all, with my two best girlfriends, Hilde and Dicke, and Tante Alice and Uncle Gui. Friends might come and go, but only my mother's arrival made a difference in our routine.

When she came she had a bedroom in the yellow house, sort of a walk-in room with a little window, but big enough for me to move in with her. I didn't like that too much, preferring the camaraderie of our joint bedroom in the blue house.

In the girls' room the three beds stood together in a ring around the wall, with a washstand in front of the window. One by one we washed ourselves at night. As we had no running water, we used a porcelain washbowl, but just the same we were expected to scrub ourselves from head to toe. The water sprayed in all directions, especially when we washed our feet, standing like herons on the floor, one foot on the ground, the other in the bowl. We shrieked a lot and snitched on each other.

After the wash, we took our slippers and hunted mosquitoes, slapping them against the walls until they were spotted with dead insects. Luckily the mosquitoes dried and disappeared until the next night. But their high whine in the dark, then the lighter-than-air settling on the skin near an ear or arm, followed by a sting, continued by a scratch which went on for days, made the pre-bed hunt imperative.

Eventually we were in bed and all the whispering began. We whispered and whispered until rudely interrupted by an adult if the giggling got too loud; then finally, suddenly, we were asleep.

——

We each had a bicycle, and as in everything else, I adored showing off. I eventually performed tremendous feats of daring and speed, managing to stand in an arabesque, with one foot on the seat, the other high in the air, while tearing down the street. We also went on long bicycle trips, and I loved best of all the isolation and silence on the wooded paths through the forest.

Another way of showing off was to dance in the garden in the afternoon. I was keenly aware that people would stop and look, and it spurred me on to give "a performance." I discovered I could make a kind of a costume for myself by taking the tablecloth from a garden table. It had a round hole in the middle for a large umbrella which fit perfectly around my waist. With a long, circular skirt, I could dance waltzes and give some impressions of a tango. Soon I wasn't satisfied with garden performances and began to dance on the dance floor of a typical café on the promenade, where a little jazz band played for *Thé Dansant*.

One afternoon, when we were having delicious cakes and coffee there, the band played and nobody was on the dance floor. The temptation was too great. I danced and danced and was in ecstasy. People gathered, applauded, and wanted more. The owners appeared from the kitchen and liked what they saw. They inquired whether I could dance there sometimes in the evening. They would put up a placard with my name on it. I pleaded and pleaded at home to be allowed to do it and at least won the promise of *one* "performance." But what would I dance?

I am sure it was a waltz, which I improvised, as I did all my "numbers." The first time I danced there, my fee consisted of a big cake covered with icing spelling out "Brigitta" and *"Erinnerung"* [souvenir]. It was presented to me with a fanfare from the band. The proprietor and his wife loved me and so did the pastry cook. I was very proud of my "salary."

My appearances became fairly regular during subsequent summers, and I would rehearse with the three-piece band for each new number which I added to my repertoire. I danced a "Pierrot," complete with white costume and red pompons; a peasant dance with lots of colored streamers or ribbons, plus tambourine; and, particularly, a "sad" dance in a black ballet tutu. I must have been ten or eleven when I graduated to fairly regular evening performances. The room would darken, the drum would roll, the spotlight was ready, while the announcer prepared the audience with a flourish: *"Fräulein Brigitta Hartwig wird nun tanzen!"* ["will dance now!"].

One night during my "black" dance, a burgher, fat and sweaty, announced in outraged tones to anyone who would listen that such a thing should not be permitted. "That poor child, so thin and sad, ought to be in bed! Not dancing in *this* place!" I stopped in the middle of my "sad" dance and told him that I was perfectly happy, that I had plenty to eat, that I was not poor, and that I wanted to dance right there! Applause broke out and the man was silenced.

By the time I finished my "summer engagements," I was earning ten marks an evening and had bought myself a camera.

My first professional engagement happened when I was chosen from Mme Eduardova's pupils to dance a little solo in *Dreimädlerhaus*, a highly successful musical based on Schubert's music and produced by Erik Charell. I remember what I liked most about my "engagement" was hearing that lovely music every night. The purpose of the solo was to present a bouquet of flowers to a singer. One night I forgot the bouquet but continued my dance just the same. When I came offstage, the manager bawled me out, whereupon my mother attacked him for scolding a child—how dare he!!

The laws in Germany were very strict and allowed only six weeks for appearances by children under fourteen. Since I was only nine, my engagement soon came to an end. But I remember that it had its reward. I was extremely attached to dolls and had seen a beautiful baby carriage in a window. It was English and absolutely the latest in design—very low to the ground, with small wheels. It was black outside and beige inside, but it was out of the question that I might have it, because it cost 60 marks. A fortune to us! I bought it six weeks later with part of the money I had earned. I found out that it was not only fun to dance on stage but useful. One could buy things one desperately wanted.

In the summer of 1928, when I was eleven, my father visited us in Misdroy. He had come to stay for a few weeks. On a gray day, a bit windy and moist, which gave us a chill between the shoulder blades, we decided just the same to go down to the beach and swim. My father didn't feel well and stayed home to rest in the garden. All of us—Alice, Hilde, Dicke, my mother, and I—set off, walking the few blocks to the beach, where the wind, the chill, and the dampness increased. We stood on the bluff looking at the sea, which looked as gray as the sky. We took our sandals off and felt our feet clammy on the wet sand.

Since it was cold we decided to swim right away and return home. Holding one another by the hand, we formed a circle in the water and jumped up and down to get warm. After a while we enjoyed ourselves and felt tingly and happy. We came running out and, shaking the water off like puppies, made a great fuss over drying ourselves.

My father came down after all and we all urged him to go in. We told him the sea was not too rough and that he would feel much better after a swim. The beach was deserted as we left him behind, but on the rise of the dunes I turned around and saw him in the sea. I made a joking remark to my mother: "Look. Papa is fighting with the waves," because his arms seemed to be waving around in the water. We both laughed since he was such a strong swimmer.

We trooped home very hungry, looking forward to lunch. We waited for my father's return but he did not come back. We waited and waited, and then felt something was wrong—a lull, a silence, something ominous. Finally someone came running to say that my father had disappeared in the sea, that he had called out, that he had drowned. It seemed completely impossible, for my father was so athletic. Then someone else came and said he had been found, he was lying on the beach, that they were trying to help him, that he was alive.

I was not allowed to go to the beach. I felt paralyzed and was silent. I pictured my father. I knew what was happening. It had happened several times during the summers that people had drowned. I had seen them dragged from the sea and tried not to watch, because it made me sick when they worked on a still figure with a dead white face so strangely in contrast to the brown body. Sometimes they even stood the body on its head to get the water out. How ill it made me, and now they were doing it to my father.

Much later I was told he was dead, that they had not been able to revive him. The only thing the grown-ups were grateful for was that he had been found, because it would have been agonizing to have his body floating in the sea and finally washed up miles away.

The impossible had happened. We were stunned and silent. My father had been taken to a Catholic chapel. My mother cried, but I don't think I did. I just remember trying to comfort her. I was allowed to go to the chapel. My father was so still, but I was not frightened. I suppose it was the stillness which was strange, the lack of movement, the incomprehensibility of death. I looked at him and felt embarrassed, as if I had intruded, intruded on his privacy. As if he were defenseless and I must protect him. Around his right ear the skin was blue; it was thought a wave had hit him, knocking him unconscious, and that was why he had drowned. Or that he had had a heart attack and been dragged into a whirlpool. The next day a sign appeared on the beach warning swimmers against strong undercurrents.

I stood looking at him. I was not conscious of anyone else being in the chapel—perhaps I had been left alone. I felt as if something was expected of me. I did not know how or what to do, but I felt I could say a prayer. I thought it was a bit presumptuous, but since my father could not do it, I must. I prayed the "Our Father" over him and then said goodbye to him. I think I made the sign of the cross on his forehead. Did I kiss him?

I wrote a letter to my mother which was supposed to be from my father and which I put on her pillow: "Dear Bille, Here in Heaven it is beautiful. Don't be sad. Your dear Fritz."

Sleeping in my mother's room that night, I was awake a long time staring at the ceiling.

I was not allowed to go to the funeral, but I visited his grave often. It had a simple cross made of two branches from a birch tree. As I stood at the foot of his grave, during the solitary visits I made on those warm summer days, I could not understand that my father was lying under that soft mound of earth.

———

When I was eleven, my mother announced that we would be going to Paris for six months. She wanted me to learn French and continue to study ballet. Some of the great Russian dancers—refugees from the Revolution—had settled in Paris and opened schools of ballet: Mathilde Kchessinska, Lubov Egorova, Olga Preobrajenska, and the famous teacher Nicholas Legat.

I believe my mother decided early on that my life would go in a definite direction in which academic learning would not play too great a role—and took me out of school frequently. She believed that I should get out—"Das Kind muss heraus"—travel, learn a language, study ballet, and be exposed to other cultures. She always regretted that she did not get me to Spain. She wanted me to see gypsies dancing the flamenco, to absorb the atmosphere of a bodega. She felt that the emotional heat and passion of Spain would have been a good influence on me as a dancer. But she did get me to Paris.

It was October or November 1928 when we set off. We were

like two adventurous tramps. Mama never felt well in the morning, and overnight journeys did not improve matters. Still, when we arrived in Paris, Mama was cheerful on our way to the hotel. It was small but exceedingly nice, very near the Madeleine. We acknowledged our room as small but elegant and in exuberance proceeded to dance a tango in the best Berlin tradition of the twenties.

Since sleep was very important to my mother, we did a lot of it, especially since we didn't have a schedule or anything fixed to do. We began to joke about it. "Now we'll sleep a little again—and again, and again," and kept encouraging each other, to dispel a certain amount of fear. Mama probably *was* afraid, having taken such an audacious step as to set off alone for Paris.

The first few days we led an encapsulated existence. Every morning we had breakfast in a café close by—croissants, sweet butter, *confiture*, and *café au lait*. It was delicious. Then we wandered around. One night we went to a movie. In those days a movie was an occasion, particularly to us, alone in Paris. It was a film starring Ruby Keeler, and had lots of tap dancing.

Often we went to Penny's—to this day opposite the Madeleine —and ate large pieces of cake which stilled our appetite for more expensive things like *entrecôte grillée, pommes de terre, une petite salade*, which we ate in various bistros when we had enough money. After a week, it became clear that Mama didn't know anyone in Paris. We were, in fact, on our own. The small amount of money we had was dwindling. Mama confided that we couldn't afford the little hotel anymore and that we had to move. She found a Norwegian pension on Boulevard St. Germain. It was in the heart of the Quartier Latin, a bit shabby, but, after being alone in the hotel, quite cozy. We shared a tiny room, a double bed, and, with other lodgers the Norwegian language. As a result, I relearned Norwegian and hardly had occasion to speak French.

After we were settled, we visited the studio of Nicholas Legat on

Place Pigalle. To my joy and relief, he accepted me as his pupil, and our life soon assumed regularity as every day we took the Métro to my class.

My immaculate-looking appearance the first morning I attended class must have given the other pupils a shock, but not Legat. The pink-and-white apparition dressed in a short white linen dress and pink ballet shoes was familiar to Legat, who recognized the Russian Imperial Ballet School uniform which Eduardova had introduced in her school in Berlin.

I, in turn, looked at the assembled pupils with amazement. They were a motley group, dressed in ill-assorted tights and tops, including dirty ballet shoes. (We had even been taught by Eduardova to clean our shoes with cotton saturated with cleaning fluid.) The pupils had holes everywhere in their black tights, especially in the crotches. It never occurred to me that this was due either to non-caring or "in-dress," and my amazement turned to pity. I thought they were all very poor and could not afford to dress otherwise. At Eduardova's, whether we were poor or not, we had to have two sets of everything. You had to sacrifice something else, but not your uniform. (Today, of course, dancers look even more bizarre, with rubber pants and woolen leg warmers.)

The studio was not big, but it was light and airy. Mirrors lined one wall, and the others were decorated with Legat's famous caricatures of dancers. Classes were very different from Eduardova's. The ages were mixed, and both girls and boys attended. In every other respect it proceeded according to the same ritual. First, barre exercises, then adagio in the middle of the room, and finally, combinations of jumps. For the last twenty minutes, the girls were sent out of the room to put on toe shoes while the boys were given more masculine exercises. When we returned, we alternated. I watched the boys with fascination when they performed *doubles tours en l'air*—sometimes askew; they flailed about in their boyish efforts, beet-red in the face, trying to master *entrechat six*. We in turn would be asked to perform sixteen or even twenty-four *fouettés*, bravely starting out but later careening around, furious at failing to stay in place.

Legat taught pirouettes better than anyone I know. He would come up behind you, ask you to assume fourth position, adjust your body, tell you to swing your arms for the momentum needed, and you then found yourself executing a perfect turn. The astonishment and joy of it! You thought you had mastered it, but he had to show you over and over again, adjusting your hips and legs. It never failed with *him*, and bit by bit you learned. André Eglevsky, also a pupil of Legat, mastered it to such perfection that he could perform four, six, eight pirouettes slowly and without a flaw.

I found it difficult at first to follow his variations toward the end of the class. He did not demonstrate them, as I was used to, but in ballet vocabulary told us the steps to be combined, illustrating with his fingers but never getting up from his chair. If we were baffled and made mistakes, it was a sign of our stupidity, and implied *disgrace* that he was obliged to get up and show us by moving about. He was a little old man but amazingly graceful, and would illustrate what he wanted us to do with perfect nimble economy. His method forced us to learn each step by name in the traditional French ballet nomenclature.

I loved best of all the adagio following barre. As with all exercises, it was danced twice, but because of the legato tempo you could develop it more fully and, by the second time around, give a decent version of it. We were always divided in two groups, and I watched the other girls closely, adopting or rejecting a particular execution of a movement. I think I had early on an affinity for adagio or slow *pas de deux*. It suited me physically and temperamentally. I had long legs, a high extension, and a flexible back—all suitable for adagio but not for fast movements. A dancer is trained in all forms of dancing, but nature dictates an individual style. One might roughly compare a dramatic soprano to the fluidity of a dancer excelling in adagio, and a coloratura soprano to a dancer executing steps with speed and brilliance.

———

Mama took me often to play in the Luxembourg Gardens, where I watched with envy as some of the children sailed their boats, busily running around the large pond. Or we walked through narrow streets to Notre Dame. Twice a week, there was an open market in front of the great cathedral, and we saw some parakeets for sale. We bought two; they were pale blue, and we found them enchanting. Their twittering made our room more cheerful. But one day we read an article on various parrot diseases, including those afflicting parakeets. We immediately became ill—but was it before or after reading the article? The damage was done. Our birdies had to go, and we quickly found them another home.

I was more than ever dependent on Mama, and if she was late returning home, I would anxiously begin to listen to the rickety elevator outside our room. Every minute which passed increased my anxiety, and she usually found me in a flood of tears.

Just before Christmas, Mama caught cold. She didn't feel well as the little party of people living at the pension danced around the Christmas tree, holding hands and singing. Christmas Day, she woke with a terrible pain in her ear. She was very ill. A doctor came and examined her. He ordered a hot poultice every few hours. I had to make it from oatmeal on a tiny single burner, wrap the gruel in a towel, and place it on her ear. During the week Mama got worse and worse, not only from the inflammation in her ear, but from the medicine to help her pain.

One day an "angel" appeared. That is how we always talked about him later. He was red-bearded, immaculately dressed in black from head to toe; a professor specializing in ears. I imagine that the doctor, seeing the desperate state my mother was in, had persuaded him to come in for a consultation. After his examination, he ordered my mother to go to the hospital immediately. At that moment, I experienced a sharp pain in my right ear. I begged him to look at it, praying he would order me to the hospital also. To my relief he said, "Yes, you too."

Since I had a middle-ear infection, my eardrum was pierced that night, but my mother was mortally ill. The next morning she underwent a mastoid operation which took four hours, apparently just in time, before the infection spread to the brain.

Afterward, Mama and I would reminisce that our hospital stay had been our happiest time in Paris, and that nothing had tasted so good to Mama as the first bowl—yes, bowl—of *café au lait* the day after her operation.

Mama and I had been so lonely and apprehensive that being in a Catholic hospital, attended to by kindly nuns, turned into a comforting experience. The priest who visited us nightly began to inquire about the "child's" upbringing, particularly when he heard that I had been baptized a Catholic. Beyond that baptism, Mama was vague. Had I received First Communion? Mama said she wasn't certain. I remember being specially dressed by the nuns and walking down the hospital corridor to the chapel, holding a candle.

After we came out of the hospital, money materialized from Berlin, probably from our friend Alice Rahmer, and we went for a few weeks to Cannes. The Côte d'Azur was bliss after Paris, the air redolent with mimosa and early spring. We walked on the promenade, and I promised Mama I would buy her a Pekinese when I had a lot of money. The rich ladies promenading with their dogs seemed to us the epitome of wealth and elegance.

The only unpleasant thing I remember about Cannes was the annual carnival, with its crush and noise. I caught a fistful of paper dots in my mouth which some exuberant reveler had aimed at me. I am sure he did not intend it, but the dry paper clinging to the insides of my mouth and throat left me with a recurrent nightmare of choking to death.

After our return from Paris to Berlin, my next professional job was as the first fairy in Max Reinhardt's production of A *Midsummer Night's Dream*. It was a famous production, and once again, what I remember most vividly was the music, this time by Mendelssohn: the Scherzo, which we "fairies" danced; the wonderful Wedding March; and the Nocturne, as night turns into day, danced by Tilly Losch. I never tired of the music and always stood in the wings to listen and watch when I did not have to dance myself.

We children had a lot of fun creeping around under the stage before our entrance. Max Reinhardt had created a mossy green forest full of invisible openings. Just before the Scherzo, a lot of steam was released, which created a marvelous effect (though it also made us cough), as if all the fairies appeared through the mist, seemingly out of the ground.

From those earnings, I bought myself a Käthe Kruse *Puppe* (a very special handmade doll), which I named Peter and loved dearly. I appeared once more for Max Reinhardt, but by that time I had been to England and considered myself grown up.

As I grew older, I became aware of loneliness, of silence and apprehension. Perhaps I was more aware of the fact that not everyone lived without a father or brother or sister. The realization that there was only my mother frightened me—it was a fear that something might happen to her. I could never still my terror when she was late in returning home—it would grow and grow until I would cry uncontrollably. I visualized her being killed, and the immensity of the thought that I would be left alone in the world was more than I could bear. I never lost that fear, even when I was sixteen, and it only began to lessen when I entered the Ballet Russe company and joined its big family.

THREE

Uncle Gui, who had connections in London, urged my mother to take me there. He would precede us and introduce us to some important people. Again I was taken out of school, and Mama and I set off on our next adventure.

In London Uncle Gui installed us in a boardinghouse somewhere in Bayswater, where we were euphemistically called paying guests. We had a small bedroom, very cold, and had to put a lot of shillings in the electric heater to keep warm. All our meals were taken in a communal dining room, where the food was pretty awful. The waiter had dirty fingernails and looked filthy. A dismal place; we did not stay there long.

To us London was an exotic city, a city with a mixture of people from all over the world. It was infinitely more cosmopolitan than Berlin. In retrospect, Berlin seemed restrictive and provincial, even in its architecture, in spite of its sophisticated and decadent reputation. In Berlin, we had felt a constant repression; in Paris, loneliness and apprehension; but in London, despite the dreary boardinghouse, we were happy. I came to love London and England more and more, and in my youth it was my second home.

Uncle Gui did indeed know important people and, if he didn't he bluffed. He took us first to Madame Marie Rambert, a formidable force in English ballet. She was famous for her exuberance. If her enthusiasm got the best of her, she would suddenly do cartwheels in class—an electrifying change from the austere classes of Eugenia Eduardova. I enjoyed being her pupil. She was a very good teacher and was responsible for developing countless excellent dancers. I remember the beauty of Pearl Argyle and Diana Gould—goddesses to a gangling thirteen-year-old girl.

Madame Rambert had a tiny theater attached to her school where she gave performances and encouraged young choreographers such as Antony Tudor and Frederick Ashton, later to become famous. She was a dedicated, courageous, and extraordinary woman who contributed a great deal to ballet in Britain.

Soon Uncle Gui took us to meet the famous dancer Anton Dolin. We went backstage to his dressing room after a performance. I was fascinated by his makeup, particularly that he outlined the shape of his lips with a black pencil. I had never seen anything like it. He looked me over and said I would have to dance for him. If I had been more knowledgeable, I might have been more frightened and awed by the impending event. Instead, it excited me. I faced the prospect in the way only a thirteen-year-old could and decided I would dance to my favorite music, the "Blue Danube Waltz."

Dolin lived on Glebe Place in Chelsea. It was a charming little street dominated by his two-story studio with living quarters in the front and back. Dolin was a forceful personality, a little king among his own circle of friends and family. His mother was very much in the picture, equally strong, very Irish, with white hair. Pat was born Patrick Healy Kay. When he joined the Ballets Russes it was Diaghilev who christened him Anton Doline (he later dropped the *e*). He had been very successful and at that time was the most famous male dancer next to his rival, Serge Lifar.

On the appointed day, I changed to my white Eduardova uniform and danced for him. I improvised with a total lack of concern or inhibition. Dolin accepted me and I immediately began studying with him. He did not have a school but only special pupils. Alicia Markova, then coming into the years of her greatest fame, took lessons with him and soon caused me to despair; everything she did was so perfect. Her body was of an ethereal thinness, which made me feel even in my boylike adolescence like a Valkyrie. Her feet, the execution of her steps, her lightness, her authority—it was all too much to bear. Dolin made one condition: I was to stop taking classes with Madame Rambert and study exclusively with him.

Mama and I soon found other "paying guest" lodgings and moved into Chelsea very near Pat, this time with a nice, easygoing young woman. I remember that we had roast beef every Saturday (or was it lamb?) and cold meat on Sundays.

London was then, perhaps more than any other city, oriented to ballet. Berlin had been the fountain of modern dance, with Mary Wigman, Palucca, Harald Kreutzberg, and Niddy Impekoven among its famous dancers. Perhaps the serious intellectual form of modern dancing suited the German soul. I could never love it the way I loved ballet, even as a child. The whole romanticism of ballet, its discipline, and perhaps even mysticism, appealed to me and was all I was seeking. For the first time, I felt that I was on the threshold of great ballet and about to enter its world.

Dolin worked with me a great deal. I had shown him proudly all my acrobatic feats, because, being unusually flexible, I could do incredible contortions. Instead of being impressed, he practically shouted that I could either continue that nonsense or study ballet, but not both. I was to stop at once and never do them again. He said I needed a strong back for ballet and that acrobatics were in complete contradiction. I obeyed and gave up acrobatics from that day.

Dolin began to work with me as a partner. He taught me adagio and *pas de deux* and the intricacies of partnering. It was very exciting to learn. It was also a very new experience to be that close to a man. It embarrassed me and made me slightly uncomfortable. And yet I knew that it also attracted me. I did my best to hide my feelings and tried to be as businesslike as Pat. He choreographed a *pas de deux* for us to the slow movement of César Franck's Symphony, and I remember the beginning of it to this day. He then announced that I was to dance with him during an engagement he had at Grosvenor House. It was pretty heady stuff for so young a girl.

London was a turning point in our life, Mama's and mine. Although we were to return to Berlin again, I knew then what I wanted and the direction I would have to take. I felt that nothing could stop me. There was only dancing and the necessary work involved in becoming a great dancer. Nothing else mattered. I also turned from a child into a young girl, with the stirrings of a young girl. I had developed a terrific crush on Pat. I adored him with a mixture of tremendous gratitude for having faith in me and a quite realistic feeling of admiration for so great a dancer and so dashing a man—dear Pat.

I don't know how my mother managed in London. I only know that at one point she gave some of her Norwegian silver to Pat for much needed cash. But manage she did, as she always had and was to do for the years of struggle ahead.

————

Anton Dolin had been asked to go to Berlin to dance in a production of Offenbach's opera *The Tales of Hoffmann*, directed by Max Reinhardt, and since I was his pupil and sometime partner, he took me along. So my mother and I were back in Berlin. The year was 1931. It was an extraordinary production and may have been Max Reinhardt's last theatrical effort in Berlin. Reinhardt had engaged Bronislava Nijinska to do the choreography. She was the sister of the great dancer. Other dancers engaged were Nini Theilade, a lovely Dutch girl who later joined the Ballet Russe;

a fine German male dancer, an ex-pupil of Eduardova; and Kyra Nijinsky, daughter of the legendary Nijinsky. Dolin had terrific fights with Nijinska. They shouted at each other across the footlights during rehearsals. Perhaps he had expected to do the choreography himself and was irritated.

Having a solo in the first act gave me the opportunity to watch Max Reinhardt directing the chorus. Young as I was, I understood his method very well, because choreographers worked in the same detailed manner. The chorus was large for the scene in which Olympia, the mechanical doll, comes alive. They were all standing in a circle around her. Reinhardt walked among the chorus and talked to each member individually, touching their heads and bodies to move them into related and apposite positions, or taking their hands and even fingers, bending or curling them until the entire chorus had an alive and disunited unity.

I also danced briefly in the second act, choreographed in the *commedia dell'arte* style. As usual, the music ravished me and I tried to hang around for the third act to hear Jarmila Novotna sing, rather than go home obediently when I was fetched by the faithful Uncle Gui. I particularly loved the Barcarole of the second act, which was magnificently staged. It had two revolving stages—the outer one clockwise, the inner counterclockwise. The illusion was extraordinary, as the gondola with Giulietta moved from stage left under a bridge (which two black-clad stagehands were slowly moving), passed a second gondola coming from upstage, and finally stopped stage center at a brilliantly lit palazzo. A wide staircase led up to an inner hall, where crystal chandeliers could be seen and, while footmen holding lit candelabra greeted Giulietta, she slowly mounted the stairs and, to the last strains of music, disappeared into the palazzo. I don't think I have ever seen anything to equal it.

After this engagement, I remained in Berlin. At fourteen, I was past the mandatory age for formal schooling. Mama made sporadic attempts to enlist private tutors. She tried to be serious about it, but neither one of us pursued it. Whatever the earnest teacher tried to impart seemed to be totally irrelevant, and soon was given up for good. I began studying ballet with Victor Gsovsky. He and his wife, Tatiana, were gifted young Russians. He was a rather flamboyant teacher, but although I probably picked up some bad habits, it was also liberating.

One of the students was Kyra Nijinsky, whom I had met during the Max Reinhardt production. She became my closest friend and, in class, my rival. She was three years older than I, and one might imagine that the gap between fourteen and seventeen was considerable, but it made no difference to us. We became inseparable and I drank in every word she said. Kyra came from an exotic, unhappy world. She had led a nomadic life and spoke bitterly of her mother, Romola Nijinsky. She was constantly boarded out and, as a seventeen-year-old, was living alone in Berlin. Kyra was convinced that she had to act in a "crazy" manner, and even went so far as to throw fits, writhing on the floor. As Nijinsky's daughter, she said it was the only way people paid attention to her. It was, she said bitterly, what they expected from her. She was very advanced intellectually, in a rather brilliant, manic way, and gave me long lectures, jumping from poetry to metaphysics to philosophy.

Kyra looked extraordinarily like her father. Her face was beautiful, Slavic, with high cheekbones and green eyes. She had the same rather thick neck as her father and held her head in the same way, tilted in a slightly suspicious manner. Her body too resembled her father's, but that was a pity. Nijinsky's stocky, short, powerful body was unfortunate for a girl. It merely looked dumpy. To make matters worse, Kyra also had a very large bust. She imitated her father in every way. Her practice clothes were exactly like his: a white shirt with rolled-up sleeves, open at the throat; black tights held up by a leather belt; and the soft dance shoes worn by men. She also used a kerchief on her head, tied exactly like her father's. She tried to dance like him and looked astonishingly similar, especially in her neck, arms, and hands. But a girl could not dance like a man, especially a girl who looked so womanly.

Kyra spoke to me a lot about her father's hands. She quoted Nijinsky as saying: "Watch a baby and see how relaxed the hands are. Round and curled without any strain in the fingers." And she would illustrate it. I have never forgotten those words and can never look at photographs without noticing hands. How often they show tension even in some of the greatest dancers. Our destinies parted us and we remet in Paris only on the eve of her marriage to Igor Markevitch. For a while we lived in a pension in Berlin. I had a big room for myself and clearly had reached the stage where a room of one's own was a privilege. Kyra and I spent many intense afternoons there.

My mother had very nice friends who owned a little miniature dachshund called Topsy. Although I was fond of Mama's friends, I frequently bicycled over only to see Topsy. On one of those visits Mrs. Cay was very agitated. Topsy had caught a mouse, which must be killed. I could not bear the thought and pleaded with her to let me have it. Finally she relented and put the mouse in a large glass jar, with which I bicycled home. The poor little gray thing, crouched in her glass cage, was trembling. I rushed to create a cozy nest, putting some rags inside, a nice piece of cheese, and some ham, but the mouse still trembled. I got an electric heating pad, plugged it in, and wrapped it around the jar. Then I discovered it was time for my class and rushed out. When I got home there was a peculiar smell in my room. The glass jar had become hotter and hotter and the poor little mouse had suffered a far worse death than if Mrs. Cay had quickly drowned it. My horror was indescribable and I could not get over my mouse "murder" for days.

Shortly afterward Mama found a nice apartment and we moved again. Mama never minded moving. On the contrary, she adored furnishing a flat and had a real flair for decorating. She very soon made it extremely attractive. We were happy to be in our own apartment, where each had her own bedroom, in addition to a living room, including a small balcony, and a fourth room, which I grandly used as my "studio." I cannot say I missed the pension, but I missed having other people around me. Now we two were alone again, and many times I came home late in the afternoon to an empty apartment.

On returning one evening, I found our front door open. I called out but there was no answer. In the entrance hall the door to the living room stood open. When I went in, I froze. The furniture was scattered, the armoire door stood gapingly open, objects were strewn. An evil presence was in the air. I turned toward my mother's room, and had to force myself to go in. I was terrified she was dead, murdered. I entered slowly. The room was an indescribable mess, but it was empty. I slowly crossed the living room again and went into my room. Here too everything was upset, but that no longer mattered to me. Suddenly my mother arrived, laden with packages. She looked around in amazement and began a barrage of questions. No, I had not screamed; no, I had not run out into the hall; I had just arrived and was too frightened to . . . Mama instantly realized what had happened. She had met two men with large bags at the ground-floor entrance. Seeing her, they had politely held the door open. She had thanked them, little realizing that they were carrying out our silver, her fur coat, my record player, and so on. Mama was furious over our combined stupidity, but both of us simmered down and were glad that nothing worse had happened. It was the first of many burglaries I was to experience, and each time I sensed the same almost tangible presence of evil.

I was engaged to tour with a small company which billed itself as the Dayelma Ballet and played mostly posh music halls. We went to glamorous places like Vienna, Budapest, and Rome. A young acrobatic dancer with an English stage name, Dinah, was part of the company and had an important solo. She had incredibly long legs and performed her slow contortions beautifully. We became good friends and shared our hotel rooms. I envied her secretly. Later she married a famous film star, Willy Fritsch, and I was not surprised: she had a lot of glamour.

It rained continuously in Vienna and I can't remember anything nice about it. But Budapest! We loved the gypsy music in cafés, although we were a bit embarrassed when the strolling violinist played too ardently in our left ear (always the left). The men seemed to be so good-looking and we had many admirers, though Dinah had more than I.

Our coffee with whipped cream (*Schlag*) was brought to our room in the morning and we reveled in the luxury. Although we were strict virgins, both aged fifteen, we were blossoming into young women. That became even more apparent in Rome. Men followed us whispering ardent Italian phrases. One night, returning from the theater, I got so enraged that I turned around, stamped my foot, and stuck out my tongue at them. Needless to say, it produced only loud laughter and was not very effective.

I remember that one of the big dance numbers was a French cancan where, traditionally, each girl has a little solo and the opportunity to knock herself out topping her previous "rival" with higher kicks, faster turns, and ending her solo by leaping in the air and then crash-landing in a split on the floor. One night I was wilder than usual because some of the girls had put itching powder in my costume and I thought I'd go mad onstage—ah well, there was nothing to be done but laugh with the rest.

———

After my Dayelma engagement I returned to Berlin and continued daily classes with Gsovsky. He and Tatiana planned to form their own small ballet company. Four girls, a male dancer, and Eva Brigitta Hartwig as the star! Gsovsky choreographed it and Tatiana designed the costumes. Its theme was "Dance through the

Ages" and began with a Gothic dance—I remember a magnificent headdress—then rather rapidly advanced through Watteau and Directoire sequences, winding up with a beautiful fluid, modern *pas de deux*. We opened at the Wintergarten in Berlin, had fine reviews, and were considered a success.

There were other signs that I was being noticed. Karl Vollmoeller, the renowned author of *The Miracle*, asked me to a party at his apartment on Unter den Linden, opposite the famous Adlon Hotel. My best dress at the time was of black velvet with a demure lace collar. I appeared in it at the party and seemed totally out of place. A chaste nymphet let loose in Sodom and Gomorrah! I wandered to a floor below, where it was extremely dark; as my eyes became adjusted, I saw couples everywhere moving around peculiarly on velvet cushions. I did not know that Vollmoeller was famous for his orgies.

One night after the performance, when I came out of the stage door at the Wintergarten, to my amazement I saw tanks rumbling by. The sky was red and people ran by shouting: "The Reichstag is on fire—the Reichstag is burning!" It was February 27, 1933. Germany was turning into Hitler's Third Reich.

———

Our engagement at the Wintergarten was followed by a tour of Italy and Scandinavia. I was considered very Garboesque by the Italians, with my long blond hair and blue eyes. Actually, their behavior was really quite harmless, with their *"Bella signorina, bella signorina."* But it began to dawn on me that I might be growing up to be beautiful. Beauty seemed to be a kind of power, a gift that you were given. Nothing to be proud of, like an achievement or like mastering something difficult in dancing, but something which obviously impressed people.

My bust began to develop in an alarming fashion. I told my mother how awful it was and asked when it would stop. She said, "You will be grateful for it later on," in the typically oblique manner in which she answered all sexual questions. Meanwhile, my body proceeded in its hormonal way and became totally disproportionate. The body of a boy with two huge globular breasts! It was not appreciated by me.

I began to love Italy, like most Northern Europeans—the warmth and the sun were a relief after the cool reticence and formality I was used to. The *pensione* in Rome where I stayed was like an instant family—friendly and affectionate. Late one night we drove to the Colosseum and clambered around inside with a full moon as our only source of illumination—it was scary, awesome, and utterly beautiful. How dark Rome was in those days before the war—no neon lights, blaring radios, and Vespas roaring through the streets. I loved all those dim, dark, narrow streets and faintly illuminated piazzas.

After Rome we went to Turin for a few performances at a large exposition which was being held outside the city. One day I took a walk up a hill and found myself surrounded by bushes with tiny white flowers which emitted the intoxicating scent of jasmine. I stood there entranced, and for the first time heard the faint sounds of Ravel's *Bolero*, which was being rehearsed in a distant concert hall.

We wound up our tour in Sweden. I had finally bought Mama a Pekinese puppy and we had to smuggle it in, since Sweden had a quarantine period for dogs. Whenever you crossed the border into another country, the train would stop and the customs officials would enter every compartment and go through the luggage. Suitcases had to be hauled down from the luggage racks, and the whole procedure created a big commotion. It was rather nerve-racking, even when you were totally innocent—and smuggling in a puppy was definitely not innocent. I sat next to the window and hid the dog under my skirt. I also pretended to have a terrible cold, and coughed my lungs out to drown the puppy's whining. My heart pounded, but at the same time it was exciting. All went well, but on our arrival in Stockholm we behaved very stupidly. On leaving the train, we carried the pup openly past the same official. We brazened it out, smiling sweetly at him; luckily, he did nothing.

We had heard that the Swedes bathed in the nude and couldn't wait to see that. They did indeed, but only the old and fat people, as we young dancers cruelly called them. Our contemporaries all wore bathing suits. We danced in some pretty crummy "theaters." I remember one place with a tiny stage where I danced alone. "Out front" were tables and chairs where happy burghers drank beer or a glass of wine. It was rather noisy, even rowdy, but it made no difference to me. I performed as best I knew how, in a way dancing for myself and trying to please the severest critic of them all: Eva Brigitta Hartwig.

———

Moving backward in time, making the mind relive adolescence and young life, is a curious experience. It is feeling pain without hurt, joy without delight, ambition without desire, speed without running, exertion without sweat. It is an echo of passion, like love remembered—love which has mellowed, forgiven, and accepted.

———

I had turned sixteen when Karl Vollmoeller proposed to my mother in a very proper manner that I be allowed to come to Venice and stay in his palazzo on the Grand Canal. I would be chaperoned by a young German couple, Count and Countess York. He, of course, would look after me. He was leaving by car, and there would be a one-night stopover in Switzerland. Of course, I was wild to go and pleaded with my mother until she finally said yes. We did stop over one night, and I put a chair under the doorknob of my bedroom. Vollmoeller laughed and laughed when he found out, and nicknamed me *Die eiserne Jungfrau* [the Iron Maiden]. He made me feel ridiculous. After driving the next day, we arrived in Venice at midnight. It was to be one of the great moments of my life.

After hurtling through various landscapes for two days, we were suddenly in a world of slow motion. It was dark as our gondola moved silently through long, narrow canals, finally emerging into the Grand Canal. We came alongside a large palazzo, where the entrance was open and a wide staircase and crystal chandeliers could be seen in the interior. We had arrived at Palazzo Vendramini! The reverse of *The Tales of Hoffmann* had happened to me. Reality was even more beautiful than what Max Reinhardt was able to create with music, lights, and theatrical magic. But then who could ever totally catch the elusive quality and mystery of Venice? Vollmoeller rented the palazzo for six months each year. He occupied the two top floors. I was given an enormous bedroom with an equally enormous four-poster bed. The next morning, when I opened the shutter, I discovered that it looked out over a large garden, with the Grand Canal beyond it. Later I saw a commemorative plaque on the wall, revealing that Richard Wagner had died at Palazzo Vendramini during a visit to Venice in 1883.

Vollmoeller left after three days, and I remained with Ruth and David York. I had been worried that I too would have to leave, and was delighted that he left me behind for another week. Our days quickly fell into a pattern. We lived in total grandeur but had practically no money between us. We ate a filling breakfast: an egg yolk beaten with sugar. After that we walked to the Hotel Danieli to take the motorboat to the Lido. During the morning on the beach, we hoped we would be invited to lunch, and usually were. If we were not invited to dinner, we ate spaghetti. The Lido was filled with rich people, ranging from the aristocracy to industrialists to artists. Everybody who was somebody tried to be in Venice in September, which meant living in Venice but spending the day at the Lido on the beach of the Hotel Excelsior.

Rich Italians who owned palazzi in Venice would arrive in their own motorboats, accompanied by two menservants with food for lunch. After they transferred to gondolas, the two men would also serve as their private gondolieri, rowing at either end of the boat in the perfect rhythm practiced throughout the history of Venice. The gondolieri, dressed in traditional white sailor suits, wore cummerbunds in the particular colors of the family they worked for—somewhat like racing colors for jockeys. For special occasions they wore a silk sash diagonally across their chest, with the tasseled ends crossed and fastened on their left hip. The color was also repeated in ribbons around their straw hats, which would fly in the wind when they rowed fast. You could always tell whose gondola it was by the colors of the gondolieri. On the Lido it was their duty to set table, put out linen, and serve the food and wine.

Days on the Lido had an indolent rhythm devoted to a bit of swimming, lazing in the sun, and gossiping. People who had neither palazzi nor gondolieri had their lunch at the hotel. One ate on the terrace and ogled other people. In 1933 Barbara Hutton was pointed out to me. She was a young, plump, pretty American who had just married one of the Mdivani princes. I had no interest in her. I did, however, have a great interest in the fact that Serge Lifar was on the Lido. His was a magical name for me—one of Diaghilev's two great male dancers who had succeeded Nijinsky, the other being Dolin. I longed to meet Lifar.

One day I swam out to a raft. Trying to hoist myself up, I scratched my legs on barnacles which were attached to the underside. My thighs were a mass of red streaks. A little later a man came swimming out, and when he was closer I was thrilled to see it was Lifar. I warned him about the barnacles and we were soon in conversation. I told him that I was a dancer and how much I admired him. Out of this chance meeting came another memorable experience for me. The Princess San Faustino gave a charity ball each year. Lifar had agreed to dance and now asked me to be his partner. I couldn't believe my ears. He wanted to do the *pas de deux* from *Les Sylphides*, and he needed a nymph for *L'Après-midi d'un faune*. We began rehearsals. I had no costumes. Princess Natasha Paley, who worked for Molyneux in Paris, gave me some dresses, which were converted into costumes We had a great success.

The ball had delayed my departure and furious telegrams began arriving from Dolin. I was to appear with him in a ballet play about a dancer, called *Ballerina*. Dolin had chosen me and rehearsals had begun. Where, he asked, was I? Of course I had by now developed a crush on Lifar, but after the ball I had to leave. My wonderful Venetian holiday had come to an end. I had had the best possible guide in David York, who taught me to walk all over Venice. I had tasted my first Alexander cocktail, a concoction made from brandy and cream, and smelled my first gardenia. I had fallen totally in love with Venice and would return many, many times—but now I had to be on my way to a less romantic place: Liverpool.

Ballerina was written by Lady Eleanor Smith, daughter of Lord Birkenhead. It was really a play with music and dancing, not in musical-comedy style, but alternating dramatic scenes with balletic interludes. The leading role was portrayed by Frances Doble, a beautiful dark-haired actress. Dolin trained her and she actually danced a *Swan Lake pas de deux*, very skillfully partnered by Dolin. The play opened with the farewell performance of a retiring ballerina, danced to perfection by Lydia Kyasht, herself a "retired" ballerina. It then showed the life of a young girl being trained as a dancer—her rise, fame, and decline. Toward the end of the play, a new young dancer appeared to complete the circle.

The balletic interludes were danced by Wendy Toye, who wore a mask of Frances Doble's face. Several other dancers participated, including Freddie Franklin. He and Wendy became prominent dancers and Wendy is today a choreographer-producer.

My role was that of the rising young dancer and I had a *pas de deux* with Dolin at the end of the play. Wendy and I shared a dressing room, which was usually occupied by her mother, my mother, and Freddie. Wendy had at least eight dance interludes to perform and kept going in and out of the dressing room. She and

Freddie were very much in love and Wendy took every opportunity to kiss Freddie: "Goodbye, Freddie dear!" "Hello, Freddie dear!" That made sixteen kisses a night. She would pace back and forth backstage before each entrance and let off steam, literally, wherever the need arose. I think she thought that the mask protected her identity and that no one realized who had fired off these salvos.

We opened in London and were a good success. Dolin had insisted that I be billed under the single name of Brigitta. That is how I first became known in London. Nicholas Legat had moved to London from Paris, and I began taking classes with him again. His studio was very large and airy—much better than the small stuffy studio on Place Pigalle. I loved him as much as ever, both as a teacher and a dear little old man. I traveled every day on the Underground for class with him from yet another "paying guest" establishment, this time on Queens Gate Road. It was in one of the rows of endless similar houses which had two steps up and, at the entrance, two columns on each side. There was nothing to distinguish one from another, block after block. Still, the location was the poshest we had lived in and the establishment the nicest. Our "hostess" was an eccentric lady never without a cigarette in her mouth, drooping from her lips like a German cabaret singer's. She liked séances, and my mother joined these evenings with enthusiasm. I attended once and never again. We sat around a table touching each other's hands with outstretched fingers. The table began to move and silly questions were asked like "Are you there?" "Yes!" banged the table once. "Do we know you?" "No!"—two bangs. But it was when the table suddenly moved across the floor with everybody trying to follow without breaking the ring formed by their hands, with chairs scraping and falling backward, that I became hysterical with laughter. I laughed totally out of control and lost control in another manner. When the hoopla subsided, I grabbed a chair and backed out of the room.

In 1932 the great new excitement in the ballet world was the formation of Colonel de Basil's Ballet Russe de Monte Carlo. Colonel de Basil had gathered together the scattered forces of the Diaghilev company, which had come to an abrupt end in 1929 on the death of the great impresario. Though many of the illustrious names of the Diaghilev Ballet did not join de Basil, he did find three extremely young, brilliant dancers who were nicknamed "baby ballerinas" by the adoring British ballet public. They were Irina Baronova, Tamara Toumanova, and Tatiana Riabouchinska. They created a sensation with their high-speed technique and young beauty. The artistic head of the company was Léonide Massine, famous primarily as a choreographer but also as an arresting character dancer. The first time I saw the company, in 1934, I was bedazzled.

It appeared that Massine had seen a performance of *Ballerina*, and through Dolin, he invited me to join the company. I was not present at the scene which took place, but I was told that Dolin was furious and accused Massine of trying to take me away from him. Massine countered by saying that it would be good for my career to join the Ballet Russe, that Dolin had nothing particular to offer me after the run of *Ballerina*, and they parted on very bad terms.

When I heard of it, I was thrilled that Massine wanted me in the company and pleaded with Dolin to let me join and not to think me ungrateful if I did. I argued that it would give me a great opportunity to develop as a classical dancer: the daily performances, the variety of roles, being literally surrounded by distinguished dancers, and concentrating totally on ballet.

Just at that time, Alexandra Danilova, prima ballerina of the company, decided to accept an offer to appear in *The Great Waltz* in a New York production. Massine renewed his offer to me, with the promise that I would be given the Danilova role of the cancan dancer in *Boutique Fantasque*. If I joined, I was to make my debut in that role dancing with him. Arnold Haskell, the distinguished

ballet critic and writer, helped me in the negotiations with the
régisseur général, M. Serge Grigoriev. The first telegram is dated
March 10, 1934, and the second April 2.

BRIGITTA HARTWIG C/O HASKELL

31 CONDUIT STREET   LONDON

OFFER CONTRACT ONE YEAR TERMS AS ARRANGED WITH DE BASIL FOR
GREAT BRITAIN AND AMERICA STOP OTHER COUNTRIES 2200 FRANCS PER
MONTH ALL TRAVELLING SECOND CLASS OUR CHARGE STOP THIS OFFER
HOLDS GOOD ON CONDITION YOU COME MONTE CARLO BEFORE 16 APRIL
WIRE DATE DEPARTURE—GRIGORIEV

BRIGITTA HARTWIG C/O HASKELL

31 CONDUIT STREET   LONDON

ALL RIGHT HURRY COME MONTE CARLO WILL REFUND TRAVELLING
EXPENSES ON YOUR ARRIVAL—GRIGORIEV

Meanwhile, Pat Dolin continued to fight against it and wrote a
lengthy letter to my mother:

66, Glebe Place
Chelsea
14th April 1934

My dear Bille,

Thanks so much for your letter. It was rather awful about *Ballerina*
but I am afraid it was expected.

The last three days have been ones of much conversation, once
more about the ballet. After many talks with Brigitta I ascertained
she would prefer to stay here and do my play than go to Monte Carlo.
This, of course, meant that I would have to be in a position to say
"Yes" or "No." The matter is now settled and my play will go into
rehearsal at the end of this month.

She leaves tonight for Scotland, to stay for the week end with
Inverclyde, and she will probably come to Berlin on Wednesday
next to stay as you suggest until the end of the month, when she must
come back for rehearsals of the play. I will send her contract with
her so that you can sign it and then all is in order.

On Tuesday next I, myself, begin a film which will occupy me for about ten days. I have a very good part to play and I also dance. They would use Brigitta in the dance with me and if she cares to do it her departure for Berlin will be delayed for about three days. She has been down at the studios with me quite a lot during the filming of the *Chu Chin Chow* dances. They have been a great success and look marvelous on the screen. I introduced her to the German director Berthold Viertel (I think this is how you spell his name). He also would like Brigitta in his film in a short dance sequence, but that is for her to decide.

I have telegraphed Massine in Monte Carlo that I regret I am unable to let Brigitta join the company now as I need her for my play. I am taking all the responsibility for this upon my own shoulders so that the only person he can be cross with is me and not Brigitta. I presume you will return with Brigitta or else arrive in time for the opening of the play. I may possibly come to Berlin myself for a day or two.

My love dear, as always, Pat

The play in question was *Precipice*, which unfortunately opened and quickly closed. As Dolin had no further specific plans, there was now no holding me back. I wanted to join the Ballet Russe more than anything else in the world. I don't think my mother was very pleased. She saw that our struggle would start all over again, just as we seemed to be doing a little bit better financially. My new salary, I believe, was about $175 a month, which I think was pushed up to $200. My mother could sail with me and the company to America for its annual tour, but only to New York and not to Mexico, where we were to open the Bellas Artes Theater and have a two-week season. Mama would have to stay behind in New York. I suppose there was no arguing with me. I could not be persuaded otherwise. I joined the Ballet Russe in London during its season at Covent Garden in 1934.

Vera Zorina was born, aged seventeen, at Covent Garden, during a heated discussion with Colonel de Basil, general director of the Ballet Russe de Monte Carlo. Two days before I was to make my debut, I was told to go to his office. I rushed down from the stage to the caverns of Covent Garden in my practice clothes, irritated at being interrupted during rehearsals. It was similar to being summoned to the principal's office.

Colonel de Basil generally adopted a paternal attitude. He did so now with me. "Brigittushka," he began, "you must now choose a Russian name." "Why?" was the natural answer. "Because, my dear, you are now a member of the Ballet Russe." I still said, "Why?" "Because, my dear," he continued, "if every member who is not Russian keeps their own name, the ballet is not Russian ballet anymore, you understand?" "Yes, but . . ." I tried. "Is no but," de Basil continued. "Here is a list of Russian names. You choose." There were twenty names on the list, all of them unpronounceable except the very last one at the bottom—Vera Zorina. I said, "That one," and gave him back the list. He squinted at it and said, "Very good, my dear." He kissed me, or rather I was obediently allowed to kiss him. I made a short curtsy and went back to rehearsal. I had no intention of keeping that name, but it stuck.

Colonel de Basil was a tall, gaunt man, usually half smiling behind his thick glasses—a smile which never seemed quite sincere. His rather syrupy way of ingratiating himself was in contrast to stories of his days as a Cossack in the Imperial Russian Army. It was hard to imagine his plump silky hands holding a gun and shooting people during the revolution.

A strict hierarchy existed in the company and a definite rule of *politesse* had to be observed. On top of the pyramid was Colonel de Basil and Mme de Basil. Mme de Basil favored elaborately made-up eyes with long individually beaded eyelashes and rouged Cupid-bow lips. She took herself seriously and expected respectful behavior from the rest of the company. For the first encounter of the day we, the younger members of the company, had to curtsey and kiss her on both cheeks. She received this as her due.

Next in the hierarchy came Monsieur and Mme Grigoriev. M. Grigoriev, as company manager or régisseur, ruled supreme in all matters, answerable only to Colonel de Basil. He was a man of immense experience and had occupied the same position with Diaghilev in the Ballets Russes. He had made himself indispensable to Diaghilev, who had trusted him completely. Grigoriev was very firm and weathered all storms, but once in a while one felt the touch of a soft heart. Mme Grigorieva, who as Lubov Tchernicheva had been a distinguished dancer in the Diaghilev company, was semi-retired. Mme Grigorieva too had to be kissed each morning. Their son, Vsevolod, was the assistant stage manager. In the event that the impresario Sol Hurok traveled with the company, Mme Hurok was given first obeisance.

The hierarchy did not mix socially with the rest of the company, except on the occasion of big parties. Even then members formed their various groups. In spite of these amenities, I had joined a barbaric island where violent storms were a daily occurrence. Jealousies seethed between Mama Toumanova and Mama Baronova. The two mothers were part of the company. Mama Baronova worked in the costume department and Mama Toumanova's husband in the scenic department. Both mothers were extremely ambitious for their daughters, possibly more ambitious than the daughters themselves. They were both excellent, strong, young dancers, and Tamara especially, a startlingly beautiful dark-haired girl.

Both girls alternately danced the leading roles, and their mothers fought fiercely over who would dance the opening performance in London, New York, Philadelphia, Los Angeles and, even more importantly, *who* would dance the premiere of a new ballet. The third ballerina, Tatiana Riabouchinska, was somewhat outside that rivalry, because her style was different. She was slightly older, was very light with a high elevation, and usually danced more special roles, often choreographed specifically for her. Danilova was impervious to these internecine wars. She had earned the title "prima ballerina" in the Diaghilev company and all the important classical roles belonged to her. To a seventeen-year-old, a dancer over thirty seemed rather old. With the unthinking cruelty of the young, I thought it quite amazing that Alexandra Danilova still danced so well. She was every inch a prima ballerina on and off the stage—always carefully groomed, makeup and hair in place, practice clothes neat and feminine, pretty bandeaus for her head, and her body liberally doused with eau de cologne.

The natural hauteur which most of the Russian ladies in the company possessed and practiced was carried even further with Danilova, who had a habit of cocking her head to one side and managing from that position to appraise you with sidelong, critical glances. You felt that you were being scrutinized physically and that every piece of clothing was being evaluated as to its suitability. Many years later, in 1943, when I made guest appearances in San Francisco with Ballet Theatre, a company of which Danilova was then a member, Sol Hurok gave me a lecture on why I should not arrive at the theater by trolley car, looking windblown, but that I should wear a hat with a veil; he cited Danilova as an example of what a star should look and behave like. He was unmoved when I pointed out that the trolley cars in San Francisco were fun and that I didn't want to spend all my money on taxicabs.

Danilova had wonderful legs—long and beautifully formed, with narrow knees and ankles. They were slender but feminine, one might almost say sexy. Her technique was not particularly strong, but she was a commanding, authoritative dancer and definitely a strong presence on the stage. I used to watch her from the wings particularly when she danced *Firebird*. It suited her imperiousness, and one could believe that this was a strange, royal, even mystical bird. But she seemed to have a special flair for roles like the street dancer in *Blue Danube* and the cancan dancer in *Boutique Fantasque*. A natural, wicked *joie de vivre* emerged in these roles, and she danced them to perfection.

Danilova left the technical fireworks to the younger generation of dancers, who knocked themselves out with daring feats of triple pirouettes on toe, thirty-six *fouettés*, or hopping on one foot *à la seconde*, alternating with double pirouettes, high leaps, dangerous lifts, etc. She came from another tradition, another generation, when these bravura displays were perhaps considered a bit vulgar. She remained regal, controlled, and never quite stepped beyond a particular style in dancing, a style which goes beyond technique and is often the mark of greatness.

When Danilova left in the summer of 1934 for New York, her roles were quickly claimed by Baronova and Toumanova. I was promised another Danilova part, the dancer in *Blue Danube*, again a role which I danced with Massine. Because of the fierce competitiveness in the company, I was regarded with suspicion. I was isolated much like a fly which has hit a spider web. I posed a threat, though I, least of all, considered myself to be such. The fact that I had been promised two coveted major roles was enough to stir up jealousy. Very few people spoke to me, because there was a language problem, but neither did many people smile at me. The Russian language swirled around me and I could only guess, when I suspected that I was being discussed, whether it was friendly or not.

One of the few people who were kind to my mother and me was the conductor, Efrem Kurtz. Although we had never met, we discovered that his wife, born in Berlin, had lived next to us on the Bleibtreustrasse. At least my mother had found a pleasant companion now. The company had a sprinkling of non-Russian members, but most of them were Czechoslovakian or Polish.

My isolation became more apparent when I tried to learn my role in *Boutique Fantasque*, in which I was to make my debut. No one would teach it to me. Undaunted, I stood in the wings and watched Danilova and Massine dance the cancan, a very fast and lively *pas de deux*, to typical Rossini music. They danced it with ease, verve, dash, and gaiety. I quavered inside. It was not the kind of dance I was particularly good at.

I spoke to our stage manager, Serge Grigoriev, but he was strangely aloof and indicated that it was my own responsibility to learn the part. I was promised a rehearsal with Massine and, meanwhile, tried to learn as best as I could from the wings, squeezed in with all the mothers who were usually grouped there watching their daughters. I finally did have one rehearsal with Massine in the large upstairs studio of Covent Garden. I was petrified, and as a result not very good. We went through the dance several times, but without a stage or orchestra rehearsal, the performance loomed in a frightening manner. The prospect seemed to have none of the possibilities of success. It was happening too fast, too differently, and in an alien atmosphere.

As expected, my debut was joyless and not very auspicious. I had seen that the wings were packed with more mothers and onlookers than usual, and felt no well-meaning emanations coming from that direction. In a way, that audience frightened me more than the audience out front. The performance came and went, at least without mishap. I consoled myself with the fact that no one knew who Vera Zorina was anyway.

I quickly settled into the daily routine—company class at 10 a.m., followed by rehearsal from 11:30 a.m. to 1 p.m. Then, after lunch, rehearsals from 2:30 to 5 p.m. Back to the theater for performances by 7 p.m.

I was soon reprimanded for my appearance. Kyra Nijinsky had converted me to her style of dressing for class, which I found very grown-up and dashing: black wool tights, leather belt, and white shirt. Someone took me aside and told me to wear a *soutien-gorge*

[bra], to wear an extra pair of little black pants over my tights and, in addition, a short black tunic. I didn't own any of these items, so Mama and I had to buy them quickly, because by this time I was ashamed that I had ever appeared the way I did in the first place.

Bit by bit, I was eased into the company. My lackluster debut had taken the sting out of the animosity and apprehension felt toward me, and I was addressed as Brigittushka, an affectionate diminutive, or the more formal Zorina, accent on the first syllable. I discovered some English-speaking members. Prudence Hyman for one, a nice British dancer who had two bad habits. When she thought she had danced well, she would say, "It was just like butter, just like butter!" And when we occasionally roomed together on tour, she would drive me mad by getting up two hours earlier than necessary and packing each single item in tissue paper.

But Sono Osato became my closest friend. She was a lovely, delicate girl born in Chicago of a Japanese father and French-Irish mother. The mixture of elongated roundness, long, narrow hands and fingers, narrow waist, long neck, small, impish Oriental face, combined with the long legs and height of her mother, had produced a little masterpiece. Her skin was of such an extreme pallor, almost greenish at times, that I nicknamed her "my little green apple." Sono was full of fun, had a wicked gift for imitation, and a very inquisitive mind. It was Sono who, during my first American tour, introduced me to American customs, including eating turkey at Thanksgiving. Unfortunately, it was in a terrible little town and in one of those nondescript restaurants, so the meal, with its dry, rubbery turkey and blob of cranberry jelly, was not a success.

———

After a holiday during August, the company reassembled and sailed for America in the early days of September 1934 on the S.S. *Lafayette*. Sono, my mother, and I were assigned a cabin in the bowels of the ship. It consisted of two double-decker bunks and a washstand. Mama and Sono took the two lower bunks and I an upper. Mercifully, the fourth remained empty.

I slept literally under the pipes which ran across the ceiling. Mama and Sono spent the entire trip in their bunks being seasick. I spent the entire trip in a state of *joie de vivre,* running around feeling marvelous, excited by the journey and the prospect of seeing America. We were allowed to visit in first class, which added to the fun. During my brief appearances in the cabin, I tried to tell Mama and Sono all about it, but they just groaned and turned their faces to the wall. Changing my clothes was an ordeal, but even that I didn't mind.

We arrived late and docked in New York at night. In the dark the monolithic city rose before us as we slowly sailed toward it. The sight was everything I had anticipated and more. I had seen the illuminated skyscrapers in drawings, photographs, even in the theater when the scenery was supposed to reflect something sophisticated and typically American—but here was the reality! It had more of a fairy-tale look than anything the imagination could dream up. I was enthralled.

As we had to continue our journey to Mexico City, we were given special permission to transfer to the liner *Orizaba,* which was sailing that night for Veracruz. Amid the babble of French and Russian, suitcases and trunks, I bade my poor mother, who had to stay behind alone in New York, a tearful farewell. I was more upset for her than for myself.

Boarding the *Orizaba* after the transatlantic liner we had just left was something like leaving a city for a village. Our cabin was on the top deck, with windows opening out to the sea and wooden slats against the sun. It had the air of a Graham Greene novel set in a Latin country. As we sailed south and the weather became hotter and hotter, the Russian remedy was to sit on deck and drink hot tea. This made you perspire more, whereupon you drank more hot tea. And so it went until we arrived in Veracruz. The weather was boiling and confusion reigned on the dock. But in spite of the chaos, trunks were unloaded, suitcases found, and the entire company herded into the train for Mexico City. The Graham Greene atmosphere continued as we rattled and chugged through the lush Mexican landscape to the high altitude of Mexico City.

I remember Mexico City then as light and fast. Taxis drove at breakneck speed and the vivid Mexican colors were in strong contrast to the usually gray European buildings. Sono and I roomed together, and she initiated me into a different form of breakfast. She insisted that we start with orange juice. The idea of having a cold glass of fruit juice first thing in the morning rather than hot tea or coffee seemed to me lunacy, but she told me it was healthy, so I got used to it. There were no warnings about water, so we drank it out of the tap and ate everything in sight like good, hungry ballet dancers. We had salads and bought ice cream from street vendors and were never sick a day.

Our season was the occasion of the opening of the new Bellas Artes Theater, the building of which had begun twenty years before and been abandoned for lack of funds. It had sunk by ten feet in the intervening years, creating a sort of moat around it. I remember the vast murals of Orozco and Rivera in the halls of the theater. They were revolutionary in theme and style, and seemed to me strange and ugly after the European paintings I was used to. Obviously I was still ignorant of different expressions in art.

We rehearsed every day and pursued our insular life within another culture and environment. I was to dance *The Blue Danube* with Massine on opening night. Learning the part took precedence over anything else. A grand opening meant less to me than to dance the Street Dancer for the first time. We did not seem to be troubled by the high altitude of over 8,000 feet during rehearsals, but opening night was something else again. For the first and last time I took a hot bath in the afternoon of a performance, thinking it would be good for my muscles, not knowing that it is the worst thing you can do. It relaxes you far too much and makes you feel like a loose rubber band. I was tremendously excited before the performance and uncautious. You can never let all the stops out during a performance—something I learned that night—but must keep some power in reserve, husband your energy, learn how to breathe in quiet moments to refuel your resources. I did just the opposite. I danced all out and, when I should have breathed during pantomime scenes, acted all over the place. Eventually I found everything turning black and was barely able to distinguish between the front of the stage and the back. Only willpower and training got me to the wings, where I collapsed in a heap with Mama Toumanova fanning me and gently slapping my face, saying, Courage, Brigittushka, courage! I had nearly fainted, but had learned a hard lesson—namely, how to pace myself during a performance, something that nobody had taught me how to do and that I had to learn from experience.

I believe the audience thinks that a performer "has fun" during a performance or, as in the case of an actor, experiences the whole gamut of emotions he portrays. That is not so. If a dancer gives the illusion of fun or total ease, that's as it should be. The audience instinctively senses security in an artist, or the opposite, strain. It transmits itself in a mysterious way, even to the uninitiated. They may not be able to express what they sense, but they are aware of the difference between greatness and mediocrity.

When an audience is disappointed, there is usually a good reason for it. And when they are elated, they have been touched by the power of a mature artist—I mean mature in the knowledge of how to exercise his art. When I'm in the audience, be it for a concert, ballet, or theater, it is always the reservoir of power in an artist, the hidden resources, you might say, which impresses me—the total security a major artist transmits. Even if the spectator can't verbalize the impact it has created in him, he knows he has been touched. The cognoscenti might talk about the various techniques involved, but this is beyond technique. What we witness is the freedom which technical mastery has given the artist.

This does not, however, mean that the artist is lost in the pure pleasure of performing. On the contrary, he is in the midst of a cerebral tracking system. He is *producing* on a highly critical level and anticipating the next sound or step. Having previously mastered through endless discipline the sounds or steps, he is now trying to *reproduce* them until the refinements of his craft please him. He knows he is capable of it, having experienced it once before, and therefore it can be achieved again. What the spectator witnesses then is an endless distillation of rehearsals, performances eventually brought to perfection.

That is where the ultimate joy for a performer lies: knowing that what he gave an audience was also his own fulfillment, his own vision of himself, composed of myriad technical problems which only he could bring under control through years of work. The problems are of no concern to the audience—indeed should not be even remotely visible—since he has at last been able to transcend them in order to give an audience perfect ease, perfect pleasure.

It takes a long time to know all these things. The artist is really celebrating a victory over himself, harnessing his inner powers to obey him at the right place in the right time. There is nothing haphazard or accidental about it. It is learned, practiced, and presented. It is more urgent, more dangerous, more immediate than the presentations of composers, painters, or writers who can perfect their art in obscurity until they are ready. It is more fleeting, because it dies with the artist and lives only in the memory of the spectator.

———

We returned via Veracruz on another venerable vessel, the *Oriente,* and on arrival in New York I had only the briefest time for a tearful reunion with my mother before our train left for Toronto. While traveling through the Hudson Valley, I stood between railway cars with tears streaming down my face, because the thought of my mother once again left alone in New York was

Above, my father and mother at the time of their marriage. Below, the en-tire Wimpelmann family in Norway. My mother is second from the left.

Top, my father with his mother. Middle, sunbathing with my parents. Bottom, with Papa in Berlin. Opposite top left, posing after my debut; right, my first billing; bottom, with my classmates in Berlin.

Robertson, Berlin

Opposite top, my mother and I strolling with Tommy in Mis-Iroy. Middle left, age fourteen with Anton Dolin; right, with Dolin in LE BAL. *Bottom, rehearsing with Dolin for* THE TALES OF HOFFMANN; *Kyra Nijinsky, second from right; author, third from left. At right, above, solo in* THE TALES OF HOFFMANN; *below, Dolin and I in* pas de *deux to music of César Franck.*

Foto H. Mederer   *Brigitte Hartwig*   Pfeil-Foto-Pa

Opposite, age sixteen in the Gsovsky ballet in Berlin. Left, with Serge Lifar, Venice, 1933. Below, picnicking with my mother near Berlin.

2//to right. Baronova, Adrianova, Toumanova, Grigorieva Zorina, Riabouchinska, Danilova, Morosova, Verchinina Osato

A FAMOUS DANCING TROUPE RETURNS

Above, Ballet Russe arriving at New York in 1935. From left, Baranova, Adrianova, Toumanova, Grigorieva, Zorina, Riabouchinska, Danilova, Morosova, Verchinina, Sono Osato. At left, with Sono Osato at rehearsal. Below, at Santa Monica; Jasinsky holding Riabouchinska, Zorina on Shabelevsky's knee, Morosova, Baronova, Danilova lying on the sand.

Four photos of Léonide Massine. Left top, in FIREBIRD. Left bottom, a snapshot. Above, with author at Piestany. Below, at Santa Monica.

Opposite above, Marlene and I in Massine's trailer; below, the Schiaparelli jacket, London, 1937. Below, curtain call for ON YOUR TOES, *London, 1937. Following page, top, BBC television in 1937, pas de deux from* ON YOUR TOES. *Bottom, still from the London stage production.*

unbearable. She told me much later that it had been one of the hardest times in her life, living in a cheap hotel off Times Square and having virtually no money for a proper meal. Even considering that one could have a room for only $2.50 and that it was 1934, our combined resources of $175 to $200 a month often allowed my mother a doughnut and coffee a day and not much else.

The company settled in for our performances in Toronto. Sono and I roomed together again and played a childish prank late one night, one particularly inviting in so staid, red-carpeted, and formal a place as the King Edward Hotel. After all, we were only fifteen and seventeen years old. I hit on the splendid idea that it would be tremendous fun to shift all the shoes which people left outside their door at night to be polished from our floor to the floor below. After the performance, we gathered as many as we could, raced downstairs, placed them before doors, and took all the shoes from that floor up to ours. We slept through the early-morning confusion, which must have been considerable.

It was in Toronto that my life took a fateful turn. I was standing in the darkness of the wings one night watching *Les Sylphides* when Léonide Massine suddenly emerged and stood beside me. Just as suddenly he passed me a tiny rolled-up piece of paper the size of a stringbean and disappeared again. I went into the lighted corridor and read it. "Do come to Western Hospital (Butthurst St.) after performance. I shall go there with my doctor. I must see you. Don't go if you see I am not alone. Don't say word to anybody."

The terse message threw me into a turmoil. Massine was a god to me—our artistic administrator, our chief choreographer, not only *our* great choreographer but, at the time, one of the greatest in the world. He was more awesome to us than Colonel de Basil and he was also a most distant person. I had never exchanged more than a few words with him. One would have to understand the strict discipline by which we lived. We spoke to Massine only when he spoke to us first. During rehearsals we stood silently and obeyed instructions. Our respect was total. What I felt was boundless admiration, total hero worship, and an infatuation without thought or hope for anything further than silent worship. Sometimes I had found his dark eyes looking at me—but no more than that. I am certain that my feelings were no different from those of the other girls in the company.

I was too unsophisticated, too inexperienced to reason out the implications of the note. All I could think about during the next few hours was that he wanted to see me.

I went to the hospital and found him in a doctor's office, where he was receiving treatment for an injured knee. It was a mark of his artistic stature that a physician was willing to see him at that late hour. It did not surprise me. We were momentarily left alone and the unbelievable happened—he drew me to him and embraced me. I don't know where the words came from, but I heard myself saying, "I love you so." Words I had never spoken to any man before. We went for a drive around a park. We sat in the back seat holding hands, and nothing much was said, if anything at all, beyond his cautioning me again not to say anything to anyone. We parted at the hotel.

Sono was waiting up for me. I don't believe I kept my promise. It was too unbelievable to keep to myself. The unreality had to become reality. Only by telling Sono could I know that the dream-like experience was in fact true. The love affair had begun, and it was to be the most excruciating part of my two years in the ballet.

FOUR

have not forced my memory to give more than it was willing to. If certain periods of my life wished to remain dormant, I have accepted it, though sometimes in amazement that great emotions left so little residue. If I had not found the proverbial trunk, which had been stored in dusty cellars and somehow survived nearly fifty years, I would not have believed what I read in the diaries I kept from 1934. First of all, they were all in German, which I thought I had ceased to speak and write long before 1938— the last year I kept a detailed daily diary. Perhaps I used my *Kindersprache* as a form of code—after all, it was a language no one else spoke in the Ballet Russe. I wrote not only in my *Kindersprache* but very often in typical Berlin slang, which like all slang is untranslatable. I have left the entries in their simplistic, teenage form because it would be false to translate them otherwise.

Also in the trunk were letters and all those tiny scrolls which Léonide Massine had pressed surreptitiously into my hand and which invariably summoned me in great secrecy to a rendezvous. I might as well have been reading about somebody else, because

I remembered virtually nothing except some vague recollections that were like a break in a dense fog. Admittedly, fifty years is a long time, and one could be expected to forget what happened so long ago. It was not so much forgetting as not wanting to remember, because each reminder, no matter how slight, was painful. After 1936 I shunned everything that could have any connections with the past—even the ballet—and went forward to another life. I drew a veil over it, which turned into an impenetrable curtain, and after several years the great upheaval of my life was buried as if it had never happened. Resurrecting it now is still unpleasant, and I ask myself, What's the point? I have persisted because it was an important part of my life. It happened when I was still young enough for it to have made a considerable impact on my future and—who knows?—on what I am today.

———

Léonide Massine was nearly forty when I joined the company in 1934—old enough to be my father. He was a slightly built man, very thin, and rather short. His most arresting feature was his large, dark eyes, which had the perfect symmetry of Byzantine mosaics: portraits of men who gaze at us with strong, black, almost square eyebrows framing huge still eyes. His whole demeanor was formal and aloof. He was very grave and did not smile easily. His hands were short and stubby, but when dancing he used them to perfection. He had a powerful stage personality. When he danced he commanded instant attention, and even in pantomime sequences he remained the focus on the stage.

I used to watch him warming up backstage, hanging on to a piece of scenery while he did his barre with concentrated absentmindedness. I could see that he was getting stiff in his joints and that his back was as unbending as an ironing board. Still, he never failed to be electrifying on the stage and never betrayed the pain he must have had, particularly in his knees, which gave him constant trouble. He had started too late to become a first-rate classical dancer or *premier danseur noble,* but not too late to become a great character dancer and, even more importantly, one of the major choreographers of this century.

He was nineteen years old when Diaghilev discovered him in a drama school in Moscow. Diaghilev was planning to produce *Die Josephslegende* by Richard Strauss, with choreography by Michel Fokine, and was searching for a boy who could dance the title role. The unusual beauty of the young drama student seemed ideal for the role of Joseph. Diaghilev suggested that he leave the school and join the Ballets Russes.

Diaghilev was still suffering from the traumatic breakup of his relationship with Nijinsky, due to Nijinsky's abrupt and unexpected marriage to Romola de Pulszky. It seems that Massine soon filled that void and became Diaghilev's constant companion. Under the special tutelage of Enrico Cecchetti, the great Italian ballet master, Massine quickly developed into a fine dancer and made an auspicious debut in *Die Josephslegende.*

Diaghilev, who probably respected choreographers more than *premiers danseurs,* always steered his particular protégés in the direction of choreography. He tried to educate them in avant-garde music and painters, and subjected them to long visits to museums— a practice which Massine later continued and advocated. He was very intelligent and quickly absorbed the cultural influence Diaghilev exposed him to.

During the First World War, after studying assiduously with a young Spanish flamenco dancer, Massine produced one of his finest ballets, called *Le Tricorne,* set to Manuel de Falla's music, with sets by Picasso. He himself danced the leading role, and no matter where he performed it, he always brought down the house with the "Farruca."

For a man so grave, he had great comic abilities and often reminded me of Chaplin. But he also had nobility and beauty. He could transform himself into a clown, a proud flamenco dancer, or be an absolutely regal Russian prince. Massine studied art, a habit he probably acquired through Diaghilev's influence. I deliberately say "studied" rather than "appreciated," because he used various styles and compositions of painters in his choreography. For instance, when he was choreographing a ballet to the music of Berlioz's *Symphonie Fantastique*, he studied the groupings and pastoral poses of Puvis de Chavannes and used them in the third movement. He never failed to visit museums and galleries and knew which American cities had notable private collections. I first saw the famous Barnes Collection of paintings in Philadelphia with Massine in 1935, when he received special permission from Barnes himself. Barnes, who had made his fortune from Argyrol, was an eccentric, bitter man and would allow only artists and students to visit his museum, because his collection had been ridiculed when he first opened it to the public. Massine particularly loved Italy and Italian painters, and I was later awakened to the beauty of Giotto in Padua and to the wonderful mosaics in Ravenna through his eyes, the eyes of a discerning artist. I believe that paintings gave him the stylistic quality of his choreography, especially in period ballets.

In music, he appeared to be working structurally from the score. In his great symphonic ballets set to Brahms's Fourth and Tchaikovsky's Fifth Symphonies, one could see the musical line unfolding. This was especially apparent in *Choreartium*, set to Brahms's Fourth. The opening theme was danced by the leading dancer and her partner, who would reappear each time the theme did. The string section was represented by the female *corps de ballet*, the woodwind and brass section by the male *corps de ballet*, and the lyrical flute passages by our airiest and most delicate dancer, Tatiana Riabouchinska. If you knew the music you could anticipate the choreography. That sounds simple but of course isn't, since Massine created movement, steps, and dance counterpoints to fuse music and dance into a creative work of balletic art.

The musicality of a choreographer always reveals itself in his work by the music he chooses and how it speaks to him. He can tame it, work with it, have it work for him, but only if he is musically trained—like Balanchine, who was a superb musician. Nothing is worse than very sophisticated music chosen by an unsophisticated choreographer. The music suffers like a wounded animal and the steps imposed on it become mere irritation. Some music is too powerful for choreography, as was the case with Massine's ballet choreographed to Beethoven's Seventh Symphony. No mere steps could keep up with the aroused imagination of the listener.

Each choreographer works in a unique way. Massine had a large book which was always beside him when he choreographed a new work. It was filled with diagrams and directions. He worked systematically, based on previous homework. He used to sit by the hour at his phonograph, listening to the particular work he was using for a new ballet. It is doubtful whether he had actual steps in mind, and although it is possible to plan them in advance, eventually they must be worked out on dancers to see what they look like and whether they are physically possible, particularly those involving partnership.

It was easy to dance a Massine ballet, not because they were technically simple, but because they were musical. The musical impulses were there, never against the grain. The ballets were not cerebral or as sophisticated musically as a Balanchine ballet, but they flowed. A dancer can feel when the choreography is musical because, rather than fighting it, he is in harmony with it.

Eventually Massine disengaged himself from his personal relationship with Diaghilev in the same manner as Nijinsky had. He married a young English dancer who had adopted the Russian stage name of Vera Savina. But this marriage does not appear to have created a rift with Diaghilev, as Massine continued in the company as one of the chief choreographers. After Diaghilev died in 1929, the original Ballets Russes disbanded. Three years later,

Colonel de Basil formed the Ballet Russe de Monte Carlo and Massine became its artistic director, chief choreographer, and star dancer. When I joined the company, he had divorced Savina and was married, for the second time, to a Russian dancer.

During the following months, our meetings were no more than occasional drives in the park of one city or another, always in great secrecy.

Do come at 6:30 to Dr. Cochran (343 South 18th Street). I shall be in this house—having treatment. You can go in.

I shall be at Dr. Resnik (184 Day State Road). Come at 6 P.M.—call for me inside at the house.

I shall be at Dr. Kendall (1263 Mackay St.) tomorrow morning. Do come at 10:15. You will find white paper on the door. If paper is not there—it means that you cannot see me at all.

I shall be at Johns Hopkins Hospital (Broadway Street at 5 p.m.). Do come if you can.

My dearest—my knee is much better. Yesterday I have done little practice. So lovely to see you even from a distance. I shall go from here to Chicago and then come to Milwaukee. All my love, my beloved one.

In spite of Massine's extreme efforts at secrecy, I soon felt the full hostility of his wife. I don't know what I thought—perhaps I was so much a part of his wishes that I didn't think beyond the moment and accepted them without question. What did I know of marriage? What did I know of the agony of a wife who begins to realize that there is someone else? Nothing. I did what Léonide wanted me to do.

Although I had received a great deal of admiration, I had never been in love, and beyond some youthful crushes, my sexual experience was nil. Emotionally I was completely naïve, unsophisticated, and, I may say, guileless, with the inability (or is it unwillingness?) of the young to reason out and foresee the consequences. I was also totally unprepared for the atmosphere I was to enter and the storm it was to create, in the center of which I was to live during the next two years. It almost wrecked me.

At Christmas and on my birthday, while we were in Chicago, I received elaborate presents from Massine. I found them slightly embarrassing—they seemed to me too extravagant. A lovely fur coat, pale brown flecked with white, which was made from parts of mink and was luckily rather sporty with leather fastenings—otherwise, had it been more luxurious, I would have been ashamed to wear it. Ashamed because it was quite obvious who had given it to me and why. The other present, equally compromising, was a watch from Cartier which was very unusual. Today we would call it Art Deco. The watch had black hands and was set in a piece of curved, pale topaz which Salvador Dali once described perfectly: "Ah voilà—des truffes en gelée"!

I was aware that I was becoming the object of discussions in the Massine household and in the company. No secret could remain a secret in the tight insular world we lived in—in any event, not after those presents. The irony was that the assumptions made by the company were totally untrue. It was all made worse when we left Chicago and Massine asked me to travel with him in his "caravan," rather than with the company. The word "caravan" sounds rather gypsyish; it was, in fact, a trailer attached to his Lincoln automobile. He employed a Russian couple who lived with him on tour. The man drove and the woman cooked and kept house. It certainly was a far more comfortable (if not cramped) existence than dashing for trains at night or leaving at the crack of dawn. Besides, it allowed Massine to have home-cooked meals and rest properly while traveling. I was now asked to join his household and sleep in a bunk in this bizarre caravan.

No matter what the company thought, it was quite chaste. How could it be otherwise, with five people living together like a bourgeois Russian family—including eating borscht—while rolling across America in a trailer? But it was hard—hard on all of us. I could not bear his wife and I daresay she could not stand the sight of me. How could it have been different? We were both forced into a position which we detested. One does things for love that one cannot comprehend having done once love has died.

It was painful. I had no one to talk to or counsel me, not even Sono. I had promised not to tell anyone. My mother was far away and knew nothing. I could only hope for a change after we returned to Europe. Massine was impervious and insisted on the continuation of our strange life. He began talking about a divorce. He was in touch with lawyers and said that as soon as the company was near the Mexican border he would obtain a divorce in El Paso. I believed him in every respect and fell deeper in love with him.

As spring approached and our tour was coming to an end, Léonide began to initiate me into physical love. It happened here and there in snatched moments of freedom. Some of it was wonderful and some of it deeply shocking, bordering on the comical, but whatever form it took, he never consummated our relationship or took total possession of me—something I could not understand. It was only weeks later, in the spring of 1935, on the night before we sailed for Europe on the *Ile de France*, that I became Léonide's lover. I realized much later that his passion had been tempered by caution. He had waited until I passed my eighteenth birthday and until we sailed for Europe, where laws about minors were less strict.

A deep emotional hurt followed. On the first day at sea, he told me that he did not believe he was the first man in my life. It should have been quite obvious that he was, since I did not react the way an experienced woman would have, but he would not listen. Later

I thought bitterly that his denial must have been motivated by the same reasons which made him wait all those months in America.

No matter how humiliating, hurtful, and frustrating our love affair was at times, nothing could diminish my feelings for Léonide. I remained hopelessly in love with him. Nor was there a chance that anything from the outside would affect my sentiments of awe, respect, and admiration. I stood every night in the wings to watch him dance, and each time learned something just by being there and observing him closely. He could literally make the attention of the audience focus on his right hand, as it slowly ascended in an arc during the closing bars of Stravinsky's *Firebird*. No one could look anywhere else except at that hand, as it reached its apex, turned, and slowly descended again, together with the last sounds of music. Watching him during rehearsals choreographing a new ballet, seeing it develop and come alive, I was proud to love him and to know that he was in love with me, even if he was rather bowlegged (which he hid by wearing ballooning black alpaca trousers as his rehearsal outfit), or even if he did look rather funny in the small formal hats he wore.

As we sailed to Europe I had plenty of time to think. My mother had returned to Berlin months ago and I would have to tell her what had happened to me. I was not afraid, because I knew she would always love me, but I also knew I would disappoint her deeply. We always rejoiced when we were together again after a separation. We would talk excitedly, relating every detail, each one totally concentrated on the other—marveling, sympathizing, laughing—utterly open with each other. I feared that an awkwardness might come between us—how could I tell her *everything*?

The past eight months had been a tremendous experience for me, some of it searingly painful. The company had been like a moving island, with its members leading totally inbred lives depending solely on one another. Even our repertoire was monotonous during those interminable one-night stands, sometimes for weeks in a row, with *Les Sylphides, Les Présages,* and *The Blue Danube* as our bread-and-butter ballets night after night. Often there was no time to stay in a hotel, and we would rush to the train after the performance and sleep in Pullmans, only to be awakened at 6 a.m. and transferred to a day coach because it was cheaper. We then pulled down the dividers between the seats and, by placing our suitcases underneath, made up a tolerable bed and went to sleep again.

It was quite a feat to transport so large a company of dancers, technicians, a full orchestra, scenery, costumes, and mountains of baggage, but it was remarkably well organized and I don't remember that we ever missed a performance. This was largely due to Serge Grigoriev, who was imperturbable and always remained calm in the midst of chaos. He could be quite terse, as when Tatiana Chamié begged him for a new costume, saying that her dress was in shreds and soon she would be naked on stage. His reply was, "That will be charming, Madame . . ." The complaint was funny, especially coming from her, because her habit was to sit stark naked in the dressing room, enveloped only in clouds of cigarette smoke. Tatiana Chamié was one of the group of dancers who had been with the Diaghilev company. To us teenagers, they were the senior members and commanded respect—although I realize now they were only in their early thirties. Most of them were married to each other and represented the respectable middle class of the company. They formed the backbone of the *corps de ballet* and danced occasional solos. As ex-members of the illustrious Diaghilev Ballets Russes, they had acquired authority when it came to re-vivals of ballets and were always consulted, since choreography has been handed down by memory from generation to generation of dancers.

There were always lively love affairs going on among the un-married dancers, and sometimes a rebellious flame would ignite among the married ones. That is why it seemed strange that my involvement with Massine caused so much whispering. (Or was that my imagination?) We had a far more celebrated instance when Paul Petroff, one of our leading dancers, fell in love with Mme de Basil. He was found on New Year's Eve in front of the elevator of the Blackstone Hotel in Chicago bleeding heavily from a stab wound. Although it created a sensation in the company, not a word leaked to the press. The culprit was discussed only in whispers, and thank God, Paul Petroff fully recovered.

Almost as spectacular was David Lichine's adventure. The black sheep of the company had been attempting to seduce a beautiful young dancer. When her regular boyfriend appeared, he barely escaped out the window and had to spend a very long time in the bitter cold of a Chicago winter on the ledge high above Michigan Avenue. David Lichine was supposed to be engaged to Tatiana Riabouchinska, but fell in love with Lubov Rostova, a beautiful half-Swedish, half-Russian girl. That *pas de trois* was the cause of much unhappiness, as was the love affair of Alexandra Danilova and the very good-looking and gentle Jerry Sevastianov, our manager, who fell in love with Irina Baronova and married her. Only Roman Jasinsky and Sono, who had fallen in love, led a devoted life and were happy together for many years.

The Blackstone Hotel in Chicago, where the entire company lived, had the added advantage of an underground passage to the theater, so that we could go freely back and forth in our practice clothes without endless dressing-undressing and re-dressing, which could amount to as much as six to eight times a day between class in the morning, rehearsals, performances, and going to bed at night. We always loved our long Christmas season in Chicago, because staying in one place for three weeks where we had so many friends who entertained us was a luxury—for us, who lived for weeks in anonymous hotel rooms and ate bad food in equally anonymous coffee shops. I remember one hostess and friend, Bobsy Goodspeed (as she was then known) with particular affection. She was a lovely-looking woman, very sweet to us all, and gave wonderful parties, which we relished.

———

After our arrival in Europe, we went directly to Spain for our spring season. Our first stop, in Barcelona, was the Hotel Oriente on the Rambla, one of the main boulevards, conveniently close to the Teatro Nacional. Massine decided to stay in a hotel outside and above the city on Monte Tibidabo. He insisted that I live there too. It was quite isolated and very quiet, and I felt lonely up there away from my friends in the ballet. After all, to be in Barcelona—in Spain—for the first time was exciting and I envied them their freedom to wander around and explore the city.

In the theater, we had our own little bullfight atmosphere. The stage of the Teatro Nacional was severely raked, slanting down toward the footlights. The wooden floor was old and had become splintered and very slippery. During the first performance the dancers slithered and fell helplessly, some of them hurting themselves badly. The Spanish audience was far from sympathetic and booed us, compounding our misery. We had to spread a ground-cloth over the entire stage, which made it a little better but hampered us in other ways. Our schedule was very hard in Barcelona. We never seemed to get enough sleep, because performances did not begin until 9:30 or 10 p.m., and since we were preparing new ballets for our season at Covent Garden, we had to stick to our early-morning classes followed by rehearsals.

Even so, we were longing to see the famous gypsy flamenco dancers, and were told we could find them in cafés and nightclubs, where they performed late at night. Massine, who had been in Barcelona before, knew where they danced, and invited a few members of the company to go slumming in the tougher parts of the city. After the performance he led us through some dark alleys in back of the theater to a nightclub. On the way, we passed a long line of sailors snaking up the steps of a dimly lit building. I was mystified to see them standing there so late at night, until I realized they were awaiting their turn at a whorehouse.

The nightclub was hazy with cigarette smoke, noisy, and very dark. You could hardly see anything at first. We found a table and sat crowded around it. There were many peculiar-looking women who circled the room. They were slim and provocatively dressed, and one of them suddenly plunked herself on Massine's lap. She began teasing and flirting with him, and when I looked closer I realized that it was a man. I was fascinated by Massine's new friend, who had long, black hair, clearly not a wig, was heavily made up, and had red fingernail polish on his nails.

We were terribly excited by the dancing. One man, very slim, jumped up on a small marble table and beat out a sharp staccato rhythm with his heels and castanets. There was a tiny stage where a group performed. They sat on kitchen chairs and accompanied the dancers with guitars, clapping their hands and singing in the strange wailing guttural and hoarse sounds of their Moorish ancestors. I had been watching a big fat woman sitting among the group and could not imagine that she would dance, but she did, looking as majestic as a Maillol sculpture and unbelievably graceful. The audience went wild. She hardly moved her torso but kicked her train with her small elegant feet in a haughty manner. She held her arms, which were generously rounded, above her head and moved them in a slow, sinuous way, while her hands produced a steady, continuous barrage of castanet trills. She was the best of them all, totally masterful in her unashamed, even provocative, maturity.

———

We had a recess between our seasons in Spain and in London, and Massine decided to take a week's cure for his knee. Like many Europeans, he believed in spas and the curative powers of mud baths. The best places were Abano in Italy and Piestany and Marienbad in Czechoslovakia. He said he would be going alone to Piestany and asked me to join him there. For the first time, I was aware of a strong reluctance to do what he wanted.

Also, for the first time in my life, dancing had taken second place. I was beginning to wake up from my romantic dream, experiencing the horrors of jealousy and seeing the outlines of a futile future. I had been in the company nearly a year and had hardly distinguished myself. My ambition, which had always been so fierce, had slackened, and our life in the company, particularly during the American tour, was too arduous for the extra study and practice needed. They had to be done every day, if I was going to develop further. I had a few solo roles and danced them no better and no worse than one or two other dancers I alternated with. In addition to my parts in *Boutique Fantasque* and *The Blue Danube*, I had been told to learn various small parts. One of the first was in *Aurora's Wedding*.

Aurora's Wedding is really a divertissement composed entirely of variations taken from Act II of *The Sleeping Beauty*. It opens with a grand entrance, when the entire company presents itself during a polonaise. It has the famous "Bluebird Variations" in it; a *grand pas* with Aurora, her prince, and six couples; the "Rose Adagio"; and many, many others. Because of its variety, it was very popular —but not with me. I hated it—to dance in it, that is. I was one of six couples and, in addition, danced a *pas de trois* with another girl and a boy. I loathed the choreography and even the music of that *pas de trois*. The *pas de six* was even worse—I always seemed to be slightly off and could not adjust to the conformity of being one of the six couples.

Over the next year, I was given solos in *Choreartium*, *Symphonie Fantastique*, *Le Cotillon*, *Les Femmes de Bonne Humeur*, and the role of the Mexican dancer in *Union Pacific*, which I danced in an inky-black wig made from tough horsehair bought at Woolworth's. Often I was pushed into the chorus, and then somehow stayed there in spite of my protests; Grigoriev always won the battle and my original contract meant nothing. Besides, I really didn't work hard enough to force the issue by showing perceptible improvement. Important solo parts, not to speak of main roles, were as zealously guarded as the gold in Fort Knox, and the assignment of such a role could come about only through injury or the sudden indisposition on the part of the original dancer or prima ballerina.

Once, because of various emergencies, I had to jump into the second act of *Firebird*, which has an extremely exposed section for the ensemble. Dancers four lines deep advanced rhythmically in formation toward the footlights, while the music assumed a menacing character. Everyone had his arms down and everyone was counting. At a given count all arms flew up for a beat, then down again. This was repeated four times but, typically Stravinskian, at uneven intervals. I had to be "talked through" pretty much like a passenger in a plane who has to take over the controls and make a landing because the pilot is incapacitated. Oh, God, what a fool I made of myself!

The only roles I think I danced well were the first movement in *Les Présages* (Tchaikovsky's Fifth Symphony), a rather strong, aggressive part; a small part in *Choreartium* (Brahms's Fourth Symphony); and *Le Cotillon*, a Balanchine ballet—but again I danced well but not great, and I was positively lousy in anything that required a degree of unison with other dancers. Such was my condition and lack of achievement at the end of my first year, and sad to say, matters did not improve in the second year.

Massine had, as usual, been very insistent. I received innumerable scrolls with urgent advice:

Dearest—the best for you is to take *plane* from Barcelona to Stuttgart and from there by train to Wien and then Piestany: the same way I go now.

Dearest—do as you think best—but please don't *meet* anybody in Paris—don't wire anyone—don't make any appointments—come straight to me.

Dearest—I do advise you to go from Barcelona—you don't need to
tell anybody why you remain in Barcelona—simply as you missed
your train—or your photos are not ready and you have probably
to wait until next train. I don't think it will be bad for my cure—
because we shall not be foolish—it is just to see you more alone and
to speak with you freely—it is now our *only chance*—I shall give you
money for your return ticket to Berlin. Barcelona-Wien is Pes. 450,
plus 13MK bed from Stuttgart to Wien.

When we parted in Spain, I finally promised Massine that I would
join him later in Piestany.

Since it was economically impossible for my mother to travel with
me, she had remained in Berlin and was waiting for me there. I
wanted to see her more than anyone on earth. During a stopover in
Stuttgart, I changed my mind, which for me was a great act of
courage, and instead of taking a train to Czechoslovakia I went to
Berlin. I arrived at my mother's apartment in a state of emotional
exhaustion, crying uncontrollably.

When Léonide called, he was astonished at my decision and
became even more insistent that I join him immediately. He asked
to speak to my mother and must have convinced her of his love for
me and his intentions for the future, for he invited her to chaperone
us. After a few days, we both traveled to Piestany. The days we
spent there together were reassuring, peaceful, and an oasis of peace
during those turbulent two years.

———

It is strange to hold the only remnant of a passionate love, which
happened nearly fifty years ago, encapsulated in three letters in the
palm of your hand. Léonide to me:

The day you left—Never in my life, I haven't thought that I could
love like I love you—Never nobody can tear from me what I
acquired with you here. The feeling and the memory of us close
heart to heart will be indefinitely vivid in me—Remember suddenly
that huge dark cloud with wonderful light ribbon which appeared

almost above our heads and sent the dark cloud away as though giving us to understand that the dark stormy cloud of our life might soon be gone too.

The next day—Some force dragged me to the place where we have met the sunset. It is about the same moment now. Coming here I stopped every place we stopped with you. I looked on the ground trying to find the trace of your feet—every place reminds me of you, I feel your breath. Now I am standing there and sun is going almost hidden behind the mountain. "You are like out of gold," you said to me looking in my face—Once you said "I love you—at least you are true person"—and you sat on the couch, it was almost dark. I looked at you and expression of your face overwhelmed me—you were like some Leonardo da Vinci paintings, so soft and so mysterious lighting was on you.

The day I left—This letter will bring you my last thoughts and last au revoir from Piestany—Brigitta—courage.

Life is wonderful—L.

The "dark stormy cloud of our life" did not go away when the company reassembled in London but hit with full force. It was as if Massine's wife scrutinized our happy sunburned faces to see whether the same sun had tanned us in the same place and at the same time, but there was obviously something more, something else which radiated from us, an irrepressible happiness, especially from me, which told the whole story. I don't know what took place between them, but our brief peace ended and our wretched, secretive life began all over again. Léonide's resolve, "I can go in the future life with no fear, no hesitation," crumbled in the onslaught.

I don't remember too much about our London season of 1935, beyond the fact that we had a very busy schedule which overlapped with the opera season while we were preparing our own. The company danced in several opera productions. I remember especially

Prince Igor. Two of our best male character dancers, Yurek Shabelevsky and Leon Woizikowsky, were terrific as the warriors in
the Polovetsian dances and absolutely flew through the air holding
their bows and arrows menacingly in front of them while exuding
an air of total savagery. By contrast, we girls wove gently in and out,
shielding our faces with veils, while the women's chorus sang the
marvelously sensuous music of Borodin.

I loved these old-fashioned ballets, like *Scheherazade, Thamar,*
and the dance interlude in *Prince Igor.* The choreography for the
women was always more or less the same—the right arm bent and
lifted up above the chin so that the elbow covered the rest of the
face from the nose down. This gesture was supposed to imply
Oriental modesty and feminine allure. We were also rehearsing
new ballets like *Cents Baisers* and *Jardin Public,* and a ballet to a
new score by Hindemith. *Cents Baisers* had a rather lightweight
score by Baron Frederic d'Erlanger and included a melody discon-
certingly similar to "Lady, Play Your Mandolin" by Oscar Levant,
a tune which was very popular then. I loved the music of *Thamar,*
with its brooding, ominous quality. In it, too, we wandered around
hiding our faces while a sad romantic plot unfolded.

In spite of Sir Thomas Beecham conducting *Choreartium,* none
of the new ballets and revivals was a hit or a favorite like *Boutique
Fantasque, The Blue Danube,* or the symphonic ballets—but one
was yet to come. Massine was planning a ballet to *Symphonie
Fantastique* by Berlioz.

Our rehearsals were either on the stage or on the top floor of
Covent Garden, where the big rehearsal room was located. One
whole side had huge windows overlooking the fruit and vegetable
markets which surrounded the theater. We were still young and
silly, and I remember that we played with oranges—that *does* sound
silly. Some of the male dancers would throw oranges up to us, and
if we missed catching them, they would crash against the wall amid
a lot of loud shrieks.

It was wonderful to be in London and to break out of our "island"—to see other friends and stay in one place. We were invited to parties, and I remember one night being told that a famous American actress was there, with the impossibly difficult name of Tallulah Bankhead. Well, we practically curtsied to her on being introduced, when suddenly she bent over and then stood on her head. Her beautiful evening gown fell from her upside-down body and, to our amazement, revealed her utterly and entirely naked. Our reaction was very strange—I would say almost prudish—because, in spite of our sometimes tempestuous lives and abbreviated costumes, we were very shocked.

One weekend, when we were visiting friends in the country, I had quite a spectacular experience. Sunday was a beautiful day and we were asked whether we would like to ride. We were all enthusiastic; I couldn't wait to get on a horse. Had I ridden before? "Oh yes," said I, which wasn't quite true. I had been *on* horses but was a totally inexperienced rider. We all rode off in stately fashion, and it was bliss. It gave me such an exhilarating feeling of freedom and power. I suddenly noticed that my horse was increasing speed—in fact, he was galloping—and I could not stop him. My efforts to control him only made it worse. There was nothing to be done except to stay on him, which I was determined to do. He tried to throw me, and he tried to scrape me off by galloping very close to a wall, but I suppose what saved me were my strong legs, which I pressed around him for dear life.

As we galloped, I saw that he was heading straight for a white picket fence. I thought, He'll jump the fence and we'll crash and then what? At the last second, he veered off and then continued his mad dash. Eventually he tired and slowed down. When we finally arrived back home, my host said laconically, "He's rather a brute, isn't he? We sent a groom along because he does this sort of thing —but the groom lost you." And so ended my riding career, but not without my feeling rather smug that I had defeated "the brute."

After our London season, Léonide invited me to spend my vacation on the Isola dei Galli, the private island he owned off the coast of southern Italy, near Positano. I am unable now to understand how I could have agreed to travel once more in triangular fashion, but then I am not eighteen anymore. I don't believe one can ever again re-experience the ferocious passion, the longing, the hope— ah yes, the hope that things will change. I had no capacity for self-denial—nor could I give up hope—nor was I ready to admit defeat.

We motored through Italy, stopping in Ravenna to admire the pure ivory throne and sarcophagus of the Byzantine Empress Theodora and the wonderful mosaics showing the Empress and her entourage. How mysterious their large-eyed, direct gaze seemed, and how perfect the splendor of their attire, which in spite of the opulence of cascading pearls, emeralds, and rubies, coupled with the utmost regal bearing, nevertheless gave the impression of an austerity. We remained for a few days in Abano, near Venice, so that Léonide could take mud baths for his ailing knee. From there, we visited Padua and Vicenza.

The Giottos in the chapel in Padua made a deep impression on me. For a dancer, who cannot express anything except through the movements of her body, there was a great deal to be learned. In the physical expression of lamentation, in the hands turned upward like birds in flight, in the raised arms, in the manifestation of sorrow of the spirit expressed silently but powerfully through the body. We stood there and looked and looked, absorbing and trying to remember every detail. The magnificent Palladian villas, and the perfection of the Teatro Olimpico in Vicenza, tiny but with the most miraculously deep perspective of the small stage—what treasures for an eighteen-year-old to see for the first time.

Before we descended to the harbor of Positano, we visited the hill town of Ravello. Was there ever a more enchanting little town, with a view for miles over the Mediterranean? How clever of the

British to have "discovered" Ravello so early; the most beautiful houses—one built on the edge of a cliff—were owned by them.

In Positano we got into a large, sturdy rowboat with an equally large, sturdy Italian fisherman who rowed us and all our luggage to the island. It took an hour and a half. I can't imagine why we didn't take a motorboat—maybe there weren't any, or maybe that would have been too extravagant. Subsequently all our provisions and mail were rowed out to us daily, except when the weather was bad and the sea too rough.

The island was primitive and had a very simple house on it without electricity. Actually, the Isola dei Galli consisted of three small islands clustered together, one of which was called Brigante. I took this to be a good omen, because of the slight similarity to my own name—but Brigante was inhospitable, rough, and volcanic when I explored it.

Léonide employed an old man who lived the year round like a hermit on the island. Perhaps he was not as old as he looked, but he was eccentric. He wore the same frayed shorts every day, but his most striking feature was his full black beard, which hung down almost to his waist and served as his shirt. In spite of his frugal attire he looked and acted extremely dignified, which gave him a marked resemblance to the Emperor Haile Selassie. Our days were spent very simply. Swimming, sunning, eating, napping, and occasionally boating around the island. I thought it was paradise and roamed around reveling in the sun and sea and freedom, and a special kind of isolation that I've always loved and which is almost magical to me.

The freedom was only outside, not inside the house. Our relationship was strained, punctuated by quarrels and scenes. Alarm clocks went off when it was considered that my time with Léonide was over and he had to leave my room. It is strange to consider why a man would want to subject two women who loved him to such an unhappy arrangement—both of whom complied in the hope that they would be left alone with him one day. I can speak only for myself, but it was a useless romantic dream in which I dissipated my love, my passion, my courage, and my capacity to think straight.

In early September we sailed on the S.S. *Lafayette* for our American tour, which was even more arduous than the previous one. For eight months we crisscrossed America and performed in a total of 120 cities, small towns, and universities, rushing in and out of trains and hotels. I remember that after Los Angeles we had an uninterrupted period of six weeks of one-night stands. We performed in El Paso, Abilene, Dallas, Birmingham, Memphis, Little Rock, Kansas City, Kalamazoo, Gary, Columbus, Louisville, Cincinnati, South Bend, Fort Wayne, Toledo, Detroit, Nashville, Montgomery, Macon, Jacksonville, Orlando, Tampa, West Palm Beach, Daytona Beach, Rock Hill, Roanoke, Philadelphia, New Brunswick, Syracuse, Hanover, Lowell, Portland, Pittsfield, New Haven, Bridgeport, Boston.

The list of towns was posted every night on the bulletin board—otherwise, we wouldn't have known where we were or where we were going. As it was, the towns blurred into one another. I am reminded of a remark of Fred Allen's: "After New York, all towns look like Bridgeport." The only familiar things at night were our well-worn costumes, the scenery, and the sound of Chopin. We often made up in classrooms, sitting on benches like schoolchildren, because the auditorium had no dressing rooms. When I traveled with the company, we had to hurry after the performance to put all those magic tubes of makeup, rouge, powder, black pencils, false eyelashes, and cold cream—all those things that transformed us into exotic creatures (which we were not)—into the special metal boxes which had our names on them so they could be packed into large trunks. The trunks waited outside, while inside everything was being dismantled and carried out as we rushed to the train station. There, everyone scrambled to find his Pullman car and his upper or lower bunk. After that was settled, some of the male dancers would repair to the club car for beer, sandwiches, and poker, which they played half the night, smoking non-stop until the club car looked and sounded like a Russian nightclub.

Sometimes, when our schedule permitted it, a notice would appear on the bulletin board that someone was giving a party for us. We would all go, eat like horses, spend the entire evening in clusters jabbering to each other in a mixture of Russian and French, and never even know the name of our hostess.

To complicate matters, I bought a dog. He was a beautiful black cocker spaniel whom I named Peter. He slept with me in my bunk in the Pullman, which could get very overheated. One night he panted so hard that I made him a compress from a washcloth soaked in ice water. I put it on his forehead, and he accepted it with love and docility and slept like a baby. For a while dogs were banned, after Massine's large Kerry blue suddenly strolled on stage during a performance and could not be coaxed off stage, to the vast amusement of the audience. But the ban was soon lifted, and we rattled on with our pets, including a pair of marmoset monkeys (they belonged to Irina Baronova's parents), which played around the Pullman car, hanging from the luggage racks by their tails and swinging from one to the next.

The big cities—New York, Philadelphia, Boston, Chicago, Los Angeles, and San Francisco—were the highlights of our tour. We longed for them as people in a desert long for an oasis. They meant good theaters, good dressing rooms, good hotels, and outside friends. One night, in Beverly Hills, I was invited with Massine and some other members to a party given by the Russian actress Anna Sten. She had just been imported by Samuel Goldwyn to play in a new film of the Zola novel *Nana*.

We were always excited at meeting famous movie stars, and one of the most famous of them all—Marlene Dietrich—was present. What a sensation! She was beautiful, she was languid, and she flirted with Massine. She murmured that she wanted to see another performance of our ballet, and when we told her that we were going to Santa Barbara, she said she would follow us. And she did. The next day she arrived in the ultimate of chic: a Rolls-Royce driven by her chauffeur but designed for only two people behind the glass partition. It had pale-beige upholstery, and attached to the mahogany interior was a crystal vase with two perfect roses.

We were just leaving for a tea given by Leopold Stokowski, who lived in the hills above Santa Barbara. We invited her to come along. Marlene was so famous at the time that Stokowski's masterful deception was simply stunning. Looking at her, he innocently inquired, "And you, my dear—are you in the ballet too?"

"Of course," she answered.

"And in what ballet do you dance?"

She glanced at us and we chorused, *"Union Pacific!"*

"I must come and see you tonight," said Stokowski.

As soon as he moved away, we immediately plotted how to get her into the ballet. *Union Pacific* lent itself ideally to our scheme, and miraculously both Massine and Grigoriev gave us permission for a bit of fun. Her famous face was not visible that night, but two of our male dancers were trembling with excitement as they carried her, shrouded in black, and carefully placed her on the stage, where she became a rail and part of the laying of the tracks for the Union Pacific Railroad.

There had been rumors that Marlene liked women as much as men. Maybe they began when she started wearing pants—even tuxedos—with such supreme panache. Her masculine attire was beautifully tailored and, if anything, enhanced her femininity and her considerable sexual allure. Or maybe the rumor began because she came to Hollywood from the wicked city of Berlin—or maybe it was based on her amoral role in *The Blue Angel*. In any event, that evening, after she had joined us in the girls' dressing room to get ready for her big role as a rail, she seemed to switch her attention from Massine to me, and we both lapsed into German, delighting in the use of the marvelous Berlin slang. The fact that no one else spoke German very quickly established an intimacy between us which shortened the time it would normally have taken to become friends. At a small party after the performance, we sang popular German songs, alternating in supplying lyrics when one of us forgot the next word. I thought she was wonderful. Not only was she spectacularly beautiful, but she had a totally realistic point of view about herself, and could be very funny in a self-deprecatory way that belied her movie-star image and made her warm and human.

After we had said good night and gone to our separate rooms, she suddenly appeared in mine. Subtly, things changed from a certain air of camaraderie to what the French call *une ambiance séduisante*. At first, I felt a mixture of amazement and curiosity, which soon turned into acute embarrassment. I didn't like what was happening and finally brought things to an abrupt halt. But in spite of it, we became good friends. Two days later, in San Francisco, I received an enormous bouquet of red roses with a card that had only one word on it: "Marlene."

Some months later we met Stokowski again, but this time as the formidable conductor of the Philadelphia Orchestra. It was a great honor to have this famous orchestra accompany us from the pit, but although we were thrilled by the sound, the *tempi* of Maestro Stokowski were a nightmare to dance to. Always controversial in his renditions, he conducted Brahms's Fourth Symphony (*Choreartium*) in the rhythm he believed in, which created pandemonium on stage. No one could execute the prescribed choreography and fearful rows ensued, both dancers and Stokowski firmly standing their ground. No dancer should demand that a conductor follow him or take liberty with the music, but the choreography had obviously been designed for a "normal" rendition, which, to say the least, was not the case in Stokowski's unusual reading of the score.

The only one singled out during that hectic rehearsal was myself. It was sheer luck that, when I came flying out toward the front of the stage, the tempo coincided with the big leaps I had to perform and, for once, dancer and orchestra were together. He stopped and shouted, "That girl is the only musical one." Everyone glared at me as if I had committed a crime. Danilova was heard to mutter, "He does not know how to conduct *our* ballet."

My relationship with Massine deteriorated, and there seemed to be little if any hope that it would change. The tensions had become worse for each of us, for different reasons. I was no longer willing to continue living in such a humiliating fashion, but I lacked the strength to break it off. I suppose until there is an irrevocable defeat, hope still struggles on.

In city after city, our personal drama was being played out cruelly, stupidly, savagely, and pathetically ineptly. After Los Angeles we embarked on six weeks of one-night stands—the most strenuous part of our tour. It was a strain on everybody and taxed the resources of the company. We never had enough sleep, our muscles became stiff from sitting in the train all day, compounded by having slept fitfully in a Pullman berth during the night.

It was then that de Basil, Léonide, and I had a serious talk. We agreed that life could not continue as it was. I was emotionally exhausted, and I daresay so was everyone involved, including de Basil; I think he had a somewhat sympathetic understanding of the situation, because he had his own marital problems. It was decided that it would be better if I stopped traveling in Massine's caravan and roomed with Olga Morosova, a soloist in the company and the sister of the very gifted dramatic dancer Nina Verchinina. Olga was a fine dancer, kind and sensible—altogether a warm, mature woman.

Was it the right thing to do? The situation became even more painful than a total separation from Léonide would have been. At least then I would not have seen him at all. As it was, I traveled with the company, roomed with Olga, but in the theater at night we re-met. During the frantic backstage activities—especially frantic during one-night stands—there was neither time nor opportunity for us to talk. Whether it was deliberately arranged or not, I felt totally cut off from any personal contact with him. I knew Léonide's routine so well and could not imagine his life being lived without me. I grieved and was in a torment of jealousy, because I knew that I could no longer exert any influence which might change our life. During the day, my emotional turmoil would abate slightly; every night, when I saw him, it would flare up again.

During this period, Irina Baronova and Jerry Sevastianov eloped, and although I was very happy for them, the entries in my diary sound melancholy: "For *me*, nothing has changed—am terribly nervous." And four days later, in South Bend: "Transformed my bathroom into a Chinese laundry. Congratulated Irina and Jerry, who are next door living happily as Mr. and Mrs." When Olga went to Palm Beach ahead of the company for a few days of rest, I felt very lonely without her.

After we arrived in Orlando, I was strolling in a beautiful park beside a pond when ahead of me I saw Léonide and his wife, walking their dog. Their union, domesticity, and the implied unconcern on Léonide's part as to my existence (had he seen me or not?) brought me to the brink. Howling inside, I ran home. Alone in the hotel room, without thinking what I was doing, I took a razor blade and cut my wrist. I had, of course, no intention of committing suicide or any thought of death. It seemed that by inflicting physical pain, I might stop the mental pain I was no longer able to endure. It was a cry for help but Massine, when he was told, paid no attention. In fact, he seemed annoyed and angry. I was made to feel that I had done something disgraceful, and I felt ashamed and humiliated. The only one who was gentle and kind was Jerry

Sevastianov, who took me to a doctor and held me on his lap like a child while the physician put stitches in my wrist.

It was the beginning of the end of my love affair with Massine. Our ultimate parting came in London during the summer season of 1936. It was ugly and wounding. Massine "solved" his dilemma by bringing another woman into his life, a woman who was to become his third wife. It took a long time for me to recover, even in the midst of success. It was less a mourning for the love I had lost than the slow healing of deep wounds.

—————

After the lamentable episode in Orlando, my colleagues were nice to me. Our tour continued northward to Boston, where my diary records a cry from the heart turned into fractured English: *"Alles scheint zusammen zu krachen und habe nur eine Hoffnung —out of love zu fallen."* ["Everything seems to crash apart and I have only one hope—to fall out of love."] After the company arrived in New York we had a few free evenings before our opening night at the Metropolitan. I saw two performances which I found very exciting. At the premiere of *Porgy and Bess* by George Gershwin we were bowled over by the marvelous score, the incredible cast, and the entire theatrical production by Rouben Mamoulian. The other was the opening night of the musical *On Your Toes*, by Rodgers and Hart. The show was of particular interest to us because George Balanchine had created two ballets for it. The first was a delicious satire on ballet, including a *pas de deux* in which the ballerina and her partner are fighting while they continue to dance in an extremely haughty manner. Tamara Geva was the star and she did a superb job. The loudest laughter came from us, who naturally were convulsed by all the in-jokes. The climax of the show was *Slaughter on Tenth Avenue*, in which Ray Bolger made a deservedly big hit. Since the plot of *On Your Toes* was that of a Russian ballet company whose impresario decides to put on a "modern" tap ballet, complicated by a temperamental ballerina and gangsters, we all had a wonderful time. The premiere coincided with the Russian Easter celebration, and several of us were invited to a big party given by Anna Roben, a friend of many Russians in New York, including George Balanchine, whom I met that night for the first time.

I congratulated Balanchine warmly on his brilliant and witty choreography for *On Your Toes*. *He* was very nice, *I* was very nice, *it* was very nice. Of course, among ballet dancers he was much admired and esteemed, but he had not yet made as decisive a reputation as he had in Europe. Many members of the former Diaghilev company surrounded him, as did his two affectionate ex-wives, Tamara Geva and Alexandra Danilova. I was curious about him and I believe he was curious about me, but for different reasons. He was only thirty-two but already had two ex-wives—not only that, but they all seemed to be very good friends. I didn't think he was particularly handsome but that he looked like most of the Russian dancers I knew: not too tall; thin, with a decidedly ascetic appearance, which is the usual mark of dancers even if they are highly sensual. But he was very nice—and that is what I remembered most. What he thought of me I do not know, but I think he liked what he saw. We did not meet again until more than a year later in Hollywood, where we were both engaged by Samuel Goldwyn.

———

Meanwhile, we were rehearsing a revival of Stravinsky's *Les Noces*. Bronislava Nijinska, the original choreographer, joined our company to stage it. It was extremely difficult musically, and the way of "counting" bars—always very shaky in ballet—broke down completely. Nijinska, who was deaf, shouted: "*Raz, dva, tri, chetyri, eh—raz, dva, tri, eh—*" on and on, and no one could get it right. I hid the fact that I couldn't count (musical bars, that is) and trusted my ears. After many days of rehearsals, I knew the music by heart and led my little group like a trusted circus horse.

One afternoon, after a particularly long rehearsal, I was late coming to the dressing room. Everybody had left and I found the large room deserted. It had makeup tables all around the walls and a rack for costumes in the middle. As I took off my shoes, I heard a noise which seemed to come from the costume section. When I took a look, our Don Juan, David Lichine, grabbed me and pulled me onto a bench among the costume racks. A terrific struggle began, which turned into a wrestling match. We were both strong, and to stop him I had to grab his hair and pull it with all my might. He finally let me go. As we stood there glaring at each other, with me safely encased in black woolen practice clothes from head to toe, I couldn't help seeing the funny side of it and began to laugh. That was the last straw for David, who fled. Opening night of *Les Noces* was pandemonium as Nijinska shouted the counts from the wings, coupled with the inherent syncopation of two pianos, solo soprano, chorus, and orchestra from the pit. I regret that I never saw that performance from the audience!

During that season I was introduced to a theatrical agent, Louis Shurr. He was well known, not only as an able and successful agent, but for his various eccentricities. He was a very small man, resembling a penguin, with a large head and a downwardly curving nose. He had a penchant for tall blond showgirls who were twice his height. When I asked him once why he preferred these statuesque blondes, he said, "Well, when I make an entrance in a club, they all look at the beautiful girl and then at the guy with her. But if I went out with a dame my size, nobody would pay any attention to two little people." He owned a gorgeous white ermine coat for the use of his current girlfriend. When that particular romance was over, he took the coat back and gave it to his new love. He was smart and he was kind, and over lunch at Sardi's he began telling me of the great career he could build for me. Nothing he said interested me—my mind was not on Broadway or Hollywood. But

I did glance at all the caricatures of the famous stars that lined Sardi's and thought it would be fun to have mine up there. We parted with the promise that he would get in touch if anything came up, but I put that possibility out of my mind.

I was too unhappy and disturbed by my private life. One does not think one will ever get over it, but of course eventually one does. The violence of first love is such that one is unprepared for the possibility that it might end. Everything is new, passionate, and wonderful, and you have nothing to compare it with, nothing to be apprehensive about. You are totally vulnerable, and the protective shield of experience has yet to grow. Shakespeare must have written his lines for Rosalind when his soul was well padded against disillusion: "Men have died from time to time and worms have eaten them, but not for love."

We sailed for Europe on the S.S. *Paris* on May 9.

FIVE

Shortly after we began our London season, I heard from Louis Shurr. He was making good on his promise. Cables began to arrive about plans for a London production of *On Your Toes*. Was I interested in playing the role of the temperamental Russian ballerina Vera Barnova? Although Shurr's previous plans for me had left me absolutely cold, this was different. I had seen *On Your Toes*, thought it a marvelous musical, and, most important of all, it had choreography by George Balanchine. To be a member of the Ballet Russe was a matter of prestige. We rather looked down our noses at revues or dancers who had one or two numbers in the *Ziegfeld Follies*. We did not consider them serious dancers, and in spite of my lack of progress in the last two years—or because of it—I was still determined to become a fine classical ballet dancer. George Balanchine's choreography became the determining factor in my decision.

Lee Ephriam, the producer of *On Your Toes* in London, called me and said, "We have seen you dance at Covent Garden, so we know you can dance—but can you act?" I truthfully answered that

I had no idea. He asked whether I would audition and sent over a script. I was given one week to prepare myself. I started by reading aloud, but my voice sounded so silly to me that my mother had to take long walks to leave me alone. I didn't find my role difficult, because it seemed like an extension of everything I had heard and lived with in the last two years.

I had learned to speak Russian, not fluently but well enough, and have always had a great facility for mimicry and imitation. I put all of that to use now and projected the Russian accent, mannerisms, and behavior onto the character of Vera Barnova by remembering some of our most flamboyant ballerinas. I thought of one evening when the curtains slowly descended on a performance of *Scheherazade*. Zobeide, danced by Lubov Tchernicheva, had just stabbed herself with a dagger and was lying on the floor. For the curtain calls she got up very awkwardly and was caught in a most ungraceful position, with her behind to the audience. When she realized that the curtain was up, she quickly turned and managed a tight-lipped bow. But when the curtain came down again, she picked up the dagger and threw it in fury to the wings. In flight it caught me on my right eyebrow, and I screamed more in fright than pain. She rushed over to me and cried, "Brigittushka! I didn't mean you—I wanted to kill *him*!" pointing to her son Vsevolod, who, as assistant stage manager, had given the cue for raising the curtain too early.

I practiced my lines on the streets, in the subway, and on buses. People probably thought I was demented, talking to myself. The audition was to take place in the Coliseum, the biggest theater in London. My mother took the bus with me to Trafalgar Square and decided that she would wait for me at the Norwegian Club in Norway House while I had my audition across the square.

When I entered the theater backstage, I was greeted by Edward Stoll, Lee Ephriam, and two other gentlemen. We trooped to the stage, which was vast, empty, and dark. Only one work light was on, which shone onto the stage, where a lone kitchen chair had been placed at the center. Out in the blackness of the auditorium the three men took their places, while the fourth remained in the wings to give me cues from the script.

The scene opened with the ballerina "lying" on her bed, singing the Russian song "Dark Eyes" but changing the lyrics to express self-admiration as she held up a mirror and gazed at herself. There was no mirror, so I took out my compact and thought a split second before I started: Well, the only one who can spoil this is you, and I began: "*Ochi chornye, Vera Barnova. Vera Barnova is so beautiful . . . Ochi chornye, Vera Barnova. Vera Barnova je t'adore . . . !*" While I was singing and trying to imitate Marlene Dietrich with a Russian accent, all I saw was my frightened face in the mirror, but I carried on. This was followed by a scene in which three characters entered, and I bravely addressed myself to an empty spot where the imaginary characters might possibly stand.

After this I could hardly believe my ears when the four men came up to the stage and said, "That was fine," and "The part is yours," and "We'll draw up a contract."

I raced across Trafalgar Square to Norway House, burst into the quiet club, and told my mother the news. We were very excited and began making plans. I would leave the Ballet Russe after the London season, we could have a holiday in August, we could probably afford a little furnished flat because my new contract was going to pay me the princely sum of fifty pounds a week, I would become a star, and so on. The possibilities were endless—we talked on and on, we were so excited. On July 9 I signed the contract, which stipulated that the opening date was September 8, 1936.

Our joy was short-lived. On August 1 I received a letter from Lee Ephriam saying that the production had to be postponed until a later date, and continuing ominously, "which as yet we have been unable to settle." This was very upsetting, since I had left the ballet and was therefore without salary, and as usual we had saved very little money. We decided to go to Berlin, where we still had an apartment but where we had no intention of continuing to live. We wanted to give up the apartment, put our furniture into storage, renew our passports, and get out.

Because of *On Your Toes*, I had not answered several letters from United Artists, one of which I reproduce because of its astonishing ineptness. Since Mr. Quarry was their publicity director, it seemed odd that he could not learn my correct name, and odder that he asked how soon I could come to London when the letter was addressed to Covent Garden. To ask me on top of this the "whereabouts" of an actress I had never heard of seemed comical.

8th August 1936

Miss Enrine Zorina
C/O Royal Opera House
Covent Garden, W.C. 2
Dear Madam,

We have received instructions from Hollywood to get into touch with you immediately, and should be extremely glad if you would let us know how soon you could come to London. Perhaps you would be good enough to cable at your earliest convenience.

We are also trying to get into touch with a Miss Germaine Aussey. If you are acquainted with this lady and happen to know her present whereabouts perhaps you would be kind enough to inform us.

Yours faithfully,
Edmund Quarry
United Artists Corporation Ltd.

After our arrival in Berlin, I was offered a short engagement for September at the Wintergarten, a music hall which changed its revue once a month. I hated to accept it, but our finances were so low and my future was even more uncertain after a second letter from Lee Ephriam, which said: "Our date for production of *On*

Your Toes in London has now been postponed indefinitely—we will let you know of a future date," etc. I took the engagement, which consisted of billing in the grand manner as "Star of the Russian Ballet," dancing a few solos, and, most importantly, being paid a good salary. I was so ashamed when both David Lichine and Yurek Shabelevsky, my friends from the Ballet Russe, passed through Berlin during their holidays and of course came to see me dance. "Star of the Russian Ballet" indeed! But they were both a bit in love with me, so they were nice and understanding.

Berlin was in the full bloom of Nazi success, putting on a display of power for the benefit of the tourists streaming in for the Olympic Games. The red flags with their black *Hakenkreuze* were flying from every building, and Nazi storm troopers filled the streets. It was a frightening atmosphere. German girls were supposed to use no makeup and wear their hair in braids. I wore mine loose and used lipstick. But after people pointed at me in an aggressive manner and derisively said, *"Ach, die roten lippen"* [red lips], I pinned a Norwegian flag on my dress, which had an immediate effect: I was acknowledged as an Olympic Games visitor, a Norwegian, the most admired of the Northern Aryans, and from then on was treated with obsequious (and insinuating) friendliness.

It was a bad time, further complicated by the fact that our passports had expired. Suppose they were not renewed—what then? My mother was a violent and outspoken anti-Nazi, and I trembled with fear every time someone rang the bell. It seemed as if every man and boy was in a brown Nazi uniform with red armbands, and we never knew what they wanted, except that it was always something in support of the Nazi Party one way or another. My mother often slammed the door in their faces, which scared me to death. Hearing about Hitler's Germany was one thing; living in it was quite another.

We had been abroad for more or less five years, living in England and America, and I began to realize how much I had changed in those years and how alien I felt in that ghastly atmosphere. Finally,

Dr. Hans Thomsen, my mother's old friend, who was still in the diplomatic service, came to the rescue and helped to speed up the issuing of our passports. The day after we received them we left Germany. No one who has ever lived even briefly in a police state can forget the anxiety of being at the mercy of rules which are arbitrary and unpredictable and which have nothing to do with inherent human rights. It was an enormous mental and physical relief when we crossed the border into a "free" land. Even at nineteen, I felt it, and it changed my attitude toward Germany—*that* Germany—forever.

———

July had been a strange month, at the end of which I had left the ballet which had been my "home" for two years and I had left Massine and irrevocably ruptured our relationship. During our London season, my mother had told me—no one else would—that Tanya, a former girlfriend of Léonide's, had joined him, and I remember feeling as if I had been hit in the solar plexus. When she and I met face to face in a Covent Garden corridor, we looked at each other, then passed in total silence. During those few seconds I was aware of a peculiar mixture of rage, surprise, and relief that it had finally happened. Her name had often been mentioned by Massine's wife in a threatening manner: "One day she will reappear" and Massine loved her and "Then it will all be over." She was telling the truth, perhaps more than she intended, because a few years later Massine *did* marry Tanya, and had two children and an apparently happy marriage.*

On July 24, Massine's new ballet to the *Symphonie Fantastique* of Berlioz had its London premiere and was a big success. I danced a solo part in the third movement, and it seems I redeemed my rather lackluster career by dancing it well, because, thank God, everybody told me I was "wonderful."

---

* *Massine was married for the fourth time in his late seventies and had another child.*

I had left the company on August 1, on a high note of expectancy for the future, coupled with an attempt to be philosophical about the past. My diary entry, written in German, says: "Will try to remember only the beautiful about him—Nature is good about that—it helps one to forget" (meaning no doubt my own nature, not trees and meadows). I was now literally footloose and fancy-free, and very soon acquired a great many dashing and aristocratic boyfriends. I became a kind of platonic libertine and enjoyed (or tried to) the sort of life I should have had between the ages of seventeen and nineteen, with "lots of beaux and lots of parties."

I was invited out a great deal and took drives in Mercedes-Benz sports cars—cars that were as beautiful as jewels from Cartier. The upholstery was invariably of pigskin leather and smelled good—the mahogany dashboard was elegant (there was always a pure-silver medallion of St. Christopher attached somewhere; it was *de rigueur* and had little to do with religion), and when Hansi or Eckardt or Talle (I even had a friend called Bismarck) stepped on the gas in their respective Mercedes, the engine went into overdrive with a sound like an accelerating siren. Louder and faster was the thing in those days. The surroundings of Berlin were exceptionally lovely, and we used to drive out of town and have wonderful meals in pleasant places, then go to movies, plays, operas, and, of course, eventually wind up in nightclubs dancing.

It was an unusually lively autumn in Berlin because of the Olympic Games—it was fun, but it was also strangely foreign to me. I found the city of my birth less familiar than London, and there was an aspect of *angst* and apprehension in the air. We often went to a restaurant called Die Taverne, which was a hangout for foreign correspondents, especially Americans, and I remember meeting William Shirer and H. R. Knickerbocker there. The talk always turned to politics, and even I, who was young, self-centered, and politically ignorant, understood the tension and seriousness of their discussions, which invariably focused on Hitler's aggressive intentions, ominous future plans, and the impending war which would ensue.

The persecution of the Jews seemed to be discussed only in a political context, because few people then suspected the magnitude of Hitler's intention literally to exterminate a people for one reason and one reason only: because they were Jews. *That* was the tragedy of the world. How could anyone believe that such a monstrous action was being planned and that sufficient numbers of people could be won over to participate in and carry out such a horror?

——

With emotions that seesawed between pain and frivolity— haunting remembrances which would not leave and came between me and any attempts I made to fall in love again—I took refuge in the only thing that helped to balance my life by taking daily classes with my old teacher, Victor Gsovsky. I had not heard any further news from London about *On Your Toes* and was developing acute anxiety about my future, a typical symptom of my inability to handle any kind of uncertainty. But when I was in the classroom all was well. If my body behaved and I had a good class, my fear and anxiety vanished and I felt strong and independent again. The obedience of my body to execute what I asked of it gave me a tremendous sense of power—the kind of power and happiness (you could almost say contentment) which nothing else could.

At this time I began to acquire the bad habit of eating, dieting, and purging. Like most dancers I was obsessed with my body and even the slightest hint of more than muscle and skin disgusted me. It went so far that when I visited the Louvre in Paris I hated to look at the paintings of Rubens, those large nudes in the room especially devoted to him, because they looked like a celebration of twisted, swirling, pink fat dancing around the walls. I am rather large-boned and was obviously meant to be a rounded female, but I would have none of it and went on one binge after another, either eating or dieting.

I finished my Berlin engagement at the Wintergarten at the end of September, when my good friend Edward James, whom I had met in London, came to the rescue with a wonderful proposition: a motoring trip together, starting in Innsbruck and driving leisurely through Italy to Naples and Paestum. Edward James was an eccentric young man about whom there were many rumors in England. One of the most colorful hinted that he was the illegitimate son of Edward VII. He had been married briefly to the Austrian dancer Tilly Losch, but I don't think that women were his real persuasion. He was a charming man, very rich, and devoted to the arts. He himself was a gifted writer and poet. He supported many artists and in 1936 had a great deal to do with the launching of Salvador Dali's career. He sponsored Dali's first exhibition in London, followed by a large party in his beautiful house in Wimpole Street. I always associate that house with the redolent scent of lilies. In the entrance hall at the foot of the stairway stood a huge bowl which was invariably filled to profusion with those delicious white flowers, flecked with deep purple, exuding their heavy fragrance.

The party was splendid and Edward had invited some of his nieces, young debutantes, to join the distinguished group of artists and writers. During the evening, Edward dramatically unveiled his latest acquisition, a new Dali. It was hidden behind silk curtains and when he pulled the cord everyone stared in anticipation. It revealed two dirty old shoes remarkably painted in minute detail, down to the splitting soles and dangling shoelaces, as if Charlie Chaplin had just discarded them. There was a baffled silence, soon broken by the uncontrollable giggles of the debutantes, who had to be led away.

———

Edward had a secretary whom he referred to only as "the Mushroom." Her name was Miss Auchade, and she accompanied us on the trip, providing us with an unending source of conversational curiosity simply because there was little else to discuss. Some people are mysterious because one cannot imagine that that's all there is, but Miss Auchade was what she appeared to be—a small, quiet woman who never said anything, did her work, was reliable, wore nondescript clothes and large hats, which made her look like a mushroom. We wondered, did she have a private life? If so, what was it like? Perhaps she was in love with Edward? We never found out, because she remained devoted and silent. Edward never stopped writing poetry and short stories during our entire trip, and kept her very busy at the typewriter.

Edward was wonderful to my mother, and invited her to join us. Before we left Berlin, she packed up our entire apartment, put the furniture in storage, and sent the rest of our suitcases to London. After the war, although the warehouse had disappeared into the rubble of Berlin, the firm sent us a long, costly bill for storage. The facts that there had been a war and the furniture no longer existed apparently made no difference. The bill also added unnecessarily: "The furniture could not be delivered as it has been destroyed by enemy attack."

Our rendezvous began in Innsbruck. We were met at the station by a big, comfortable Bentley driven by Edward's chauffeur. The next morning we drove to Verona for the first stop of our Italian journey.

While Edward worked with the Mushroom in the morning, Mama and I rushed around visiting museums and churches. I nearly spoiled the trip for her by insisting on dragging her to obscure places, and insisting that there was a particular painting or fresco which we *had* to see. I would run around in the darkness of a church and finally locate what I was looking for high up in the corner of the ceiling—something the art books I lugged around did not indicate. While I stood in adoration in front of a master of the Sienese school, she nearly cried from fatigue, frustration, and boredom. It was not that she was uninterested in art, she just preferred it at a more leisurely tempo and in small doses. She certainly did not appreciate the relentless thoroughness with which her daughter lectured her on Cimabue, Giotto, and the hands of Carlo Crivelli. I was in ecstasy in Florence, but I daresay Mama was rather worn out.

There was only one mishap. An hour after we had left Florence, my mother whispered that she could not find her gold cigarette case, which she must have forgotten in her hotel room. It was very embarrassing (to me *enraging*, since she always forgot something), but we had to turn around and drive back. At the hotel everything was turned upside down while we waited in the car. Suddenly my mother turned to me and said, "Please don't say anything, but I've just found it." When Edward returned from a fruitless search, she managed to say grandly, "Never mind—let's go. It will show up . . ." We set off again, with the entire staff of the hotel standing outside with long faces. She never told Edward the truth, and neither did I.

Things simmered down a bit in Rome when I was felled by the flu and had to stay in bed. Edward went ahead, and we followed by train to Naples a few days later. Then we all drove to Amalfi.

Oct. 12. In the evening at Positano I looked over to the Isola dei Galli, where I had spent my vacation the year before with Massine. It lay far in the distance—like a part of my life—such a beautiful place, like a rough, craggy diamond in the sea. It could have been—I tried not to think about it.

Our leisurely Italian sojourn was at times troubled, because I was anxiously awaiting news about *On Your Toes.*

Oct. 13. Called London because I hadn't heard a word from [my agent], which drove me to despair—but understood very little. Afternoon tea with Mrs. Frost, sister of Lord Grimstorp, who owns the Villa Cimbrone. She herself has a perilously situated villa, which is built against a cliff. When you stand on the balcony to admire the magnificent view, it is best to keep your eyes on the distance because below you is an absolute chasm!

We visited the beautiful beige-pink temple in Paestum and drove home via Salerno in streaming rain and thunder. The following day we were in Naples, where Vesuvius gave us an awesome spectacle. Day and night, fire burns into the air from the crater and is seen for miles, especially at night. It is utterly spectacular and beautiful to watch, until one grasps the reality of the volcano's terrifying destructive power. We stood on the rim of the huge crater watching the cracks through which the lava flowed slowly, like pure, hot gold. It made me understand how the people of Pompeii died: not from the liquid fire, from which they perhaps could have run away, but from the rain of ashes, which suffocated, destroyed, and buried every living thing.

When we visited the ruins of Pompeii, the guide refused to allow me (I was underage) to enter a special section of excavated rooms because the walls were covered with highly erotic frescoes. I walked up and down on the crude cobblestones waiting for my mother to emerge and thought, Is there really anything new under the sun, even in Pompeii? My mother reported *not*.

Finally, we went to Capri and stayed at the Hotel Quisisana. I did all the things that are fun to do on that beautiful island— swimming at the Piccolo Marina, cocktails in the piazza, visiting the Blue Grotto, and acquiring an Italian "admirer," who followed me around indefatigably (on one day from 5 p.m. to 1 a.m.), begging me with his eyes for a rendezvous and singing beautiful songs ("*O Sole Mio,*" no doubt). On October 21 my past intruded; I remembered in my diary: "Today the ballet sails on the *Ile de France* without me. *Ile de France*, the boat with so many memories —Léonide, Chevalier." (This refers to a hilarious moment during a storm when an elaborate basket filled with fruit and candy tipped and fell into Maurice Chevalier's lap, showering its contents all over him and the floor.)

Soon we left, with poor Rafael, my admirer, following me to the boat. Italians can be very dogged when they pursue a woman. There is some aspect of what the French call *pour le sport* about it. They carry on as if one were the only woman on earth, but when they fail they're quite good-natured about it, because even they know it wasn't a very serious attempt in the first place. One year, when I was taking the cure on the island of Ischia, I was alone and knew no one—so I ate all my meals in solitary splendor. You always have the same table and therefore the same waiter. Mine, who was very polite and efficient, did a lot of hovering about. He began his strategy with: "Such a beautiful woman alone on this beautiful island," and he offered to show me some delightful spots, and so on. I said, "Thank you so much," with exquisite politeness and, I hoped, an air of finality, but no. He continued, undaunted, during the next few days and, quite unconcerned about other guests, pantomimed like a lover in an old-fashioned ballet the pitter-patter of his heart. At that point I thought it best to tell him that my husband, who was arriving the next day, was certain to want to see those special sights very much. He stopped his pantomime in midair and withdrew. The following day we saw him in the corridor, and I called, "Roberto! I want to introduce you—" Which is as far as I got, as he disappeared around the corner faster than a MIG jet.

On October 28 we arrived in Paris and stayed at the Ritz. What bliss! Mama and I loved it all the more after the awful experience of our first visit to Paris, when I was eleven. We reveled in its luxury — not luxury in an opulent manner, but in the sheer joy of total well-being. I had a room under the mansard, with a huge brass bed, overlooking the Place Vendôme. The beauty of it at twilight filled me with happiness just being there—watching from the window; waking up in the morning to *café au lait* with croissants and con-

fiture (only the French make that marvelous slightly tart cherry jam); the scent of perfume everywhere, knowing that you could wear as much of it as you pleased and no one would quiver a nostril disapprovingly; the extreme elegance of shops, which made me want to explore them all and made me feel more feminine. It was *séduisante*, the seduction of my senses.

I found a little piece of paper in my diary dated 30/10/36: "Miss Hartwig, Ritz, fitting Wednesday, 3 p.m." It is written under a printed heading:

SCHIAPARELLI

POUR LE SPORT

POUR LA VILLE

POUR LE SOIR

which tells a story. In 1936 Paris was the undisputed fashion center of the world. The great houses of *haute couture* were awesome and dictatorial. Women watched for their latest edicts in magazines, adjusted their bodies, and tried to dress accordingly, even if they couldn't afford the real thing. As war and revolution influenced clothes, so were the designers influenced by the painters and artists who lived and created in Paris before World War I, right through the twenties and thirties. The opulence of the costumes of *Boris Godunov*, which Diaghilev presented in 1909, were as significant as Surrealism twenty years later. I once saw Dorotea Tanning in a dress which her good friend Max Ernst (both Surrealist painters) had designed for her. It had an embroidered snake coiled around her exposed breast, in which her own nipple became its beady eye.

To go to see the new collection of Chanel or Balenciaga required an invitation and was as exciting as going to the opening night of the opera—maybe more so. I was particularly drawn to Schiaparelli's designs. I found her daring and theatrical, and with impeccable taste. It was Schiaparelli who introduced the perfume *Shocking*, whose flacon was made in the shape of a female torso. Shocking Pink became known as her particular color, a shade between red and pink which she made famous.

Edward James knew "Schiap" (as she was known to friends) and introduced me to her as *"la danseuse ravissante du Ballet Russe"* and *"la future grande vedette de Londres"*—grand introductions never hurt. I remember her as having somewhat heavy features, as dark-haired and Latin-looking—a handsome woman with an aura of masculinity. She was quite formidable and brusque, but we got on very well. When I saw the collection I instantly fell in love with a full-length evening gown and dramatic matching cape. It was a magnificent color of midnight blue—a blue as in a moonlit landscape by Edvard Munch. The dress was deceptively simple, with braided matte gold straps, but its sensation lay in the way it was cut on the bias and outlined the body. The cape's only adornment was embroidered shoulders—much like a bullfighter's jacket. I thought how perfect it would be for one of the scenes in *On Your Toes* (if it was ever to come off). After all, Vera Barnova was an eccentric ballerina and should look exotic and absolutely smashing.

Since all dresses were made to order, the ritual of taking my measurements now began. It resembled having a modern physical. One lady kept a chart and pencil, the other measured every inch of my body up and down, sideways, crisscross, from the neck to the nipple, from the nipple to the waist, under the armpits to the waistline, from the waistline to the crotch, to the midcalf, to the ankle, around the neck, and even around the forehead in case I ordered hats. The slightest detail or oddity was noted and duly written down with extreme exactness; and while all this was going on, you were expected to stand up straight and not slouch. You were also expected to be available for numerous fittings. Those fittings were attended by several seamstresses who were all engaged in the execution of the dress and a *directrice* who acted as an overseer. Sometimes Mme Schiap herself appeared, but that was rare and made everybody very nervous. You had to stand still, not fidget, and not complain, and, above all, not point out anything that didn't seem right. It was considered unnecessary, since it invariably had been noted long before it had been noticed by you. It was almost as if you didn't exist—people talked across you, snipping, pulling, and pinning—and you were only a body inside a creation. If you were pricked by a pin and made a sound, the ladies looked up in surprise, so completely had they forgotten about you.

I recklessly ordered two more "items" that I could not resist—a black wool jacket embroidered most delicately with small gold palm trees at the pockets and a pink satin evening jacket edged with tiny glass flowers complete with flexible green leaves. That jacket was really a work of art; I have kept it to this day.

I gained the courage to order these clothes because *On Your Toes* was once more assuming reality. Lee Ephriam had just telegraphed me that he expected it to open at the end of January in the Coliseum. Rehearsals would start three weeks earlier.

Edward introduced me to his friends in Paris and several times took me to the house of the great hostess and patron of the arts Comtesse Marie-Laure de Noailles. There I met many artists who became my friends when we met again in New York during the war. I became particularly fond of Pavel Tchelitchev, the eccentric and gifted Russian painter and set designer, though in the beginning he frightened me with his sharp, devastating wit. It was Pavlik who described someone with a paunch as looking "like a pregnant mosquito." I also met Vittorio Rieti, composer of many ballets for both Diaghilev and Balanchine. He had beautiful Italian good looks and was a very gentle man. We had dinner with Dali at Maxim's, which was always a wildly difficult affair, because his use of surrealistic imagery, coupled with a thick, rolling Spanish accent, made it almost impossible to understand him. We also had a memorable dinner with Natasha Lelong (Princess Paley) and Russie Sert, the second wife of the Spanish painter José María Sert, whose first wife had been the famous Misia.

Russie Sert was one of the most beautiful and fascinating women I have ever seen. She was Russian-born and the sister of the legendary Mdivani princes. She was young, but her hair was white, and I was told it had turned overnight when her adored brother, Serge, was killed in an automobile accident. It is hard to describe beauty and fascination. It depends on what a woman does *with* it; it depends not so much on the individual perfection of her features as on the interplay of those features. Russie Sert had the largest, most beautiful eyes I ever saw, including Garbo's—but like Garbo, there was something boyish and angular about her. She wore rough stones on several strings around her neck, except that the stones were rubies and emeralds, which enhanced her look of a barbaric princess. She was quite indescribable. Since her brother's death, she had lost interest in living. She chose to die by not eating. A year later, she was dead.

My diary has a curious entry for November 1, Paris: "Made the acquaintance of Igor Markevitch, who is slightly mad, and who reminds me of Kyra Nijinsky in temperament. What is even stranger is that he knows her and said that Kyra has long, blond curls, which I find crazy, *and* that she expects a child!" Igor Markevitch was a young musician and, as was well known, the last protégé of Diaghilev. It seemed to me an extraordinary coincidence that he should later marry Kyra, the daughter of Nijinsky, who was the love of Diaghilev's life. Kyra and Markevitch visited us in our mansard room at the Ritz, where Kyra, my mother, and I had a noisy and excited reunion. Igor Markevitch wound up on his knees in front of my mother, kissing her hand in an excess of affection. Kyra did not have golden curls, nor do I know whether she was pregnant, but soon after she did marry Markevitch and had a son. We did not see each other again until after the war, in Rome, in the early fifties. By that time, she was divorced and earning a living as a saleslady on the Via Condotti. She was haughty about her job and as maniacally brilliant a conversationalist as ever.

We returned to London in November and Mama began hunting for an apartment. At last she found a furnished flat which we could afford at Fountain Court on Buckingham Palace Road. It was tiny and we bumped into the furniture, but it was better than all the other places we had lived in. I had always loved London, but this time, after Paris, it struck me how much of a man's city it was. In London, men seemed good-looking even when they were not. Their clothes fit better, their hair was better cut and groomed, nothing in their apparel was new-looking, and they took delightful and audacious risks in choosing lilac socks or a scarlet lining for a coat and wearing soft felt hats (chocolate brown) with the brim tilted down to the eyebrows—all with panache. In 1936, it was *de rigueur* for men to change into dinner jackets in the evening, and women wore evening gowns. It made dining out or going to the theater more festive and elegant.

We were total Anglophiles and followed enthusiastically all the royal happenings. Speculations about Mrs. Simpson had become public, the Prince was now King Edward VIII, and the unbelievable event of the abdication was about to happen. No one could speak of anything else. The night of the abdication speech, we were invited to a dinner party where we all listened to the broadcast. When the speech was over, a silence fell over the assembled guests. My mother and I began to speak, but no one would answer or comment. Things had taken a fatal turn, a turn so shocking that no one wished to discuss it further.

The next year, we were in London for a happier event, the coronation of King George VI. I was lucky to be invited to sit on a grandstand directly opposite the entrance to Westminster Abbey. The colonial empire was still in its glory, and I remember particularly the Indian cavalry in their magnificent uniforms and white turbans, riding on black horses with leopard-skin saddles, holding decorated lances aloft. The maharajahs seemed to me the most romantic and glamorous symbols of the empire. Their wealth and opulence were famous, much like the extravagances of the Russian Grand Dukes in their time. One night I saw the Maharajah of Jaipur in the Savoy Grill. With him was a beautiful actress, Virginia Cherrill. Her pale-blond, exquisite beauty was enhanced by a dazzling display of sapphires. Looking at her, I dreamed, *That's* what I wish for—to have a big, beautiful sapphire ring one day.

———

When I see from my diary that I flew back and forth to Paris, sometimes for only twenty-four hours, I am amazed. It seems so long ago that I almost equate the period with the Wright brothers. The fact that I flew over just for a fitting with Schiaparelli or to get a permanent wave with Antoine (my favorite hairdresser) seems to me incredible. It was considered rather sporty to fly, and it was Spartan compared with today. The stewardesses were severe, and dressed in uniforms and did *not* inquire whether you wanted a martini or champagne. You sat strapped in your bucket seat and did not wander around. I remember once flying in a plane whose motors were totally exposed; they looked like sewing machines. Still, we took off, we flew, and we landed, and in those days I was never afraid—only excited by the wonder of getting up in the air.

In December in London I awaited the start of rehearsals, and I met Dwight Deere Wiman, the debonair and charming American producer of *On Your Toes*, who was to play a great part in my future career. I began working with Lina Abarbanell, who had come over from New York to "coach" me in my first acting role. Lina had been a star and a big hit in *The Merry Widow* in her day. She was small, dark, and vivacious, with two spit curls curved in front of her ears. She was hardworking and had an incredible amount of energy, and she was tenacious in bringing me up to her standards. We became good friends and continued to work together on many shows and films. I seem to have spent the month of December 1936 in building up and tearing down. I took lessons with my beloved teacher, Nicholas Legat. I went on one crazy diet after another: the whole day long nothing but buttermilk—or nothing but vegetables—then eating to my heart's delight—then being disgusted with myself—Turkish baths. I must have had the constitution of an ox to have survived all that.

Just before Christmas, I was invited with two other couples for dinner and the theater. Things went a bit sour right from the beginning, when I refused the offer of a drink. While everyone got slightly high and ate a big dinner, I ate sparingly and, to top it off, asked for an apple for dessert. Nothing seemed to be as amusing as that request—an apple! Instead of accepting my explanation that I was "in training," they began to tease me. When we got to the theater, they bought a large box of chocolates and handed it around during the play, and again I refused. By the time we went to a nightclub for supper, the teasing had turned into a challenge—if I would eat a whole Baked Alaska for four I would win £25. I had no idea what Baked Alaska was or that it consisted of layers of cake and ice cream encased in baked meringue. I was so thoroughly irritated by then that I accepted the bet. My real motivation was the £25—a lot of money before Christmas. I packed in the dreadful dessert, and the only concession I asked was to get up and dance before finishing it off. The man who made the bet gave me my reward with ill grace, before I rushed to the bathroom. But I returned home triumphant with my £25.

I was still concerned with who would be my classical ballet partner in *On Your Toes*. I was hoping it might be André Eglevsky. We had met two years ago in Paris when we both studied with Nicholas Legat. He was a very good-looking and nice boy who became a marvelous dancer and partner. Unfortunately, de Basil wouldn't let him go. I finally saw a young dancer at the Café Anglais, got his address, and he was engaged. He became Jack Donahue's understudy and danced the ballet *Zenobia* with me. Finally, on January 7, we had the first official rehearsal of *On Your Toes*. Gina Malo, Olive Blackney, Eddie Pola, Jack Donahue, and I read through the script. After waiting for five months, poor Jack Whiting, who was starring in the part Ray Bolger did in New York, caught the flu and couldn't attend.

The day we started rehearsals I entered a whole new world. I discovered that even though we worked very hard, we could also have a lot of fun. It was my first introduction to American show-biz humor—easy banter and informality, not taking yourself too seriously, the absence of a hierarchical structure. Nobody had to be kissed unless you wanted to do so, and genuine affection among cast members made daily working together a pleasure. I was immediately recognized as an absolute natural to play a joke on, but even if I was often the "straight man," I loved it. After the gloom of the last months in the ballet, I was happy with the gay camaraderie and thrived on it.

My co-star, Jack Whiting, was an attractive, easygoing person. He was married to Bess Whiting, a warm, lovely woman with premature white hair. Bess had previously been married to Douglas Fairbanks, Sr., and was the mother of Doug Jr. One night she brought her son backstage. There he stood, the epitome of a movie star, tall, handsome, and elegantly dressed in a dark coat with an astrakhan fur collar. He was then the ex-husband of Joan Crawford and exuded charm, the kind of charm he has to this day, completely natural and unselfconscious. Bess, Jack, Doug, and I became good friends and saw each other frequently outside the theater.

I was dieting with a vengeance now. "Jan. 10. Heroic buttermilk-day!" Then depression.

Jan. 11. A very quiet day—no class. I don't rehearse because Abarbanell is in Paris. I can't believe in this show anymore—this constant, endless waiting after the hard work in the ballet is intolerable—and no class because of my legs. My muscles have to have rest and nothing but massage—so I went to the British Museum, then in the Turkish bath, where I decided that a buttermilkday helps a lot in losing weight—another 5 pounds and I'm O.K. At night, to the movies.

Jan. 14. Finally, "we seem to be getting somewhere." Ephriam called to say there would be a rehearsal tomorrow—it seems to me it's about time! In the evening, to a concert—very, very good. Saxophone Concertos of Glazunov and Debussy—wish I heard more music. Met Bunny Tattersal of the *Daily Mail* and went out with Ellen Mosner and Otto Clement, a very nice man who talks a great deal and *very slowly*—a type like Von Sternberg and Vollmoeller.

Jan. 15. Rehearsal at 11. Read through the play again. Then Jack Donahue and I rehearsed, because he will play Morosine, my temperamental partner. Tried out the *Zenobia* ballet—not bad—he is very strong.

Jan. 17. Rehearsal also today (Sunday) and buttermilkday. Love rehearsing the ballet. I very much hope Donahue will be good. Afterward went through the whole play—it's beginning to get some shape.

Jan. 19. First rehearsal on the stage of the Palace Theatre. All the chorus people sat in the audience—got my first "laughs" from the dialogue—it's such fun. In the evening, saw the second act of *Gisèle* at Sadler's Wells with Margot Fonteyn—very good, but not as good as Markova. Nijinska was there with Pat [Dolin]. Very sweet to me—also lots of fans from Covent Garden.

Jan. 20. At 10, practiced the *pas de deux* for an hour with Donahue—went very well—then in the Gaiety Theatre all day. Everything goes so well I'm almost afraid, I have so much fun—tried on costumes.

Jan. 22. Rehearsal at 11—before that, looked at costumes—now tired but happy at home. I find Jack Whiting very, very nice and sympathetic. I know I always have to have something "romantic" in the theater and he is exactly right for the role. Jack Donahue is nice—but *too* nice—*also* right for Morosine, so I can play my scenes better. Today the blue foxes for my costume were chosen.

Jan. 24. Buttermilkday—rehearsals only in the afternoon—everybody was wonderful to me. Mrs. Whiting and Wiman—I would say almost too much praise. In the evening, Abarbanell came for dinner and we worked afterward together—then played Halma for hours.

Jan. 25. Rehearsals—what else at this point? Terrible, poor Legat died—I am so sorry—going to special Mass for him in his studio.

I got quite a shock when I entered the studio for the funeral service. It had always been a place of immense activity—dancers, music, and noise—but now the big hall was silent. Legat was lying on a bier in the middle of his studio surrounded by the symbols of his life's work—empty bars on the walls where countless dancers had practiced, and all his caricatures of the dancers he knew, loved, and had satirized affectionately. The piano was closed, and the dancers and friends (Agnes de Mille among them) huddled against a wall which was almost entirely mirrored, in front of which Legat had conducted his classes sitting on a stool and tapping his cane loudly, beating time. I approached him and kissed him, and I thanked him silently for all he had taught me.

Jan. 26. Rehearsal with Donahue—then he went through the whole play. I can only say: "I enjoy it all tremendously!" [in English].

Jan. 27. Tried on shoes at Raynes—tried on costumes at Mrs. Bowes—looked very beautiful—then rehearsals. What can one write about that? We always go through the whole show—my role goes well. I am a little afraid of *Zenobia* because of Donahue [Jack Donahue was not a professional dancer, which gave me concern]—otherwise O.K. *Slaughter* [*on Tenth Avenue*] gives me enormous pleasure. I can really let go [what I meant was spend all my pent-up energy]. If only Jack Whiting had more temperament—he keeps worrying about his hair falling into his eyes and brushing it away during the most passionate part of the dance. Lina Abarbanell is sweet—she always comes and gives me good advice. Otherwise, I gab a lot in Russian with my partner—gave half an interview—paid Equity—and now I have to go back to rehearsal. I pray to God that the premiere will go as well as the rehearsal. Then I shall be content.

Jan. 29. Rehearsals at the Palace—then lunch at the Ivy with Vera Nemchinova and Anatole Oboukhov, both great dancers from the

Diaghilev company. Talked Russian the whole time; made me very happy that I could still speak it that well. Then again rehearsal. Today press people were there and photographers—Mrs. Wiman—Mrs. Henson, all severe critics, but they were enthusiastic. It's beginning to get complicated because Ephriam wants to talk to us about my future! Abarbanell and Wiman on the other side want me for New York for a play. Then there are Louis Shurr and Goldwyn. Well, and then there is de Basil (who wanted me to come back to the ballet). Had a letter from Olga today that Léonide is all right—traveling in his trailer with his wife and secretary!! So that's that. [Last entry in English.]

It was indeed getting very complicated, because my reputation was rising on both sides of the Atlantic. Sam Goldwyn, who in Europe was regarded as the most distinguished independent movie producer, was, according to my agent in New York, "interested" in me. Among all these as yet vague offers, the possibility of doing a new show with Wiman interested me the most, returning to the ballet the least. But I knew that all these plans hinged on one thing—whether or not I made a success in *On Your Toes*.

Jan. 31. Buttermilkday—slept badly. Had nightmares [English] before I went to sleep because of the show. Everybody expects and predicts such a success for me that it scares me. Otherwise, rehearsals at the Gaiety—Jack Donahue's waistband broke in the middle of the adagio so that he stood there nearly naked among the howling chorus girls.

Feb. 1. Raced around the whole day—in the morning, in the Gaiety right through the show. Then to Annello [ballet shoes]—then Vega [shoes]—then more dress costumes—then Scala Theatre—then Nathan's [costumes], and then Palace rehearsals—have a very beautiful star dressing room next to the stage—my own dresser, telephone, etc. All my "dresses" are wonderful—especially the Schiaparelli evening dress and the costume with the blue fox! The ballet costumes absolutely sweet and the striptease girl with hair like Garbo—but still very choruslike *à la* "burlesque girl"! It was so exciting to be again in full makeup! Dear God, if I'm not a success—what then? Because I have everything, beautiful costumes, a role just made for me—and, in spite of all the running around, I'm not even tired!

Feb. 2. First dress rehearsal. Went quite well—I personally was very dissatisfied—didn't act as well as I have—danced dreadfully badly—and anyhow it was so peculiar in the bedroom scene—had to kiss Jack Whiting, which I found so embarrassing—have no idea after all how to kiss on the stage.

Feb. 3. It was very exciting this afternoon—the public was present and liked it a lot. They died of laughter over Olive Blackney, who is such a marvelous comedienne. All my scenes went very well until the change from the striptease girl into the ballet costume, but *Zenobia* went without a hitch, which gives me a lot of confidence. Wiman and Henson were so sweet to me—one can't imagine it—Henson: "I am so happy to have worked with you—and always keep your head as small as it is now." Received long, long letter from Louis Shurr with big prospects for Hollywood.

Feb. 4. Again dress rehearsal—but went for myself only, so la-la—Douglas Fairbanks was there and Pat Dolin came later—but that didn't help, either. I'm glad that the premiere is finally tomorrow—this tension is unbearable.

Feb. 5. What a day—but first things first. Slept late—then played all the rumba records [apparently that was soothing!]. Mama and I went nearly mad from nerves. Then I went to church—truly, God was with me yesterday. Then to the doctor and hairdresser, then into the blue Schiap cape and to the theater. My dressing room was filled with flowers, telegrams, costumes, and a thousand things—Doris [my dresser] found everything so glamorous, which pleased me the most—then Toi-Toi's for good luck, and suddenly I was on stage singing "*Ochi chornye.*" Everything went the way I hoped—every little thing. The success was enormous—people poured into my dressing room, I simply couldn't speak—everything trembled in me. Violet Tree said she had seen Bernhardt, and even against that she thought I was wonderful—oh my! People whom I didn't know congratulated me. In the Savoy Grill, big applause—then to Leslie Henson's, more people. The most beautiful day of my life. My mamile and I sat holding each other by the hand like two children. Everything was really like a dream—so beautiful—(and more). My God, what an evening—flowers—people—congratulations—Wiman—Henson—Fairbanks—Cochran—Asher—hundreds of people, and I was honored at the Savoy Grill!!!

It was theater tradition to go to the Savoy Grill after a premiere. I had been there many times before for supper and always had to wait until the haughty *maître d'* showed me to a table. This time, when I came through the entrance, the whole room started to applaud. I quickly turned around to see who was behind me, until I realized it was for me.

Feb. 6. Today Saturday. The reviews are fabulous. All kinds of people call to congratulate—my bathtub is an ocean of flowers. Very good performance. A man came from Fox films and wants to make a test.

Feb. 7—Sunday. Slept and slept. Wrote letters—read reviews—all good. Someone rang and asked me for an interview. "It doesn't suit me very well today, but maybe tomorrow?"—that's Zorina! Then I went to church, where I felt overwhelmed by happiness, joy, gratitude for all that God has given me.

Feb. 9. Took photos the whole day in the theater until 4:30. In the evening, big party in the Café de Paris for Wiman and Lina—so sad that they had to leave already—but the party was divine. Wiman absolutely wants me to come to New York for him and a new show.

The day after the opening brought a great many offers from Hollywood, New York, London, and even Berlin. A long, long letter arrived from UFA, the prestigious German film company. Herr von Reiht wrote congratulating me on my big success—the news of which had even reached Berlin: It should be of interest to me, a *German*, that a *German* film company also had an interest in me and would I kindly inform him whether I had had other offers from foreign companies and would I not prefer working for a German company? A rather *"Deutschland, Deutschland über alles"* letter.

On Your Toes was a big hit opening night and had excellent reviews. But in spite of that, it had a curious history. The "stalls," or the people in the orchestra seats, loved it. Often that particular audience would come back again and again to see the show. But apparently it was too sophisticated and ahead of its time for the large general public who usually filled the mezzanine and balcony. They didn't "get it" and stayed away. Perhaps they were offended by the show's theme, satirizing the Russian ballet and a prima ballerina, introducing a jazz ballet and gangsters, making fun of an impresario who might have been modeled after Diaghilev. It was a supremely irreverent show, witty both in dialogue and in the choreography by Balanchine. Those who knew the dead earnestness of ballet and the backstage feuds and jealousies were convulsed with laughter, especially during the *pas de deux* of the *Zenobia* ballet, but I don't think that the truly devoted English ballet lovers at that time wanted or could accept such an attitude. Of course, Diaghilev had done satirical ballets, Lord Berners and Satie had written satirical scores, but perhaps *On Your Toes* went too far for ballet aficionados, without having the sanction of being presented by a ballet company. And so we missed a crucial part of the audience. Sophisticates alone cannot support a show; the vast general public does that, and unfortunately they didn't come in sufficient numbers.

The euphoria of opening night continued. Every day there were new offers and inquiries from film companies, requests for interviews, or photo sessions for magazines with "Anthony," "Sasha," or with Cecil Beaton—all the things that happen when you have made a big personal success. But already, six days after the opening, there were doubts that *On Your Toes* was really the big hit we had expected.

Feb. 12. Am angry because our business is not as good as it should be with such a marvelous show. Terrific performance tonight—people became nearly hysterical over *Zenobia*. Louis Shurr has asked for too much money—$1,000 a week for my first film for Goldwyn—well, we'll see.

Feb. 13. Matinee and evening—got a completely crazy love letter from a woman and was invited to open a boys' school—*I*!! of all things! Burst out laughing. Duke and Duchess of Kent in the audience—it was marvelous.

Feb. 15. In the evening went to Lucienne Boyer's premiere at the Café de Paris. [She made *"Parlez moi d'amour"* famous.]

What fun it was to go dancing in nightclubs, especially if you were flirting with someone. That moment when you got up to dance close together to really dreamy music. To this day I am transported back to the "400" when I hear Cole Porter's "Night and Day" or "I've Got You under My Skin," songs which were all the rage in 1937 in London. The Café de Paris was equally special, although not as intimate as the "400." It had nightly shows with big stars, either French, American, or British—even Noël Coward appeared there after the war. The Café de Paris had a central staircase, from which people made "entrances," pausing at the top for a second and then slowly descending. Men were always dressed in black tie or white, and women wore long or short evening gowns. When a British woman is beautiful, she is really beautiful. Who has ever been more lovely than Lady Diana Cooper or Vivien Leigh or Merle Oberon?

The British Actors Equity Association wrote me on February 17, 1937, about the overpayment of six shillings. I reproduce it as nostalgic testament to the slightly redundant but exquisitely polite manners of bygone days.

Dear Miss Zorina—

When we approached you regarding membership of Equity prior to the production of *On Your Toes*, we were unaware that you had previously joined the Association under the name of "Brigitta." We have, therefore, brought your membership up to date as from the date of your last payment, and, of course, you remain a permanent member.

Had you not been an old member you would have been subject to the new rule, and been made a temporary member as a visiting artist. It was for this purpose that we charged you the usual £6.6.0. The sum owing to bring your membership up to date to the end of this year was £6.0.0. We are, therefore, returning the balance of 6/-, which our representative will hand to you when he calls at the theatre on Friday evening.

We trust that this arrangement will be satisfactory to you.

Alexander Korda called me one morning asking if he could see me. I said I couldn't come out to Denham Studios, and so he said he would come to the theater that evening. In my dressing room after the performance, Irving Asher (who also wanted me to take a test) appeared just as I was waiting for Korda. He talked and talked, when suddenly Korda entered. They stared at each other. Asher said, "Well, we'll fix the contract tomorrow," very friendly, and Korda said, "Oh, I just came to say hello." But that wasn't why he had come and it was really very funny.

My diary continues:

Feb. 23. Was fetched in a Rolls and driven out to Denham Studios to Mr. Korda, who proposed a 50–50 deal with Goldwyn and already has two films in mind for me. After our conversation, I was driven back in the Rolls. That night, following the performance, with the Queensberrys and Merle Oberon, who is sweet, at the "400."

Since I can't bear to sign contracts, I procrastinated endlessly. Sam Goldwyn wanted to sign me to a long and exclusive contract, with a starting salary of $750 a week. My first part would be in *The Goldwyn Follies*, a high-budgeted Technicolor movie. I wasn't really interested in making movies and balked at signing a seven-year contract. I was still primarily committed to being a dancer and could not see a career without it. But George Balanchine had been mentioned as the choreographer for the movie, and that was a decisive point. One of my drafts for a cable to Louis Shurr has survived:

AGREE TO GOLDWYN OFFER BUT MUST HAVE RIGHT IN CONTRACT TO APPEAR IN PLAY AS PER WIMAN'S OFFER. ALSO MUST HAVE GUARANTEE OF WORKING WITH BALANCHINE IN FIRST PICTURE. ZORINA.

It was only after George Balanchine was signed by Goldwyn to produce two ballets for the picture that I signed my contract—and not before a clause was added giving me the right to return to the stage after my first movie.

On Your Toes closed after only two months. We were to take two weeks off and then play for a few weeks in the suburbs. It had been a wonderful time for me in every way. Some very funny things happened during the show that I remember to this day. For instance, Jack Whiting and I played a scene together in which I had to try to seduce him. I was sitting on a small bench covered with rattan weaving. As I pulled him down and said in a commanding fashion, "Sit down," he crashed through the bench and wound up with his bottom on the floor and his feet dangling over the frame of the bench. He just sat there while the audience and I howled with laughter. It got worse when he tried to stand, with the bench sticking to him. I finally pulled it off, yanking with all my might. We couldn't continue for five minutes.

It was good to laugh and it was good to have had success. I only hoped it would come again. When the curtain descends after the last performance, one never knows. As perhaps all performers do, I have often stared at the curtain as it hit the floor, separating me from the audience in a particular kind of finality, and silently prayed, Please, dear God, soon again.

———

The next few weeks would have unnerved a hardier soul than I. I was asked to make a screen test for Samuel Goldwyn, and I was pressured to do so by my New York agent, Louis Shurr, as well as by an emissary who had lately arrived in London—A. C. Blumenthal, nicknamed "Blumie." No one seemed to know quite what he did besides being rich. He was kind and had lots of time on his hands. He liked nothing better than to take a pretty girl out to supper and seemed to know everyone in New York and Hollywood, including, obviously, Samuel Goldwyn, for whom he seemed to be "scouting."

The closing of our show was very upsetting; it had not run long enough to make our financial situation really secure. Alexander Korda had shown considerable interest in me and had a very distinguished reputation as a filmmaker. The idea of continuing to live and work in London, where I felt more at home than anywhere, appealed enormously to me. As for UFA, Herr von Reiht renewed his efforts to get me to come to Berlin for a test. I knew I didn't want to do that, but I was in no position to turn things down, so I strung along and stalled and said maybe, while he painted rosy pictures of a big role which would make me a star. These were all possibilities, but the real and immediate task I faced was to make the test for Goldwyn. I couldn't seem to wriggle out of it. I had been before a camera only once and it had been very unpleasant. It was during our first Paris trip, when I was eleven. I had a little part to play in a movie and at one point was supposed to cry. But I couldn't. Everybody stood around and waited for me to start, and the director got very angry, but no matter what he or my mother said, I *could not* cry. It was awful and humiliating, and I thought I never would do that again. Nobody asked me to cry in the Goldwyn test. It was: stand there, look beautiful, smile, turn around, and, of course, dance. Only the dancing was easy—the camera and I never fell in love. It must have gone well, although in my diary I don't sound too happy.

March 13. Saw the test in the morning. Everybody was very enthusiastic—Blumenthal and Silverstone said it was the best test that they've sent to Hollywood. I personally didn't like it very much. Have a German accent and have not been well photographed. But the dancing was very good.

To my delight, the producers decided to play *On Your Toes* for two weeks each in the suburbs of Golders Green and Stratham. Since the engagements were not to start until the end of March, I decided to go to Berlin after all and do the test for UFA. I was very happy to see my former teacher Victor Gsovsky again, and we worked together a few times, preparing for the test. He escaped to France and survived the war teaching in Paris, but we never saw each other again.

March 24. The whole day test at UFA. Sang, danced, and talked—have discovered that I have gotten very fat again—now I'll begin to diet. Kirchoff directed—was very nice. Uncle Gui was there the whole time.

Ever in the role of proud stage mother, Uncle Gui was really the architect behind the scheme to get me to UFA.

March 25. Drove to Neubabelsberg, UFA Studios, with Hans and Olga Biernath [my cousins] to see the test. Quite good—in some ways better photographed than in London. Shopping in the afternoon, then out to Königs Wusterhausen [a suburb where the Biernaths lived] and spent the night there. Harald [another cousin] is very nice and grown-up. Talked for hours with Olga—the poor thing has gotten so thin because she has love problems. Slept well and was awakened with great noise by Harald.

Politics had not yet entered our lives. Granted, it should have, since we were not children anymore, but I was no longer *eine Berlinerin*. I had lived in London and been twice to America, and perhaps I enjoyed the role of being brought back by UFA after having starred in London. Our reunion was mostly that of cousins who had liked each other since we were children. As with Gsovsky, it was the last time we were together before the war separated us. Over forty years passed before I met my relatives again and could pick up our common family bonds with affection.

————

I returned to London and described the Channel crossing as wonderful: "Calm sea, blue sky, and sunshine"—a rare occurrence. We opened in Golders Green on March 29, and I thought the performance good but with "no spark," but we improved and turned into a success all over again.

April 1. Matinee (in Golders Green)—a lot of actors were there. Ivor Novello came tearing into my dressing room and cried, "I am Ivor Novello—let me tell you that you are absolutely marvelous!" and so on. Later, a party, which Mr. Henry Horn, head of Seagers London gin, gave—he has a beautiful old house—not so surprising, since Lord Nelson gave it to Lady Hamilton! We were very excited, since we heard that the show might go back to London.

April 2. Thank God it is certain about the Coliseum—am beside myself with happiness. Telegram from Louis Shurr that Goldwyn is very enthusiastic about my test—very glad about it.

We reopened at the Coliseum on April 19, and for the third time had a big success. I continued with lessons at the Legat studio and recorded: "Everybody is amazed how thin I am." (Oh, that eternal obsession with *thinness*!) That week I had tea at the Savoy and a long talk with Colonel de Basil, who wanted me to dance in the ballet, at least from time to time. He also promised me, because of my success in an acting role, more dramatic parts in the ballet.

My mother went to Norway for a well-earned rest, particularly from me. I think she sometimes got tired of being called "Mami" by everyone and longed to be someone in her own right. What I missed most was her presence—talking to her, making fun of things, or letting go—because *that* was one thing I did only with her. We talked everything over, and I never had any secrets from her. Well, almost none. We differed on many issues, but never seriously. She still found me too *gründlich* [thorough and serious], and I could not understand why she became irritated when I was fired up by a passage in Plato and wanted to read it to her. "Later, darling, later," she would plead. She visualized me as a terrifically beautiful Ziegfeld girl with flowers in her hair, and she would say quietly, "Do you have to pull your hair back so severely? Wouldn't it be softer and prettier with some curls?" On the other hand, with unerring instinct, she would discover the chink in the armor of a beau she didn't approve of. Nothing escaped her. She would sweetly smile, sigh, and then say, "Yes, he is *very* nice, but what a pity he has such ugly hands." And that was usually that. But we loved each other better than anyone else, so in the end none of her criticisms mattered.

One of my admirers at the time was Alfred Beit. He was tall, blond, handsome, and very rich. He was also somewhat pompous. Since my aim in life was not to marry a rich man but to make a lot of money on my own, richness per se did not overawe me. Alfred took me to his country house and introduced me to his sisters. He had a fantastic greenhouse, and I admired the rows and rows of orchids—but he would not give me one. I can understand it now—because it probably was a rare orchid—but at the time I was offended and considered it mean. On returning from the country, we went to dinner at an Indian restaurant where Alfred ordered chicken curry. I must say he treated the Indian waiter rather grandly: "Now, my good man, don't give me that stuff that you call curry here. I've been to India and I know the real thing." Well, they must have given him the hottest imaginable dish, because beads of perspiration began trickling down the side of his face and he became absolutely purple. Still, he didn't give up, and finished his meal—which showed true character.

Edward James invited me to come to Paris, which (my diary records) I regarded as a prima—Berlin slang for first-rate—idea. It also records that at the Ritz I spent a wonderful evening dancing for hours with an acquaintance I had met originally in Berlin, Hansi von Welzceck. He was a racy, elegant young man, very good-looking, with a scar which ran from his hairline to between his eyebrows. I don't think it had anything to do with fencing and Heidelberg, but it did give him a rather sinister, romantic look. Our flirtation was not serious—but briefly wonderful. Both of us knew that our future lay in different directions, and I sensed a social snobbery in him—a snobbery which I possessed about other things. It was the same as with Alfred Beit. Among all these friends, I had not yet met anyone with whom I could talk about music, ballet, or the arts. Flirting was fun, but in the end other things were more important to me.

Even in the thirties, I was becoming more and more involved in television. Britain was far ahead in its development—much farther than Europe or America. As early as 1936, Dolin asked me to dance a *pas de deux* with him for television. When we looked at the result, it resembled an old silent movie flickering in black-and-white dots. But by 1937 it had improved remarkably. "May 21. The whole day out at Alexandra Palace for television of *On Your Toes*—worked under the hot lamps until our tongues hung out." The show turned out to be very successful. I was then asked to make some solo appearances. Blithely I borrowed some costumes from my friend Wendy Toye and improvised. "Everybody was so pleased that they want me back in May."

I now set about it more seriously, dreaming up some proper dance solos, and began rehearsing at the Tiller Studio. (Does anybody remember the Tiller Girls? They were the British version of our Rockettes.) I chose Chopin and Grieg and decided to do a classic ballet solo to Chopin and choreograph to Grieg. "As the music suggests Spring, a nymph in the forest awakes and dances, costume transparent *à la* Botticelli."

May 7. Television—everything went perfectly. All the directors were absolutely mad about my dance to Grieg's *Spring*—I've rarely seen such enthusiasm. They want me to become a permanent television star and to dance for them as often as I can. The producer Mr. Monroe brought me home and altogether they made a lot of "fuss."

I appeared again in my own "original" choreography and can only add that I would give a lot to view those dances today.

May 14, 1937

Dear Miss Zorina,

I have received so many congratulatory messages regarding this production that I would once more like to thank you very much indeed for the really grand performance you gave. I feel that, with your assistance, we definitely made history, as *On Your Toes*, in addition to being the first musical comedy to be televised from the London Television Station, was the first London theatre production we have had the privilege to present with the original cast. I do hope you did not find things here too much of a strain.

I am very much looking forward to your appearance here again on Tuesday 1st June from 9.00–9.10 p.m. and I should be very glad if you could arrive at 7.30 p.m. on that day for rehearsal. As arranged, I should be very glad if you would dance the "Elegiac Melody" as your first item, and finish with the "Blue Danube" waltz, which, as discussed, you are now going to do on points.

D. H. Monroe

May 15. Between matinee and evening saw Kyra [Nijinsky Markevitch] again with her baby. So funny after all these years. She did some very interesting *numérologie*—very true about myself.

Kyra started off by saying that the numbers 2, 11, 22, and 29 are very significant for me, in both a positive and a negative manner.

Ominously, to prove her point, the notice went up in the theater that we were going to close on the twenty-ninth.

Ever since I had made the test for UFA during the first week in April, von Reiht had pressured me—at first, with great promises and flattery, then in rather heavy-handed fashion. He wrote that a great deal of interest *had* been *generated* by my test, and he now urgently needed to know whether there was a possibility of my making a film prior to my departure for America. I was to answer precisely what my obligations were.

1. With whom did I have a theater contract and for how long?
2. With whom did I have a ballet contract and for how long?
3. With whom did I have a film contract and for how long?

I tried to answer with the same Teutonic thoroughness, while at the same time stalling, since I had in fact signed no contracts at that point. My hemming and hawing produced another letter in which von Reiht applied Machiavellian sympathy coupled with outrage that I should be treated in such an "embarrassing" way. He urged me, in a "purely friendly manner," to get my contracts settled. In any event he found all this unnecessarily complicated, because if a manager, after all those weeks, *still* did not have a signed contract, something must be wrong, etc. This was followed by dangling bait in the form of a starring role in a film entitled *Daphne and the Diplomat.*

Since I myself was the sole cause of the delays by waiting until I was sure that Balanchine had *really* signed with Goldwyn and that I could do a show for Dwight Deere Wiman after the completion of my first film, von Reiht's letter did not bother me. I wanted to go to America and I wanted to work with George Balanchine. I also wanted to get back to the stage once I'd made the movie. The next day I received a cable from Los Angeles:

BEAUTIFUL HERE. THINK WOULD BE GOOD IDEA IF YOU CAME TO
HOLLYWOOD MIDDLE JUNE BEFORE CONTRACT STARTS AND DISCUSS WHAT
WE DO AND HAVE MUCH FUN STOP PICTURE MEANS VERY MUCH FOR YOU
WANT YOU TO BE BIG SUCCESS. BALANCHINE.

May 28. The whole Ballet Russe was in the audience—Lulu, Sono, Gala, Ismailoff, etc. They thought it was marvelous and were really, truly impressed. That was the greatest thing for me, that *they* have seen it and found me good. Olive and Ben invited us to the Café de Paris—we had a "wild party." Harry Richman, who was performing there, was very funny, and we all had a swell time.

The Coliseum was much too big a theater for us, and although the loyal fans of the show came to see us again, we did not do sufficient business. We closed after six weeks—this time for good—on May 29. I had decided to go for a "cure" to Marienbad, so that I would be as healthy and beautiful as possible for my Hollywood debut. After all, it was daunting to be touted as "the new European discovery of Mr. Samuel Goldwyn," who had never seen me except in a test. Supposing he didn't like me or was disappointed in his acquisition? Strange to think that I would be so concerned about my appearance at age twenty! I arrived in Marienbad on June 4 and stayed for two weeks, following a strange regime under the strict guidance of Dr. Porges. When I left Marienbad I had "lost 1 stone and weigh 8 stone 3 now."

On June 23 we sailed on the *Normandie* to America. For the first time, Mama and I went up the steep, canopied gangplank marked I CLASS, being greeted by waiting officers and stewards and escorted down to our large double cabin, which was beautifully appointed with twin beds, dressing table, deep armchairs, and a full private bathroom. As soon as the steward left, we were ready for our exultant tango, which we always danced when we were happy, feeling like two adventuresses who had succeeded in realizing their wildest dreams. Our cabin was so elegant and life aboard so luxurious that it never occurred to my mother to be seasick, nor was she seasick ever again in the future. Traveling first class definitely cured her. She ordered champagne and caviar and enjoyed every moment. Meanwhile, I paraded around in my new Schiaparelli clothes and basked in the admiring glances of fellow passengers. Those five days had all the ingredients of adventure and a promising future— New York, the Superchief, and finally Hollywood.

SIX

Our return to America on this occasion was so different from previous visits. No more dingy hotels, grubby coffee-shops, or bus rides. We were met by limousines, escorted to lunch and dinner, and loved our suite in the Waldorf-Astoria. I discovered that its twin towers were more exclusive than the rest of the hotel, with apartments for celebrities (Cole Porter lived there permanently), the super-rich, and royalty. I had seen little of New York on previous visits, because the Ballet Russe routine centered on the area between the old Metropolitan Opera House and our modest hotels in the Times Square theatrical district. To my delight I discovered how beautiful and unique New York really is, with its wide avenues stretching for miles straight into the sky without obstruction, just as the crosstown streets stretch out between the two great rivers of Manhattan island. What a city! I loved it from the start.

I was just a European discovery of Samuel Goldwyn's, but that was apparently enough to create press interest in New York. Blond Scandinavians were still at a high premium. The morning we docked, reporters swarmed aboard and I had to pose sitting on the rail for the traditional "cheesecake" shot, with my skirt up to the knees, and smiling from ear to ear; but when I asked where the term "cheesecake" had originated, no one knew the answer. My Russian stage name and my background as a member of a Russian ballet company created confusion. Since I had made a hit in the role of a Russian ballet star in *On Your Toes* and was soon to be cast as a temperamental ballerina in the film *Goldwyn Follies*, everyone assumed I was Russian, and for years I patiently explained the origin of my stage name. I still do. Meanwhile, in order to dispense with the quandary of whether to address me as Miss or Madame, people simply called me Zorina, which was fine with me.

Although I had never been really poor, I had been aware of the constant struggle for money. Well, now I didn't have to eat Baked Alaska on a bet, and the only value to having been strapped financially was that we appreciated the luxuries that came our way like gleeful children. Every new acquisition gave us so much joy, but was invariably coupled with "Can we really afford that?" or "Is this really happening to us?" Although the seven-year Goldwyn contract still frightened me, it did ensure a settled future.

Dwight Deere Wiman threw a debutante party to which I was invited, and I recorded in my diary: "The boys cut in on the dances and one asked me, 'Do you come from school?' and I said, 'Yes—only on two weeks' vacation!'" (Actually, I wasn't much older than they were.) Our first American Fourth of July weekend was spent mostly swimming and sunning on Long Island.

We left New York on July 7, stopped for a few hours the following day in Chicago, and continued on to Los Angeles. Everything was exciting, even boarding the Superchief for Los Angeles. Black porters, immaculately dressed, stood at the entrance of every carriage as we walked down the platform on a special red carpet. We were politely shown to our compartment, and when the door closed, Mama and I excitedly looked around. It was large and very comfortable, with two sofas which could be made into beds at night. There was a soft knock at the door, and a waiter appeared, asking us at what time we would like to reserve our table for dinner. A certain curiosity was in the air about who was on the train. People looked searchingly at you to learn whether you were a movie star, or at least a potential one. We in turn were looking for the Gary Coopers and Carole Lombards as we discreetly peered into compartments on our way to the dining room. Since this was the most publicized means of transportation to the West Coast and Hollywood, some important person was always on the Superchief, the Concorde of 1937.

I was very conscious of the stares and tried to behave in a worldly and nonchalant manner to make myself more intriguing. I languidly spoke to my mother in three languages—French, German, and Norwegian—sometimes combining all three in a single sentence. We discussed our fellow diners in wicked terms and had an absolutely marvelous time. The trip was very restful, so different from the ballet days, as we traveled across America, seeing the landscape change and, best of all, being out of touch for a few days. It was considered positively tacky to leave the train at the final destination, Los Angeles, and the special stop of the train in Pasadena was invariably well publicized. There we were met by Louis Shurr, Blumie, photographers, and reporters, and taken to the Beverly Hills Hotel.

My notions of Hollywood changed considerably on my first night, when I was invited to dinner by the Goldwyns. I was very nervous and dressed in my best Schiaparelli evening dress—black, with the sensational pink satin jacket. To my relief, Sam Goldwyn was extremely gracious and flattering (as I told my mother later, *Vollkommen hingerissen*—roughly translated as "totally bowled over"). I don't know what I had expected—some overblown vulgarity perhaps—but I found the house elegant and Mrs. Goldwyn racy and very chic. A big tennis star was there, Perry Shields, and also a movie star, Errol Flynn—but that doesn't seem to have impressed me very much. Blumie, my escort, and I stayed until one in the morning talking, and then we went for ham and eggs to Trocadero, the famous nightclub.

The next evening Blumie took me to a big party at Jack Warner's, head of Warner Brothers studios. It was even more like my preconceived idea of Hollywood—a very rich house and lots of movie stars. My diary listed Charles Boyer, Dolores Del Rio, Fay Wray, Gilbert Roland, Constance Bennett, George Cukor, Ernst Lubitsch, and Mervyn LeRoy as being "very uninteresting"—which sounds like sour grapes on my part. Probably I was not important enough for anyone to pay attention to me—especially someone belonging to another studio. Still, the party was an eye-opener.

The following day, Monday, July 12, I went for the first time to the studio, where I lunched alone with Goldwyn, who was "so-o-o nice and so-o-o enthusiastic." I met the scriptwriters of *The Goldwyn Follies*, Anita Loos, John Emerson, and Dorothy Parker; our director, George Marshall; Omar Kiam, the dress designer; Richard Day, the set designer; and two important ladies, Mme Jane, head of wardrobe, and Nina, head of the hairdressing department. Then I was sent to a dentist, Dr. Hartley, to have caps put on my teeth. (The most memorable thing about him was that he immediately told me that he took care of Garbo's teeth.)

My first week in Hollywood did not turn into a "dream of glory." From the moment I stepped into the Goldwyn Studio, I was turned into an object and was scrutinized from head to toe. The makeup department discussed my face as if it were disembodied: "I think we should pluck the eyebrows, they're too thick. Don't you think the nose is too straight? Makes her look too classic. Put some shadowing along the bridge and under the tip to make it more curvy and pert. What about the mouth? Too wide—go easy on the sides and build up the upper lip—give it some heart shape. Boy, those teeth—I think they're going to give us some trouble.

The left front sticks out a little—that's going to give her a shadow
—well, we'll see in the test. And tone down the chin—too strong—
will make her look hard. And those moles on her left chin—tell
you what, cover this one up and give the other one a little brown
dab—it'll make her look piquant. Of course, her forehead is too
high, but let's talk to the hairdressing department about that. Hey,
Nina, can you take a look at Miss Zorina here? Okay now, try
different hairstyles—loose, pinned-up—you know, and keep it soft,
especially around the forehead . . ."

I was washed, shampooed, curled, combed out, pinned, unpinned
by the hairdresser, and plucked, patted, and powdered by the makeup man. I emerged looking like Ann Sheridan or Betty Grable,
certainly not like me. The costume department measured my body
and supplied one "gown" after another until I was ready for a test.

When Mr. Goldwyn saw it, he shrieked, "What's that spot on
her chin?"

"A mole, Mr. Goldwyn."

"Get rid of it! What's that shadow on her front tooth?"

"It's a shadow from the tooth next to it, Mr. Goldwyn."

"Well, have it fixed!"

I was sent to Dr. Hartley again; he ground down another perfectly healthy tooth and capped it into porcelain evenness. I next
went to a dermatologist, who burned off my moles—and left me
with two big Band-Aids on my face. I thought I was going to be
made beautiful in Hollywood; instead, I looked a perfect mess after
one week.

On the domestic front, my mother was luckier. She found a
small, pleasant house, with a lovely garden, at 513 North Camden
Drive in Beverly Hills. We took a lease on it for six months. It
became imperative that I learn to drive and buy a car. It was not
a matter of extravagance but a sheer necessity, in order to get
around. I took to my driving lessons with gusto and soon imagined
myself an expert driver. I bought a small black Buick and was so

proud of it I could have kissed it every morning. One day I was so careful about closing the door that I left half my finger in the crack. The pain was unbelievable. Now I had a bandaged finger in addition to my patched-up face.

Thank God, I was soon released from all the fuss the studio made about my appearance. I could now start rehearsals for the ballets, which were to be filmed first. George Balanchine came for a visit soon after we moved into our house, and invited us to dinner at his place. Aside from our introduction the year before, he and I hardly knew each other. He had made his mark in the Diaghilev company with several ballets, especially *The Prodigal Son* (Prokofiev) and *Apollon Musagète* (Stravinsky). Everyone who was knowledgeable about ballet, including me, ever since I had danced in his ballets *Le Cotillon* and *Le Bal* (in the repertory of de Basil's Ballet Russe), knew he was *the* emerging choreographer, and that Diaghilev's death in 1929 had only momentarily delayed the impact he would make universally in the world of ballet. Someone once asked me, "What did he see in you?" He probably saw in me when we first met—a beautiful blond girl with big blue eyes—a kind of precognition of the type of girl he was susceptible to. Forty years later he said in an interview: "Brigitta was nice dancer and beautiful girl." *That's it*. Why else would he have cabled me, a virtual stranger: COME EARLY TO HOLLYWOOD. WE'LL HAVE FUN. And, on my part, why did I make endless difficulties about my contract until I was assured that Balanchine had definitely signed to do the choreography for *The Goldwyn Follies*? However, our interest in each other took on different dimensions very quickly.

Our first dinner at Balanchine's house marked my entrance into a new Russian "family." He had brought not only his own dancers from New York but two of his closest Russian friends, Nicholas Kopeikine, who was an excellent pianist and played for our rehearsals, and George Volodine, who tripled as friend, cook, and general assistant. Other Russian friends soon became part of this group, which, in its way, was as exclusive as the upper echelon of Hollywood. It included the composer Nicholas Nabokov, his wife, Natasha, and their young son, Ivan. Later Vladimir Dukelsky, a.k.a. Vernon Duke, arrived from New York. Though Russians tend to be clannish, this group did not make me feel like an outsider but surrounded me with affection—mostly due to Balanchine, who was kind, gentle, and a marvelous host. Three musicians from the Goldwyn studios soon joined the inner circle. All of them were working on our film—Alfred Newman as the conductor, and Edward Powell and David Raksin as arrangers and orchestrators. Eddie gave a memorable dinner party one night—memorable because it included two composers of wide divergence, Arnold Schönberg and Richard Rodgers.

Arnold Schönberg and his wife were recent refugees and had settled in Hollywood, soon to be joined by a great many other German giants of the artistic world (such as Thomas Mann, Bertolt Brecht, and Franz Werfel). When I met Schönberg, I was too ignorant to know that I was being introduced to one of the greatest composers of the twentieth century. I was still rooted in Tchaikovsky and Brahms, and my musical education with Balanchine had not yet begun. Of course, I knew the music of Richard Rodgers—not only knew it but loved it—but we had never met, even though I had appeared in *On Your Toes*.

Without my realizing it, my future took a big step forward that night. Dick Rodgers told me months later that he and Larry Hart, who were under contract to Metro-Goldwyn-Mayer at the time, had browsed around in the script department and found a Hungarian play that Metro didn't know what to do with. It had been a big success as a straight play, but the plot was unacceptable to the Hayes Office, the powerful watchdog of American movie morality. It concerned a bachelor, thoroughly fed up with his tricky girlfriends, who says, "The only way I would ever marry is if an angel came down from heaven." Well, she does and all hell breaks loose, because under any circumstances she always tells the truth and unwittingly proceeds to ruin his life. Rodgers and Hart loved the play and managed to get permission from Metro to make it into a musical. The search for the "angel" was on. Dwight Deere Wiman, after seeing me in *On Your Toes* in London, had suggested to Dick and Larry that they write a small part for me in their upcoming musical. After meeting me that night, Dick sent a telegram to Wiman in New York: SMALL PART, HELL—I'VE JUST FOUND THE ANGEL.

My personal relationship with Balanchine developed rapidly, perhaps because we were both Europeans working for the first time in Hollywood, drawn together through common experiences, discovering a new environment, and sharing a love of music—things of which friendships are made. We began to entertain each other, either at his house or at ours, with my mother and George alternating in producing wonderful meals—because, in addition to his many other talents, he was also a superb cook. He and my mother quickly became friends when they discovered their mutual passion and vied with each other in preparing special dishes. My mother's *tour de force* was Norwegian caramel pudding. It had very few ingredients: a quart of heavy cream, twelve egg yolks, and sugar. The result was something akin to eating pale beige satin tempered by the slightly burnt taste of caramelized sugar. Oh my! This was clearly my mother's *pièce de résistance*. In those days caviar was still comparatively cheap, and for special occasions George would present us with a five-pound tin, which we would put in the middle of the table, then spoon the caviar liberally onto our plates. It was accompanied by black bread with sweet butter, but never mixed with chopped egg and onion. George considered that a sacrilege. I was introduced to vodka poured into tiny tumblers. George told me to toss it down in one swallow, then to eat, and then more vodka. My mother frowned on the vodka, but I never became more than slightly tipsy, because I ate so much caviar. In fact, I eventually got quite sick of it, like a child let loose in a chocolate shop.

Our professional relationship fell immediately into place when we began working together. The discipline of ballet is unlike any other in the performing arts. From the earliest days of study, a pupil obeys the teacher, then executes to the best of his or her ability what has been asked—never complains, objects, or protests, but strains to perform the steps in class or while working with the choreographer. Balanchine found much to change in my style and technique. He not only choreographed *on* me and *for* me but began to teach me in class and during rehearsals. Although not aware of it at the time, I was in the process of becoming a "Balanchine dancer." Without illustrations it is difficult to explain, but it mostly involved the hip—as if I was learning to move sideways after having kept my body straight up and down. He corrected my hands and concentrated on my feet. "Caress the floor, use the foot like a hand," and a hundred other directives. He made me over completely, a process which was to continue during all the years we worked together.

Balanchine's leading dancer, William Dollar, was to be my partner in both ballets. We started rehearsals immediately, several weeks in advance of the actual filming, and were given a big dance studio with attached dressing rooms, one for girls and one for boys. I was blissfully happy being part of a company of dancers again, taking class every morning and working with a great teacher and choreographer.

We had been rehearsing for three weeks when an assistant asked me for permission to put something in my dressing room. I pointed to the girls' room, and he said, "No, *your* dressing room." I told him I had no other. He was shocked and insisted we go out together so he could show it to me; there in the dressing room building, a big sign had my name on the door. I had been assigned a suite all along. It consisted of a living room, bedroom, dressing room, and shower. It even had a little kitchen. I was amazed and thought, Why did Mama and I have to rent a house? We could have lived here! It was far too grand and isolated. I continued to dress with the girls.

Bill Dollar and I were rehearsing a *pas de deux* every day and were perpetually dieting, hungry, and cranky, as Balanchine urged us to get thinner. (Not easy to do with all those wonderful meals, whose cook wanted me to eat his creations while the ballet master wanted me to be thin!) One morning, Bill and I felt superb, full of beans and happy—we both had a secret. Unbeknownst to one another, each had bought a big coffee ring, thick with icing, raisins, and nuts. I had eaten mine literally at one throw, and Bill had done the same. There wasn't a crumb left between us! But for the sake of the camera, we couldn't afford to do that very often.

For the first ballet, Balanchine had chosen Gershwin's *An American in Paris*. The death of George Gershwin from a brain tumor shortly after our arrival in Hollywood had been a great shock. I remember how excited I was when told in London that he was to write a new score for *The Goldwyn Follies*. I very much admired his music, especially after seeing the marvelous Mamoulian production of *Porgy and Bess* in New York. All of us felt his loss in a personal way. Balanchine suggested to Goldwyn that Vladimir Dukelsky be engaged to finish the songs which Gershwin had been unable to complete, in addition to the music for a ten-minute ballet. Dukelsky and Balanchine had met in Paris when both were creating ballets for Diaghilev. Dukelsky had branched away from classical music and had written the lovely song "April in Paris" under his simplified name of Vernon Duke. He now joined the Russian "family," completed the score, and worked with George on a second ballet which was planned for the film.

I could see how differently from Massine Balanchine approached choreography. His impulse was always music, rarely art or literature, but music. He played a piece over and over again on the piano until it was entirely in his head. He had no scraps of paper, no diagrams with choreographic notes, but would begin choreographing by lightly touching a dancer's hand and telling him or her how or where to move. He was certain what he wanted but sometimes stood still as if listening to inner music and visualizing dance movements. There was no sign of rapid re-creation of preconceived ideas, but the unfolding of steps and patterns born at that moment from inner impulses. For an inexperienced choreographer, it is a nightmare to have dancers standing around waiting to be told what the next step is. Or worse, trying choreographic sequences which do not work out. The dancers are polite, but they sense very quickly whether a choreographer is in command or not. George's "silences" were always pregnant with ideas ready to emerge into action—with him it was merely a process of selection.

George effortlessly became a master at filmmaking, a field in which he had never worked before. Even then (he was thirty-three at the time) there was a quiet authority about him which he never needed to stress. He was calm, he guided people, he never raised his voice or lost his temper. He knew what he wanted and exuded confidence. He had enthusiasm and was able to transmit it to those he worked with, and although he was respectful to the technical experts—whether they were cameramen, sound men, cutters, or grips—he led them quietly into better, easier, or more effective ways than they had planned. He always seemed to have a solution to a problem and conspiratorially pointed it out, never offending anybody but, rather, producing sighs of relief. The mastery of his craft made him flexible, so that if something didn't work out either in choreography or concept, he simply changed it.

Balanchine worked with great foresight. Rather than choreograph a full ballet from beginning to end, as he would have for the stage, he choreographed with the camera in mind. When sitting in a theater, you have only one view of the stage: straight ahead. But George planned all the action with camera angles in mind. It was a source of amazement to me that Balanchine had a complete grasp of film technique right from the start. We began with *An American in Paris,* which George made into the story of an American visiting a world exposition. This gave him the opportunity to show pavilions from different countries. When the sets were ready, we moved our rehearsals to the huge soundstage, where they were erected. We rehearsed each section in each pavilion, moving from one to the next all over the soundstage, which was as big as a football field. Balanchine timed the sequences with a stopwatch. Since the total ballet was approximately ten minutes long, each section lasted only a few minutes, some less, with transitions of only a few seconds. It was a charming and lively ballet and worked perfectly—"Like a Swiss watch," as George said, using his favorite expression.

We were ready for shooting to begin when the "great Goldwyn" sent word that he wanted to watch a final rehearsal. We all assembled on Stage 5 with our fingers crossed, and he walked in with a group of men for his "inspection." There was much hustle and bustle while stagehands scurried around for chairs and set them up in front of the first pavilion. When Mr. Goldwyn and his party were finally seated, George gave the order to start. We began to dance the first sequence, which lasted two minutes, when George called, "Cut!" Goldwyn was surprised to be told that the next sequence was at the far end of the soundstage. All the chairs had to be picked up; then the party moved and settled down again. The next sequence was even shorter. Again everybody moved. When this had happened for the sixth time, Goldwyn was thoroughly put out. He turned to the nearest stagehand and bellowed, "Do *you* understand this?" The man quaked and stammered, "No, Mr. Goldwyn," and Goldwyn stomped out, followed by his group. Word came down swiftly from his office that the ballet was canceled.

It seemed incredible to us that so astute and experienced a filmmaker as Goldwyn could not visualize the total ballet. An amateur might have had problems in following our rehearsals, but Goldwyn? He didn't seem to realize that George was way ahead of the game in choreographing for the camera and not the theater. So he threw out almost four weeks of work.

A great deal of maneuvering went on behind the scenes to avert an expensive and needless catastrophe. Goldwyn called me at home that night and said that he found my "dancing wonderful, but there was too much ballet." I then proceeded to plead the case as if I were at least an assistant producer, and told him how popular ballet was becoming in America, privately hoping to God that Balanchine and Goldwyn would reach a compromise. But no, what Goldwyn wanted was *modern* dance and ballet together. George was furious and disappeared. We knew where he was; the studio did not. Since production of the movie had begun, Goldwyn capitulated after a stalemate of two weeks. He did scrap *An American in Paris*, but he then gave Balanchine carte blanche, with the added promise of no further interference in future ballets.

We decided to use the "stalemate" period to drive up the San Bernardino Mountains to Lake Arrowhead—Mama, George, and I in my car; Natasha and Ivan Nabokov and Nicholas Kopeikine in the other. I was under the impression that I was an accomplished driver by then and raced through the Los Angeles traffic like a Keystone Kop. George and my mother endured it until we began our mountainous ascent, at which point George asked diplomatically whether he could drive the perilous curves to "test" my new car. I reluctantly handed over the wheel. We arrived safely at dusk, and after dinner George and I went for a long walk. It was a beautiful night, with the lake looking mysterious in the dark and huge pines silhouetted against the starlit sky.

We spent a few days enjoying ourselves—boating on the lake, eating, laughing, and having long, long talks. George was easy to talk to and very wise, and we seemed to understand each other right from the start. He was also funny in the typical Russian manner. Many of my Russian-born friends have a way of speaking and making puns, outrageously butchering the English language in the process, but with George it was something else. He defused one's unspoken and less noble sentiments by taking away the connected guilt and making one laugh. I remember his saying after we had attended a very good performance: "Is awful when is bad, but is also bad if too good—then it is depressing."

He could be withering in his comments: "Awful stuff," but totally generous when he admired something. In those days of making a film for the first time, he was enchanted by Busby Berkeley, the dance director of all those superb Warner Brothers movie musicals. He loved the pattern that Berkeley created with a hundred girls. "Looks like toy we used to look through when I was child," meaning a kaleidoscope. He was mad about "big, beautiful American girls" and said admiringly of one of his dancers: "Wonderful legs and big, strong ankles like horse," making an image of a Percheron, in strong contrast to his later preferences of wanting his dancers to be *"thin* like needles." We spoke much about Russia and the last hard years before he left in 1924. He told me he walked for miles carrying salt he had saved to exchange for some potatoes with peasants in the country. He blamed those years of deprivation for the tuberculosis he later developed, and told me how he had cured himself in a Swiss sanatorium by eating half a pound of butter every day—straight—and gaining fifty pounds. The very idea of getting all that butter down made me gag, but he just shrugged and said, "If you have to do, you do."

Of course, I could never hear enough about dancers, especially in the Diaghilev company, and what he thought of them. When I wanted to know whether it was really true that Nijinsky jumped *that* high, his answer was: "Yes, many dancers like that in Russia." He would illustrate for me the incredible technical feats of Messerer, a dancer then famous in Leningrad. "Here nobody can do those things" (and the truth is, we never *did* see such things until Nureyev and Baryshnikov defected). Balanchine blamed a lack of training for the dearth of male dancers in the United States. Of course entering a boy of nine in a ballet school was practically unheard of in 1937, especially in America—but not in Russia, where ballet was and is as highly regarded as theater and opera. There it is considered an honor to be accepted in an academy, and it is really not a wonder that Russia has produced such extraordinary dancers considering the system involved. To be specific: boys and girls are auditioned and carefully screened when they are around eight years of age. Only the best are accepted. It's pretty much like building a racing stable. They are evaluated for posture, conformation, bone structure, knees, ankles, feet, and neck (long or short)—much like a young foal at a horse auction in Kentucky. From the day they enter the school, which is a boarding school, they have daily classes in music and ballet in addition to their regular schooling. This education and training will continue until graduation at eighteen, culminating in a "debut." The work for the dancer will of course continue more intensively, but the major point is that there will have been uninterrupted training for ten years. The financial burden of this specialized education was originally provided for by the Imperial Court, just as it is now provided for by the Soviet state—in a long tradition. It is rare in our system that a family can afford that kind of expensive, sustained education. In other words, there is no magical reason for the extraordinary dancers we have welcomed from Russia other than the plain, hard facts of economics and education.

This is what we talked about and what I learned from George in 1937, concepts which he introduced and implemented through almost fifty years in his own school. I wanted to know more about Diaghilev. What was he like? "He liked asses, wonderful asses" was the answer. "He would sit at rehearsal and admire the behind of a boy." When Diaghilev was displeased with some group choreography, he said it was "like fire in whorehouse." Of course these anecdotes were not meant to diminish Diaghilev's enormous contribution to ballet, but were, rather, a heterosexual's disdain for Diaghilev's preferences, because George was not a man without prejudices. He looked at male dancers as instruments for his choreography and could be extravagantly admiring, as if describing a statue of Praxiteles': "Tall, beautiful man." Even at the age of seventy-eight, I heard him angrily speaking of a choreographer: "He ruin my wonderful dancer with his stupid steps," implying that too much stress was placed on one particular male dancer, risking injury. He guarded them jealously, because exceptional male dancers are rarer than female.

Balanchine preferred to talk about women, the ballerinas of Diaghilev's company: Danilova, Nikitina, and Doubrovska, that wonderful, long-legged, elegantly elongated trio he used in *Apollon Musagète*, which marked the first artistic collaboration between Stravinsky and Balanchine, a collaboration which was to become an enduring relationship of fifty years of work, mutual respect, and friendship. In 1929 Stravinsky said, "I cannot imagine more beautiful choreography for my music than Balanchine's."

Bit by bit I began telling George of my two years with the Ballet Russe. It was easy, in the sense that he already knew from Diaghilev's company what that insular world was like. I did not need to explain very much. When I told him about Massine, he was not censorious or shocked but gave me love and understanding. In spite of my frivolous London nightclub life—having a lot of admirers, going out, dancing—I was still raw and wounded, and fearful on a deeper level. My relationship with Massine had been too traumatic, and had made me literally incapable of trusting and giving myself in love to another human being. I had to mend, to recover, to heal, and to forget—as if it had been a serious illness. This took a long, long time. Yet I knew what I had been in love with was what I still respected and loved—a great artist, a man who knew music and art, and a great figure in the ballet world.

It seemed more than strange that I should meet such a figure for the second time in my life. But this time I knew with absolute certainty that I would not be hurt again. I knew George was good, and I felt safe and protected when we were together. He had something trustworthy and priestlike about him, and I felt that by telling him of my past I would be forgiven. I called him my mystical Prince Myshkin and became utterly, completely, and totally devoted to him. This feeling never changed, no matter how much our lives were altered. Even so, in 1937 George knew that I could not yet return the intensity of his feelings—feelings which were becoming quite obvious to both of us. I knew this, and he accepted that it would take time.

The ballet which had been planned as the second ballet was now pushed forward to be filmed first. Of course Goldwyn got his way, combining "modern" dancing and ballet. What he meant by "modern" in 1937 was something like the terrific tap dancing of Eleanor Powell or the sublime dancing of Astaire and Rogers; he did *not* mean the Martha Graham kind of modern. One also has to remember that ballet was definitely not yet widely popular in the United States. I am certain that in the late 1930s the average person in America thought of ballet as something bizarre and foreign. What Balanchine was doing—and perhaps immodestly I with him as his instrument—was presenting ballet for the first time to the vast audience of moviegoers as something palatable, something beautiful and not difficult to understand. In retrospect, I must say that Goldwyn had foresight, taste, and courage, because in *The Goldwyn Follies* he presented both opera and ballet, of course neatly balanced with the Ritz Brothers (lesser versions of the Marx Brothers), but nevertheless "cultural."

The new ballet we embarked on was based on a Romeo and Juliet theme. The dancers were divided into the warring Montagues and Capulets, represented by tap dancers versus ballet dancers. This gave each group the opportunity for technical display. Bill

Dollar and I were, of course, the starcrossed lovers. When the set was ready it nearly gave Mr. Goldwyn another attack of apoplexy. What he saw was a Neapolitan-like street with a narrow upward perspective. Balanchine's whimsical touch of stringing laundry between the houses was not Mr. Goldwyn's idea of what his opulent Technicolor movie should look like. He brightened somewhat when, at a signal, the laundry disappeared in a flash and the "Dance War" began. By the time he had seen the lovely *Romeo and Juliet pas de deux* George had choreographed for Bill and me, he was mollified.

———

George came for dinner and told us about his new, mad idea for the next ballet. We hope it will please "our Goldwyn!" He began with: "There will be marvelous, beautiful, big stage, round, with Greek columns on each side like Palladio; then, in the back, statue of big white horse. Poet comes and sees beautiful Undine [water nymph] coming out of pool." I interjected, "Pool?" "Yes, pool, covered with beautiful white flowers. She slowly, slowly comes out of water—will be *very* sexy with wet material clinging to her body—then she will dance on water, and poet watches and falls in love with her. Then lots of girls appear and they dress her in beautiful ball gown. She dances with poet. Then big storm starts, wind blows like mad, and we discover her on the horse. Then the wind blows all her dress away and she slides slowly, slowly from horse and in her little tunic and bare feet she goes back to lily pool, and slowly her body disappears in the water until only her head is visible, and then she puts her cheek on the water like pillow and she is gone like sun disappearing in ocean."

George looked at me triumphantly; I was both fascinated by his story and thunderstruck, wondering how it could be done. As it turned out, it became a kind of classic of filmed ballet with marvelous visual effects. In time to come, I was awestruck not only by his choreography but by his capacity to visualize images. The realization of these images in practical terms never defeated him. On the contrary, their difficulties were always solved by him and no one else, through simple solutions. When technical people made cautious objections, he always brushed them aside and proceeded to illustrate in terms that were perfectly logical and to him very simple. "Just *do* and will be okay." Or a triumphant: "You see!" would be his typical reaction when something worked out exactly as he had said it would. If anyone was dubious, he would explain things like a father patiently teaching a child, at the same time transmitting his enormous confidence and enthusiasm.

His main artistic springboard, particularly for complicated abstract ballets, was music, but when he worked for films, he thought in terms of the visual impact first. It was his imagination which was limitless, and thank God, he had the capacity to make his visions visible to us.

August 3. Rehearsal for the jazz part in *Juliet*. Balanchine is so interesting the way he mixes ballet and tap and how he shows it to Bill Dollar—gives you an idea what a marvelous dancer he himself must have been.

August 13. Today was a big day. Goldwyn saw the *Romeo and Juliet* ballet in rehearsal *and*—what joy!—was delighted about it—*at last*!! In the evening I drove high up above the Hollywood Bowl and listened to Lily Pons trilling.

August 14. Was annoyed with George today because he shortened the *pas de deux*. He said Goldwyn wanted it so that the public would see more of me, which didn't seem to make much sense. George was so touching, called me later and said, "If I cut something from, I cut something from me."

August 15, Sunday. At Goldwyns' with George for tea and dinner in his Beverly Hills house. Virginia Bruce very beautiful—Tilly Losch and some others were there.

Sunday was the Hollywood day for play. I was invited to swimming pool and tennis parties, or I should say, "grandly casual Sunday-afternoon get-togethers"—no one was nobody, everybody was somebody. I remember swimming or playing tennis but feeling vaguely that it must be an honor to be there. I just sat and stared at famous people. Strange to see Charlie Chaplin with a tennis racket, an ordinary older man obviously involved with a brash and attractive young woman named Paulette Goddard. Reality became unreality and disappointing ordinariness. One saw "powerful" figures: Jack Warner, who had a silky, dark-haired wife who seemed to wear emeralds even at the pool. Or the deceptively easygoing Charlie Feldman (during that period one of the most important agents in Hollywood), married to one of the most beautiful women, Jean Feldman. Or being briskly taken care of by Frances Goldwyn, who amazed me one day by telling me that she herself, and no one else, gave "Sam his manicure." What a strange image that was—Frances bent over her husband's cuticles. But she *was* very devoted to him and apparently spent her life in taking care of every detail to make him comfortable. Goldwyn, on the other hand, ran his own ship. He had a lot of charm in spite of his lower-jaw-jutting-forward ugliness, and in spite of his famous malapropisms, being ignorant in some ways, instinctual and shrewd in others. He always showed good taste, inviting new talents, whether actors, writers, composers, or a relatively unknown like Balanchine, to come out to Hollywood to work for him.

He had a passion for what he called "warmth." Over and over again he would say, "Zorina, it's got to have warmth"—as if he were invoking the sun to spread a soothing ambiance. I liked him, although at times he pursued me rather more ardently than I wished. I simply wasn't interested. Power as such meant nothing to me. My ambitions were different—not better, but different. For one thing I didn't like Hollywood. I didn't like its values or absence thereof. I was disappointed by its lack of architectural cohesion. Only the majestic palm trees, lining the residential drives of Beverly Hills, seemed right. What was ludicrous were the various architectural styles next to each other. They created the same appearance of unreality as a movie set does. It all seemed so artificial that I finally longed for pelting rain and a change from the ever-shining sun.

The higher up you went in the social stratum, the worse it became. Conversations were "industry talks" heavy with sales, hits, properties, previews, and premieres. Agents were powerful and "handled" stars. It's funny to think that the people who lead pedigreed dogs at the Westminster Kennel Club shows are also called "handlers," but then that's star business, too. The people I was fond of were the technicians, who were true professionals. Anyone connected with the technical or artistic aspect of making a movie was interesting to talk to. They knew their jobs, took pride in them, and were absolute experts in their field.

My happiest times during my six months in Hollywood were in the dance studio, working with Balanchine and the company—dressed in practice clothes, taking class, rehearsing, sweating, and having a sense of achievement. Filming the ballets was another matter and became excruciating at times. Though the ballets on film lasted only about eight to ten minutes, they took a week to film, due to different camera angles, special effects, and the particular story of the ballet.

A dancer is used to performing with a controlled burst of energy —giving a performance which might last anywhere from ten to twenty minutes at a stretch, depending on the particular length of the ballet. In preparation for it, the body must be warmed up like a well-tuned engine. First, a barre, then stretching exercises, followed by a few jumps and whatever steps need last-minute practice. The main thing is to get the muscles warm and keep them warm until you are ready to go on stage. Dancers take their legwarmers off only minutes before the ballet begins. The process of moviemaking made this ritual extremely difficult, if not impossible. I had to be at the studio even earlier than dawn to make up, practice, and get dressed, in itself a complicated procedure. Head-dresses must be securely anchored with what feels like a million hairpins, or they fly off at the first pirouette. Even one loose strand of hair can be a nuisance if it gets caught in your eyelashes. Costumes have to be tight, and in 1937 we did not yet have all the marvelous materials which stretch with the body—so I could hardly breathe.

Putting on toe shoes in itself requires a little ritual. First you break them in, make them "comfortable"—each dancer has her own routine—then, without tying the ribbons, you slide your foot in, wriggle around, stand on your toes until it feels right, and finally tie the ribbons, tuck in the ends, and take a stitch with a needle and thread so the knot won't slip out. After that, you're ready to go, but in moviemaking that's when the real trouble starts. The soundstage was vast and invariably draughty. Preparations for ballet sequences were always elaborate and time-consuming because of the space involved, moving cameras either on tracks on the floor or high above on cranes. The synchronization necessary to coordinate the cameras at the precise moment with shifts in light, including the difficulties for dancers of hitting the spots designated by the cameramen, demanded split-second timing on the part of the crew. We rehearsed and rehearsed (that was all right, because at least we kept warm). It was worse when purely technical matters had to be taken care of—such as a new setup, or adjusting the huge lights above us, or changing the film in the camera— which meant long waits. You tried to hop around to keep your muscles flexible and warm, but after some hours of dancing and stopping, waiting, dancing and stopping again, everything began to pinch and hurt, and you began to pray for the lunch hour to be called, or, better, for the day to end.

Sometimes our own timing would go off. I remember a difficult sequence involving my partner Charles Laskey and myself. It was going perfectly until the cameraman called, "We'll have to take it again," for some technical reason, and we became so dejected that we made one mistake after another. Normally you forget pain on the stage, but here the sequences were too short not to be aware of aching feet, costumes which chafed, and hairpins which drilled into your scalp.

Another problem was the floor. The man in charge would carefully mop and polish it before each take, making it as shiny as a mirror but also dangerously slippery. I would then have to wet my toe shoes and put resin on them; this would throw the poor man into fits, because it made white streaks on the floor. The argument ended when I pointed out that if the audience noticed the streaks I made I had failed to captivate them in the first place and that he had better let me get on with it and at least dance well instead of falling down. No, it wasn't easy, and the person who agreed with me completely when I said that filming was the hardest thing I'd ever done was the great skater Sonja Henie, who experienced the same problems filming her ice-skating routines.

Something that fascinated me was looking at the daily rushes. The viewing room would fill up with everyone connected with the previous day's filming. Not only the actors or performers, but the director, cameraman, sound man, makeup man, and hairdresser, all the way down the line. They would look at each sequence with great concentration and see absolutely nothing but their own particular aspect of work. The room would be alive with whispered comments, every one specialized. The makeup person would agonize over a "shadow on the nose" that nobody else had noticed, the hairdresser over a wisp of hair out of place, the cameraman some imperfection in his work, and each wanted the whole sequence redone. The only one who kept a grip on things was the director, who had the last word anyway. Once a very difficult scene had gone well for me, when to my dismay the sound man said we had to take it over. In agony I asked why. He said, "I heard your stomach growl." That's when you burst into tears.

August 16. Mama has bought a horse! You would think we are rich as Croesus. She is in seventh heaven. The horse is a thoroughbred and sweet—rode him in the afternoon and Balanchine watched. In the evening George and I went to the recording session of Alfred Newman, and I became angry because George whispered in my ear, "What awful music," and then said to Newman, "Very good." Saw the test for *Romeo and Juliet*—adagio was beautiful, but the costume for jazz section awful.

———

I spent one Sunday in bed doing a "milk cure" (one of my lose-weight schemes). Below me in the kitchen I could hear noises made by George and Volodine, both covered in aprons, running around preparing a Russian dinner. Once in a while George came upstairs for a visit. We expected Al Newman, Eddie Powell, "Dima" Dukelsky, and our ace cameraman, Gregg Toland, and his wife. George had formed a friendship with the shy, elusive, and brilliant cameraman. A few years later Toland became famous for his deep-focus photography, which means, in lay terms, simultaneous focus of foreground *and* background. Toland used this technique brilliantly in *Citizen Kane* and *The Magnificent Ambersons*, two films he made with Orson Welles. Cameramen did not have the status then that they have today, and all the glory went to Orson Welles—but with a deep, respectful bow to Welles's genius, I believe Gregg Toland was a major innovator in film technology.

———

August 23. Received a wonderful present from George, a marvelous gramophone and radio, and those things are enormously expensive. I was so touched. Had to go to the studio at midnight and stayed there until six in the morning.

August 24. Slept until one, then practiced in the studio—fittings for clothes. Watched *Traviata* with Helen Jepson and Charles Kullman. [These Metropolitan Opera stars filmed one scene from *Traviata* for *The Goldwyn Follies*.]

August 25. Class, rehearsal, costumes, test, and dinner in the studio; afterward we rehearsed again. Bill and I to record "taps" [tap dancing],

Preceding page, top and cen-
ter, rehearsing ROMEO AND
JULIET pas de deux with Wil-
liam Dollar for THE GOLD-
WYN FOLLIES; bottom,
rehearsal group with Balanchine.
Above, tap-dancing sequence
choreographed by Balanchine.
Left, film version of ON YOUR
TOES, 1939.

Above, the set for the Undine *ballet,* THE GOLDWYN FOLLIES.
*Following pages, top left, Balanchine during filming; bottom left, emerging
from the lily pond; right, dancing on the glass surface.*

Opposite top, I MARRIED AN ANGEL, *two poses with Dennis King,
1938; center, honeymoon ballet by Balanchine; below left, with another
"angel"; right, surrealist ballet by Balanchine. Above, breaking up at dress
rehearsal with Audrey Christie and Charles Walters.*

Left top, 1940 film I WAS AN ADVENTURESS, *with director Gregory Ratoff and Balanchine; center, in same film with Erich von Stroheim and Peter Lorre; bottom, rehearsal with Balanchine. Opposite top and center left, rehearsing the Black Swan ballet for this film with Balanchine on camera boom; center right, with Lew Christensen; bottom, relaxing on the set.*

Above and right, with Gary Cooper on the set of FOR WHOM THE BELL TOLLS. *Opposite top, director Sam Wood, Akim Tamiroff, the author, and Gary Cooper; below, with Gary Cooper and Sam Wood.*

In Igor Stravinsky's ELEPHANT BALLET *at Madison Square Garden.*

but that was very complicated. We wore earphones with long lines through which we could hear the music, but of course not the "taps," so we were never together. Oh, God.

August 28. The whole day on the set—tried on clothes, shoes, sandals, ballet shoes, stockings, tights, etc.—then all we did was the balcony scene and the kiss between Romeo and Juliet. We were both so nervous that our lips trembled. Dinner with George. He showed me his techni-film—excellent. [Balanchine had his own camera and made his own film during our actual filming on the set.] Then we talked and talked—he is so dear.

August 29, Sunday. George fetched me at three to go to Goldwyn for one of those Sundays. In the evening Goldwyn screened *Broadway Melody* with Eleanor Powell, and I was so surprised when he got up at the end and said, "It has no warmth, no charm, and, Balanchine, I want you to do for Zorina one or two minutes real ballet because I believe in it now after seeing *this*"—finally, finally, after weeks Goldwyn has come around.

August 31. Sat around again and filmed the ending of *Juliet*, where I had to execute sixteen *fouettés* six times from different angles—that makes ninety-six *fouettés*! Afterward my knees felt like macaroni.

September 1. Shooting had to stop today because Bill Dollar has a rash and they are afraid I might catch it—no rehearsal. Had dinner with George in the Café Lamaze. Then we went to his place and somehow we had a quarrel because he told me about his girlfriends. Of course it was my fault, because I wanted to know; then everything became very dramatic and I never wanted to see him again. My *rimmel* [mascara] began to run and it burned terribly, and I went home, ate ice cream, and felt fat as a barrel.

September 2. George called as if nothing had happened—we should go and try on wigs. He came and was very sweet—I was still "dramatic." But he told me a funny Goldwyn anecdote: Goldwyn was absolutely thrilled by *Traviata*. He kept congratulating our conductor, Al Newman, over and over again, and after endless explosions of joy he said to Newman, "Do me a favor, congratulate Eddie Powell on the orchestration!" Mr. Verdi would be so pleased.

A memorable Goldwyn malapropism occurred two days later when Goldwyn visited us during a ballet rehearsal. We stopped and he said, "You know, I saw a wonderful film last night, *One Hundred Men and a Girl*, with Deanna Durbin and that wonderful conductor Dostoevsky." We all said, "Dostoevsky?" and then the pianist tried to help by saying, "You mean Stokowski?" "No, no," said Goldwyn, "Dostoevsky—" We had a terrible time trying not to break up.

Great efforts had been made to film a big close-up of Juliet following Romeo slowly with her eyes. Balanchine and Gregg Toland kept experimenting with lights and placed huge klieg lights at my feet which shone directly up into my face. As the camera slowly moved in front of me, I looked into those lights and just below the camera lens. We rehearsed and rehearsed it and then shot it several times, until both George and Toland were satisfied. The end result was beautiful, but staring directly into the klieg lights had burned my eyeballs, literally. When I woke up the next morning, I felt as if someone had thrown a handful of sand into my eyes. In addition to being very painful, it was also very frightening, because I thought I had hurt my eyes permanently. This all came together and proved to be too much for me.

September 12, Sunday. Woke up with swollen eyes—felt miserable. Took my car and drove off—almost to San Diego. When I came home at night, George was waiting for me, and suddenly without reason I broke down and became hysterical. Dr. Hirshfeld had to come and give me an injection.

In addition to battling my weight and trying to keep it down to an abnormally low level, I was also having cyclical problems. Within the twenty-eight lunar days, I had really only two peaceful weeks in which I felt well. The week before my period, I would begin to blow up and retain as much as five pounds in fluid, which added to the accompanying depression. After that, I was often in severe pain, sitting around miserably with a hot-water bottle pressed to my pelvis. Many female athletes suffer from this problem and it doesn't stop them. In fact, I always felt better after hard exercise and a good sweat, but it certainly was a debilitating and terrible nuisance, which became aggravated in Hollywood, because what I had previously managed in relative anonymity now became, so to speak, a public matter. I found it humiliating to have everyone scrutinizing me, because I was in a business where beauty is paramount. The wardrobe people noticed that my weight was going up and down. The cameraman watched to see whether I looked well, and Balanchine whether I danced well. It became a kind of vicious circle: the more drastic the measures I took, the sicker I became. Beauty is a gift, but it can also be a burden. People begin to talk about you as if you were a garden—"Look at those beautiful tulips," or a house—"Isn't that staircase graceful?" You become an object, which creates the kind of bitter internal anger that makes you want to scream like a child: *"I'm* in here and I want to be loved for myself."

September 14. Half in bed, half out—still feel rotten. Goldwyn came for a visit—was very dear and nice.

It has been suggested that Goldwyn was in love with me. It may seem strange to put it that way, but I have absolutely no recollection of any such emotion, beyond realizing that he had a "crush" on me, or that he saw the possibility of "star" material, or that he, a middle-aged man at that point, could momentarily lose his head over a beautiful young woman. I did not take it seriously. He *was* exceptionally nice to me and he seemed to care, qualities which mattered a great deal more than expressions of passionate love. *That* would only have embarrassed me, and he must have realized it. However, it is rather flattering if a very powerful person is in love with you—doors open, carpets unroll, secretaries smile, direct lines—no waiting, but that's all. I was interested in other things and always have been. I wanted to succeed, but my end goal was not money and power but to be good at what I did. I had unlimited ambition and drove myself hard. Shortcuts through bedrooms never occurred to me. Either you have talent or you don't, and if you have it you don't need to. That people fell in love with me was nothing unusual but an accepted fact. That may sound fatuous, but nevertheless it was true. I too developed crushes, but they soon ran their course and sometimes I would shiver with disgust that such a thing had been possible in the first place. At this point I was only interested in Balanchine. He was goodness personified to me, the only one I trusted, could confide in, be comforted by, and whose love I believed in.

The set for the *Undine* ballet is worth a detailed description. It was as handsome to look at the first time I saw it as it was on film. George had achieved exactly what he had described to me weeks before. Space was beautifully used, so it had a truly architectural quality, with different levels and a deep perspective culminating in a magnificent statue of a white horse modeled after one by the painter Giorgio de Chirico, who often used Greek antiquity as a theme. The double row of columns which curved and embraced the set enhanced the feeling of fantasy, so that when the poet appeared and gazed in wonder at the pool, covered with water lilies, one could well imagine him being in awe of a strange landscape into which he had wandered.

Gregg Toland and Balanchine understood each other from the beginning. They had tremendous respect for one another and began to collaborate in total harmony. Balanchine suggested that a trench be built and the camera placed below floor level in order to get the elongated view of dancers achieved in the theater, where the stage is on a higher level than the auditorium. That is the reason why dancers look so much taller on the stage, because the audience is looking at them from below. If the camera, in the studio, stands on the floor, the lens is roughly on a par with the chest and therefore foreshortens the legs. Toland thought the trench idea wonderful and promptly had it constructed and lowered the camera into it. I believe it was the first time this was ever done. Huge airplane propellers were placed in various positions "offstage" to be turned on for the storm sequence. The pool in the center of the set was quite deep, filled with water, and real water lilies floated on the surface.

As the water nymph Undine, I was dressed in the flimsiest costume imaginable, made out of sheer gold lamé. When it was wet it was not only flimsy but transparent, which embarrassed me quite a bit. But that was exactly what George had planned—"Will be very sexy"—and it certainly was. The sequence involving the pool took two days to film. Long shot, medium shot, close-up, and different angles, so four duplicate costumes were made, as well as an extra wig. After each take, I was enveloped in a bathrobe, coddled and patted on the back, and then I changed into a dry costume. But since I had emerged from the pool and was therefore supposed to be wet, I would stand in a basin while a propman with the largest sponge I'd ever seen would squeeze it out over my head in order to match the next shot.

I was fascinated by the expertise of the crew. Nothing was ever an unsolvable problem. The logistics of the pool sequence were ingenious. I stood in the middle of the pool on a small platform only big enough for my feet. The water reached up just below my shoulders. With the cameras rolling, I would take a deep breath, bend my knees, and carefully disappear below the surface, wait for a slow count of ten until the water settled on top, then slowly straighten up and emerge. Once I was out at shoulder level, the platform on which I stood rose like an elevator until my feet were at water level. By a camera trick, the water dissolved into a glass surface and I began to dance.

Diving below the water was no problem, but staying down, even for a count of ten, was. My lungs, which were full of air, made me pop up and I had nothing to hold me down. We had to stop and find a solution. I said that I needed something to hold on to under water, then it would be easy. The crew consulted and went to work, standing in the water affixing two handlebars to each side of the platform which I could clasp and release easily.

That problem was solved, but a new one arose. The lilies were floating around on top, doing their own thing, no matter how carefully I lowered myself or rose up out of the pool. The script girl, who watches these things like a hawk, said we could not match shots that way. While I sat shivering in my bathrobe, the crew went to work again and wired each lily firmly to the bottom. I thought they were marvelous. There was absolutely nothing that was impossible for them. Even my wig was completely waterproof, with every curl lacquered in place. Goldwyn constantly came on the set to watch, and hovered over the nervous makeup man who was trying to fix my mouth. "I want her lips voluptuous," he insisted. The next problem arose when I began dancing on the glassy surface of the pool. With my body dripping water, my bare feet began to slip and slide, so George changed a few steps, and I moved very, very carefully!

When we came to the part in which Undine is discovered on the white horse in her beautiful ball gown, we faced another challenge. I wore a fly-away version of my costume so that when the "storm" started and the propellers were turned on full force, my costume would literally fly away. Well, it wouldn't. Even though the wind generated by the propellers was coming straight at me and nearly blew me off the horse, some piece of my costume would stick tenaciously and ruin the take. We must have filmed that sequence thirty times, until finally it all came off in one perfect take.

Toward the end of the ballet, when Undine re-enters the pool and slowly sinks down into the water, Balanchine wanted a close-up of my face as a large tear rolls down my cheeks. We tried and tried, but the tears stayed brimming on the edge of my eyes. At last, thanks to my technical friends, a beautiful, heavy teardrop made out of glycerine rolled slowly down on cue.

The very last sequence of the ballet ends with the poet gazing toward the pool, where the nymph has just disappeared. He runs toward it and, half lying, stares down into the water, trying to get a last glimpse of her. When Bill Dollar, dressed as the poet in black velvet, with white ruffles at the neck and cuffs, filmed that sequence, he lost his balance and plunged headfirst into the pool. As everyone screamed with laughter, poor Bill emerged dripping wet. The cameras had kept going, and George thought up an opportunity to revenge himself for the *American in Paris* fiasco. When the ballet was cut and edited, he tacked on that ending and Goldwyn was invited to the viewing room to see it. He arrived with his entourage and was absolutely delighted, until he saw the splashy ending. When the lights went up he remained silent, true to his promise of non-interference. After all, he could not afford to have his "mad" choreographer walk off again in the middle of the production. He was greatly relieved when George confessed his joke and ran the real ending.

All in all, the ballet showed the enormous ingenuity of Balanchine. From his first funny, wild, seemingly unrealistic description of this ballet, he demonstrated that he had the capacity to transform his imagination into cinematic reality. He dispelled the concept of the artist as a dreamer and proved he had the practicality of a *master craftsman*, something he was to repeat over and over in the future. It was a quiet power, which made an indelible impression on me in 1937.

With the ballets finished, I now began filming my "acting role." There was a plot line to *The Goldwyn Follies*, and there were many famous entertainers and stars of that period who wove in and out of it—Adolphe Menjou, Andrea Leeds, the Ritz Brothers, Edgar Bergen and Charlie McCarthy, Kenny Baker, Helen Jepson, Charles Kullman.

My part was absurd, and it seems to me I did little more than do as I was told—to speak, to look, to act, to sit, to walk, and so on.

In addition to Mr. Potter, who was a dialogue director and whose job it was to work with inexperienced actresses like me, another young man would occasionally appear at 513 North Camden Drive to rehearse the next day's scene. His name was Garson Kanin. He was very sympathetic, and I'm sure he thought the lines I had to speak were as silly as I did. But we rehearsed them earnestly just the same. I had a sketch to do with the Ritz Brothers and didn't have a clue what the jokes meant, like: "Do you know Zorina?" "Sure! I have it for breakfast every morning!" Playing a scene with Edgar Bergen, the brilliant ventriloquist, and his "puppet" Charlie McCarthy was quite astonishing. Although I was fully aware that I was talking to an inanimate, wooden, mechanically operated manikin, it still was uncanny how riveting Charlie could be and how totally engrossed one could become staring at that funny, impertinent, wooden face.

One day Sam Goldwyn came to watch with Gary Cooper. Cooper was a great car buff and had the most beautiful black Duesenberg, which I passionately admired. Once, when I was trying to park my own car, I slowly—slower than a snail—crunched into the side of his black beauty, peacefully parked in front of his bungalow. I was absolutely mortified and expected the most dreadful scene. Instead he made light of the nasty long gash, and I never forgot his kindness.

Although the ballets were finished, George stayed on to oversee the final editing. He was in complete charge of it, which was a rare concession on the part of the studio. When the "acting unit" went on location to Lake Arrowhead, George took a few days off to be with me. It was now October and the air was crisp and beau-

tiful at the lake. At times it seemed like a vacation, though it wasn't
for me.

October 2. At eight o'clock in the morning by motorboat to work.
Was made up outside. Sat around the whole day and was not used.
Long walk with George and a drive to Big Bear, where we found a
sweet restaurant. An English lady who brought us wonderful tea told
us without charge her entire life story.

October 5. George was as sweet as always. We cooked dinner together
as if we were married and ate by candlelight. He peeled onions and I
set the table—adorable. [I find this a hilarious entry in my diary—I still
prefer to set the table rather than to peel onions—who wouldn't?]

October 9. Worked with Adolphe Menjou. In the evening we had a
mad dinner—Balanchine cooked and we had heavenly caviar and vodka
and were very gay afterward.

October 10. Worked the whole day with awful stomachache [I wonder
why]. At night very sad goodbye from George.

October 11. George has left. Talked to him early in the morning—he
sounded very sad and said, "Eh—don't look at the makeup boy."
Received beautiful red roses and a telegram: JEG ELSKER DIG ["I love
you"]—the sweet one.

When George left Hollywood, the lights went out. In the last
four months the major part of my life, both working and private,
had revolved around him, and he had become more and more
important to me as teacher, guide, mentor, and closest intimate
friend, my soulmate—somehow there is no better word for it. I
loved him, but not the way he loved me. George loved with all his
being, all-consuming, passionately, romantically, and inevitably
tragically. No one could quite match it. Certainly not I, not then.
I had my own battles to fight, physically and emotionally. I had a
film to finish and work to do in a role which at best occasionally
amused me, humiliated me, and most of the time bored me to
death. All I dreamed of was to finish the film and leave for New

York. Hollywood was not for me. I desperately longed to be back on the stage and in New York. The big question now was, Would Goldwyn let me go and do a musical with Rodgers and Hart and Balanchine?

Douglas Fairbanks, Jr., and I renewed our friendship in Hollywood. He was living in the beautiful beach house his father owned in Santa Monica. To own a house on the beach was obviously a status symbol, and the rich and powerful, like Louis B. Mayer, Norma Shearer, and Douglas Fairbanks, used these houses as summer residences and second homes. Most of them were close together and there was quite a bit of "dropping in" and visiting, in contrast to the more formal lives everyone led in Beverly Hills. It was lovely and cool at the beach, and one could still swim in the ocean in late October. I do remember, though, a very frightening experience when Doug and I were swimming. The undertow, with its inexorable strength, kept lifting and then propelling me in huge swells toward a pier jutting out into the sea and away from Doug. I had visions of crashing against one of the pylons and then drowning like my father. It took all my strength to swim away to the beach, where I lay puffing, utterly exhausted, like a beached seal.

At that time Douglas was very much the glamorous bachelor about town and it appeared that everybody was in love with him, especially Marlene Dietrich. And why not? He was charming, good-looking, and very dear—all the things he still is today after nearly fifty years. I met many of his friends, particularly Norma Shearer, who lived next door. She came to dinner one night, and I thought she was lovely and ladylike; she was very kind to me, who at that point was practically a nobody in the world of her stardom. On another occasion David Niven came with Hedy Lamarr. She sat informally on the floor and was incredibly beautiful, with blue eyes and black hair. Then there was Merle Oberon. With the exception of Vivien Leigh, I don't think I have ever seen a more enchanting face, with her almond-shaped, delicately upturned eyes, small mouth, and lovely smile. It's strange to me why I thought these women far more beautiful than the masculine movie idols of that or any other period. There is something natural about a beautiful woman—it's her business to be beautiful, it's feminine; whereas a really beautiful man is somewhat off-putting. A "beautiful" or very good-looking man seems never quite at ease with his looks, taking on somewhat the ludicrousness of a peacock.

David Niven did not belong in that category. I simply adored him. He was most urbane, sweet, and elegant, and seemed the epitome of a witty, understated Englishman. He was also an impeccable storyteller. It didn't matter whether one had heard the story before—one's pleasure was in the way he told it. He made merciless fun of himself and used any situation, whether private or professional, that might have a bit of ridiculous humor in it. He remained unspoiled all his life, no matter how big a star he became. (We met again many years later when my husband, Goddard Lieberson, and I, David, and Hjordis, his beautiful Swedish wife, were guests on the yacht of producer Milton Bren and his wife, Claire Trevor. The six of us sailed for the weekend to Catalina Island. The yacht had only one cabin, so that we the four guests had to sleep on deck in sleeping bags. I expected that Goddard and I would sleep at one end and David and Hjordis at the other. But no; four sleeping bags were lined up side by side. It didn't occur to me to get undressed below—I simply wriggled around inside my sleeping bag and took off my slacks, etc. I was no sooner settled than an immaculate apparition towered above me—David in silk pajamas, with a silk dressing gown sashed at the waist, very handsome slippers on his feet, holding a sleeping mask. He folded his dressing gown neatly beside him, took off his slippers, and slid into his bag. When I woke up at 5 a.m., there he was next to me, sleeping peacefully with his mask on.)

November 12–13. Decided to fly to New York at eleven o'clock in the morning. Rushed around like crazy to get everything in order and flew off. I woke up in Pittsburgh and had to leave the plane because the weather was so bad that we could not land in New York, so had to continue by train.

I made this mad dash because I was desperate to do the new musical *I Married an Angel,* in which I was to play the lead, with two ballets choreographed by Balanchine. Flying in those days could sometimes be arduous. I must have been in transit more than twenty-four hours, on a trip that now takes four hours by jet. A clause in my contract with Sam Goldwyn giving me permission for a leave of absence seemed very shaky and my agent did not succeed in obtaining my release. Goldwyn was in New York, and negotiations between him and Dwight Deere Wiman looked as if they were about to collapse. I was hoping that if I could plead my case personally with Goldwyn I might succeed.

My whole philosophy about issues that really matter, whether private or professional, is that if you feel strongly enough about them you can and will succeed. A passionate conviction gives you a blazing kind of energy that cuts through obstacles. I wanted to go to New York, to the stage, to ballet, to George, to my life and my work, to everything I loved.

In the end, Goldwyn and Wiman compromised by agreeing that this was only a leave of absence and that my contract with Goldwyn was otherwise to continue unchanged. Thus, I would be allowed to return to New York and star in *I Married an Angel.* One cannot imagine the power a studio, or in this case an independent producer like Goldwyn, had over one's career. Had I not received permission, I could have been suspended without pay, not only from making films, but from any kind of employment— Broadway, ballet, or radio. I think Goldwyn finally relented because he was about to enter into a lengthy litigation over studio rights with Mary Pickford, Douglas Fairbanks, and Charlie Chaplin, the other three shareholders of United Artists. He was forced to cut back his own productions and release his films through other studios. Those actors and actresses he had under personal contract were loaned out with very little say about it, and in my case no say at all. I never made another film for Goldwyn but was loaned out to one studio after another. I remained chained to my contract until the seven years had run out, though I begged to be released. Whatever success I later made on Broadway was promptly ruined by another bad film for which I was "on loan."

As I look back on that particular trip to New York, I realize it was a turning point. I had temporarily won my battle, but it must have been galling to Goldwyn, a proud man and one who was used to getting his way, that in my case no matter how he painted the future, or the considerable care he had taken in the past, it was no use. Becoming a movie star had absolutely no appeal for me. In his view I had rejected him and everything he so passionately believed in. Of course, that was hardly my intention. I just knew that I could never succeed in movies because the camera embarrassed me. It is a matter of temperament: I had talent in the theater but not in movies. The enormous freedom I felt on the stage—the confidence, the conviction that I was good—completely deserted me in front of the camera. The minute I heard the awful noise of the clapper and the assistant yelling, "Quiet—roll—camera," I froze and loathed the whole damn procedure. The process which gives screen actors so much comfort—knowing that they can repeat a take or do it over and over—drove me mad. The dialogue lost all veracity and the lines became more and more ludicrous to me from repetition.

In all fairness, it is also true that I never had a part in which I might have been good and never worked with a really great director. Being European, I was invariably cast as a Russian or European vamp parading around in sexy clothes and having lines which deliberately added to my accent. The only time I had a real chance was when I was given the part of Maria in *For Whom the Bell Tolls*, but that turned into a sad, ugly story which I will describe later.

The one who thoroughly enjoyed Hollywood was my mother. She could not understand me. We had a lovely house, a car, financial security, and wasn't the climate wonderful? She could ride her beloved horse every day—all luxuries we had never known before. What was the matter with me? she asked—baffled and annoyed. She had made friends, a little coterie of European exiles who were beginning to make Hollywood their home. She begged me to buy the house we rented—we could have had it for $12,000. Paulette Goddard's mother, who was in the real-estate business, had told her it was a very good buy—but I would hear none of it. The idea of owning a house threw me into a panic. Poor Mama. At her point in life it was right. She never let me forget that I could have had *that* house, *that* garden, *that* property for so little, but for me at my point, it was wrong. It seemed to me that in Hollywood all I did was get in and out of cars, or sit in a chair while people fussed over me, or wait around on the set. So much time was wasted, but there was no time for a class or even doing a barre alone. I was as restless as a caged tiger—a tiger who lacked the necessary narcissism to succeed in movies.

———

December 1. The first preview of *The Goldwyn Follies* in Pomona. Mama and I were fetched by a studio limousine—the drive seemed endless. When we finally arrived, there was hardly a seat left and we had a lot of trouble getting in. The film seemed much too long and I didn't find anything special about me.

December 2. Big party at Edmund Goulding's. Marlene was there—*very* affectionate and gossiped like a schoolgirl with the Countess di Frasso about Douglas. Fritz Lang was very nice to me. I screamed with laughter over David Niven's stories. Met Ronald Colman, Loretta Young, Benita Hume, Brian Aherne, William Powell—charming and very gay evening.

I was obviously having "a ball" that night. At twenty that can be a lot of fun, especially when the men involved are charming, good-looking movie stars. But I seemed to generate drama and gloom in New York, where George realized that he had fallen deeply in love with me. He was very sad, he missed me—when was I coming back to New York?—what was I doing? Did I miss him? Yes, I missed him— No, I was not in love with anyone— No, I could not leave until I got the green light from the studio —we were still redoing some scenes, and publicity and photo sessions—I was hoping to be in New York by Christmas—but George became sadder and sadder.

December 16. Filmed the whole day—a new scene with Menjou and a lot of "close-ups." In the evening, went alone to see *The Blue Angel* with Marlene, and found it dreadful. Then I drove around in a completely silly way—all the way to the beach and back to Beverly Hills. When I got home, George called and it was still very sad.

On December 17 I went to the studio to say goodbye. Sam Goldwyn was very nervous, and started to cry when I left. I could scarcely believe it. I left Hollywood without a twinge of regret. I was starved for New York. I missed the theater, the opera, the ballet, concerts, museums. I longed for winter, cold air, even snow. I had never previously been six months in a place where it didn't rain, and I relished Fred Allen's joke: "California is a great place to be if you happen to be an orange." Fifty years have made an enormous difference, and Los Angeles is now one of the most dynamic and exciting cities in America. It wasn't then.

In conjunction with the premiere of *The Goldwyn Follies*, Goldwyn had insisted that I do a great deal of publicity. Our first stop on the way to New York was Chicago. I was delighted that Chicago was windy and bitingly cold, and even happier that the Ballet Russe was in town for their season. Of course, I went the first evening, dressed to the teeth in my new mink coat and mink hat. All my ballet chums surrounded me when I went backstage and gave me a terrific welcome.

After two days, we left and arrived in New York on the morning of December 24. My mother and I moved into the Ritz Tower at Park Avenue and Fifty-seventh Street, and lived there on and off for years. At last we were back in New York, happy as could be. It was Christmas Eve. Soon I was going to start rehearsals for *I Married an Angel* (a necessary reminder to myself so that I could permit my conscience to enjoy a period of leisure). George, my dearest George, gave me the most beautiful earrings from Cartier. I was worried that he had spent too much money, but he shushed me. It was like a gesture from a Grand Duke of Russia.

December 27. Spent hours getting a special hairdo for the opera. George took me to *Tannhäuser* at the Met; it was absolutely wonderful.

December 29. Supper with Louis Shurr. He introduced me to Howard Hughes, who danced excellently and talked an enormous amount of nonsense.

I accepted one dinner invitation from Howard Hughes, expecting to be taken to the equivalent of Maxim's in Paris. After all, he was a genuine American multimillionaire. Instead he took me to the grill of the Hotel Lexington, which I considered very *déclassé*. He ordered lamb chops and spinach for both of us. Afterwards we went on to the Maisonette Russe at the St. Regis, and I was mortified to see the condition of his old overcoat when the hatcheck girl tried to help him put it on. The lining was in shreds, and it was so torn and threadbare that he had difficulty getting his arms into the armholes. I considered him too peculiar for words.

SEVEN

The year 1938 began with a marriage proposal from George, signaling the beginning of a very stormy period. I have tried to feel myself into the young woman who was so single-minded and in many ways so tortured. George was the only one I cared about, but as I confided to my diary, "I can't lie that I am madly in love with him, but perhaps that isn't necessary—he is such a good human being and has everything spiritual that I respect." The years between my immature twenty-one and George's thirty-four seemed like a lifetime. After two marriages and lots of girlfriends, George knew what he wanted and I, after one catastrophic experience, did not. The idea of marriage scared me to death. So I said, "Let's wait," words which triggered high drama in George's emotional nature. He became exceedingly depressed, jealous, withdrawn, and finally announced with a tragic expression that he "was losing one pound a day—*no*, there is nothing you can do about it." He exasperated me with his mournful air of resignation. After all, I had not turned him down but only asked him to wait for his sake as much as for mine.

George's suffering when in love stemmed from the depths of his Russian soul, and I strongly suspect was part of his imagination and genius. Several of his ballets have as their central theme the idealized, unattainable woman. George put women on a pedestal, where they don't necessarily want to be. Women don't want to be idolized, which can be dehumanizing. Women want to be loved for themselves and, above all, on an equal basis. Maybe in the depths of their psyche they want to be taken care of, but so do men. It can become oppressive to be adored too much—even suffocating. Perhaps this was at the root of George's comparative failure with women. He was the first to point out that all his wives had left him, not the other way around. And to the best of my knowledge, they all left in friendship and with continuing, unabated affection for him.

When he loved, he loved too much—or maybe we (though I should not presume to speak for others) loved him not enough. His keen judgment failed him in love because he used to make fun of marriages whose partners differed considerably in age. "When *he* will be seventy, *she* will be only twenty-nine—can you imagine?" Yet in his subsequent marriages the age gap became wider and wider as his wives became younger and younger. How we lose our better judgment when we fall in love! No one expressed it more succinctly than Noël Coward: "Loving is better than being in love. If you can cross that bridge, you're in for a long run." I *had* crossed it, and loved and respected George with all my heart, but I was not *in love* with him. While I was trying to adjust to the impact of so many new experiences, he remained violently in love. At this point, most inconveniently, I developed a tremendous crush on Orson Welles.

The Mercury Theatre, a brilliant new repertory company, was the theatrical event of the 1937–1938 season. It was founded by John Houseman and Orson Welles, then a precocious and brilliant young actor/director/producer from Chicago. Welles, only twenty-three in 1938, already had an impressive theatrical background. He started in Ireland, aged sixteen, as an actor with the Gate Theatre in Dublin. He went on to act and direct in New York, including an all-black production of *Macbeth* in 1936. On stage, he had a dynamic presence and a beautiful vibrant voice, which he used to great effect, especially when playing Shakespeare. He also had impeccable diction, which is not always the case with American actors. He was tall and handsome, with unusually wide, set-apart eyes and a full, sensuous mouth. The only feature which prevented him from having classical matinee-idol good looks was his nose, which was somewhat too small and upturned. Years later I was a witness to a flurry of excitement at London's Heathrow Airport. A British official came rushing up to a departure gate carrying a box and urgently called out, "Mr. Orson Welles's nose has to be on Flight 355." What on earth was going on? It turned out that Orson was to play Cyrano de Bergerac and had had an extra-large nose made for him in London.

In 1938 he was a romantic-looking man, somewhat Byronic, with one quizzical eyebrow slightly raised, and often laughing in a special throaty way. I think we would call him "sexy" today. In any event, I don't think he cared at all for matinee-idol roles but was totally *un homme engagé* in liberal causes. I heard him make a political speech in which he said he did not like the word "tolerate" in the context of "putting up" with something we don't like. He made a strong point and said acceptance rather than tolerance was what we should strive for. He directed *Julius Caesar* with a political slant toward the events which were on the verge of explosion in Europe. It was a brilliant production without scenery or costumes, but with platforms on different levels on the stage and unusual lighting effects. The actors wore nondescript clothes and uniforms, and Welles wore a long coat reminiscent of the long overcoats typical of German army officers. It was amazing how topical this "modern" version of *Julius Caesar* was. By shutting out all extraneous matter, the production became totally intense theater.

The first time Balanchine and I went to the Mercury Theatre we saw *The Shoemaker's Holiday*, which we found very amusing, well acted, and well directed. Afterward, we were invited by Cecil Beaton to a party in his apartment at the Waldorf. All the cast were there, including Martin Gabel, Joseph Cotten, and of course Orson Welles, but I was particularly impressed to meet Lillian Gish, who was very sweet and charming. It was not until a month later that I saw the production of *Julius Caesar*, which completely bowled me over. In the next few weeks, I went to see it twice and became as infatuated as a schoolgirl with Orson and the brilliance of the Mercury Theatre productions and ensemble. I found Orson just as magnetic offstage as on. We saw each other occasionally, and one night he invited me to a dinner party at "21" which included the famous actress Mrs. Patrick Campbell. I remember that we were late and all eyes were on us when we arrived. I was terrified when Mrs. Campbell insisted that I sit next to her. She was a formidable lady and famous for her sharp tongue. She lowered her voice an octave and boomed at me: "My dear child, since *when* have you been so beautiful?" I truthfully replied, "Since 7:30." There was a roar of laughter from the great lady and from everyone else at the table. It was considered a very witty reply. No one suspected that I was simply being literal, remembering that I had made up my face at 7:30 p.m.

A most memorable event for me was the annual March of Dimes ceremony at the White House. To me, a European, it was very exciting to be driven in a limousine to the White House, preceded by a police escort with screaming sirens. To meet the President and Mrs. Roosevelt was quite unforgettable. I felt that Mrs. Roosevelt had the same position as royalty in Europe, so when we were all lined up for our introduction, she must have been amused when I curtsied, but she could not have been nicer and warmer. I remember the President as a tremendous dazzler—exuding ease, broad smiles, and, *yes*, showmanship. He sat behind a desk as we were ushered into a special room to watch him broadcast to the nation. The room was packed with technical crews, and we were all jammed into a fairly limited space. During the broadcast, I was absolutely amazed to see Franklin Jr. and John Roosevelt in a silent but vigorous wrestling match, which ended with John on the floor, shirttails out, and Franklin racing down the corridor. They were twenty-one and eighteen at the time, and their conduct was un-believable to me. I couldn't wait to tell my mother all about it.

It was an exciting New York season. I heard Toscanini conduct Verdi's *Requiem* in an electrifying performance, never equaled again—at least not for me. Although he conducted in a passionate manner, characteristically slashing the air with his baton in large, circular motions, his left hand often rested in elegant military fashion on his hip. His enormous energy was always under control, without any display of self-indulgence.

As the premiere of *The Goldwyn Follies* approached, I had a phone call from Samuel Goldwyn. After we talked a while, he said he found my English much improved and asked what I was doing at that moment. "Why, I'm reading Shakespeare." "What the hell are you reading Shakespeare for?" "But, Mr. Goldwyn—for diction!"

Most of my diary references to Balanchine in those weeks reveal that he was unhappy over my refusal to commit myself to marriage:

February 18. Mama, Lina, George and I went out for dinner and I began demonstrating "The Big Apple," when my chair tipped backwards and I landed on the floor. . . George is *so* tragic, it is almost unbearable. He is a Dostoevsky angel, but I can't feel anything when he acts like that.

The Goldwyn Follies opened in New York the next day and Volodine, who had gone to the movie house when it opened at 9:30 in the morning, reported that the ballet got applause and that the house was packed. That evening George and Edward James took Mami and me first to the Sert Room, and then to a party given by

George's close Russian friend, Lucia Davidova. George looked very sad, but everyone else seemed to enjoy it.

February 20. Went to see the *Follies* with Mami and Edward James. Thought myself better than when I saw the film in Pomona, but found it boring toward the end. In the evening at the Metropolitan Opera saw a very good ballet by George, *Serenade.* It was the best ballet of his I have seen and everyone danced very well.

This ballet remains, forty-eight years later, one of the most beautiful Balanchine ever choreographed, mysterious in its simplicity and starkness. Though it is danced to utter perfection by some of the great dancers of the New York City Ballet today, it was equally arresting in 1938. What was not so obvious then was that its many choreographic innovations heralded the dawn of a wholly new direction in ballet.

February 25. Dinner with Orson Welles. I have never enjoyed anything more. If I never see him again, I shall always remember it. How we talked and understood each other. He is wonderful and for the first time since Léonide I felt my heart pounding and hands trembling.

I found myself totally bedazzled by Orson Welles. He was charming, erudite, and had marvelous ideas about the theater and what he wanted to accomplish. I admired him enormously and had all the symptoms of having fallen head over heels in love. Orson was as imaginative in love as in the theater. On days when we did not meet he bombarded me with telegrams, spaced to arrive every few hours. But our attraction to each other remained platonic and short-lived. Orson was married, and though we never talked about it, I understood that there were problems. While our respective careers raced forward, our stormy interlude passed, as work and success created storms of another kind.

———

I now realize that my incessant activities as a social butterfly were a cover for my real self. Underneath there was a totally puritanical persona. I still believed in the Latin dictum *laborare est orare*. (I had copied this out on a piece of cardboard, decorated it with colored pencils, and hung it over my bed when I was a child of eleven.) No wonder I was engaged in a constant internal battle and was paying a high price in self-loathing. Somehow "enjoying myself" could be permitted only after lots of hard work; this was the only way I could be happy. My credo became, Be strong, independent, work hard, and nothing can touch you. In sensuality lay perdition. A typical diary entry in this period reads:

Dreadfully unhappy. Raged, cried, and finally went to the Ansonia Hotel, where I settled myself down on one of those "beds" in the Turkish bath. Outside, there are magazines and newspapers full of photographs of the "beautiful Zorina"! Walter Winchell writes in his column almost every day about Zorina's legs being more beautiful than Dietrich's, while here I am sweating in this hotel. If they only knew— it's disgusting!

It really was a strange dichotomy, the public image of Zorina and the private me. A massive publicity campaign for *The Goldwyn Follies* was in progress and there wasn't a day that I did not see an image of myself in some paper, magazine, poster, billboard, or ad, posing, smiling, gorgeous, artificial. It should have made me happy, but it certainly did not. On the contrary, I think it made me self-destructive. Freud said: *"Die, die am Erfolg erscheitern"*—"Those who are shattered by success." Or, in plain English, some people can't take it and are destroyed by success. But why? One can only conjecture. It can be deeply upsetting to be constantly on display— always on your best behavior. One sees it in children who are drilled for special occasions and, when the ordeal is over, they immediately misbehave, doing outrageous things in order to break the tension they've been under.

The cause perhaps is being forced to do things one doesn't want to do, day in and day out. After all, that aspect of a career has nothing to do with the actual work and performance. It is the strain of becoming not only a public figure but public property. People do become proprietary when they have paid to see you. Every performer needs an audience, but outside the theater the relationship of performer, public, and press can be very upsetting. It takes a very calm and stable person—the antithesis of the artistic temperament, which is apt to be high-strung and nervous—to handle the impact of public adulation. Many artists have indeed been "shattered" by it.

I was unable to put my self-imposed dictum into action. Though I worked on voice and diction with Lina Abarbanell and took classes at the School of American Ballet, it was not enough. What I longed to do, but was prohibited from doing contractually, was to work with George. He was working on new ballets and choreographing for operas. While I watched George in rehearsal and saw his work in performances—beautiful ballets like *Serenade*—I wrote: "This is the time I should have danced—while I'm young—but no, there I sit, miserable, and cry in the darkness at the thought that I haven't danced for four or five months." Not to dance, for a dancer, is sheer hell.

Balanchine's new position as choreographer for the Metropolitan Opera was not a happy period for him either. He was often criticized by the important ladies of the Met. "Ignorant old women," George called them, especially when they were outraged by his *Aida*. Instead of the traditional ballet, he dressed, or rather undressed, the dancers and made them do barefoot acrobatic dances after ancient Egyptian bas-reliefs. He further ruffled feathers with *Orpheus*, when he staged the entire opera with dancers, placing the singers in the pit. It was absolutely beautiful, with costumes and scenery by Tchelitchev, but drew heavy criticism. Finally George resigned his position in disgust. But not before stating his opinion in no uncertain terms in *The New York Times*.

A marvelous team assembled for I Married an Angel on the first day of rehearsal. Richard Rodgers and Larry Hart, who were responsible for one hit after another, seemed to have done it again. We were enthralled as we listened to the score, the wonderfully witty lyrics by Larry set to the lilting and endlessly inventive melodies of Dick Rodgers. Will anyone who ever heard it forget "Spring is here, why doesn't my heart go dancing?" Then there were Balanchine, who had done two other shows with Rodgers and Hart; the brilliant young director, Joshua Logan; and a cast which consisted of Dennis King, Vivienne Segal, Audrey Christie, Chuck Walters, and a man who became my dear friend, Walter Slezak, son of the famous Wagnerian tenor Leo Slezak. We sat in a circle on the empty stage, with only a work light above us and a piano on the side. Josh Logan faced us, and Dick and Larry paced around listening. We read through the play, sang the songs, and at the end of the day felt very happy about it. We were on our way at last and nobody was more excited than I.

The role of the angel was one of those dream parts which are practically foolproof. How can you fail when, for your first entrance, the stage goes dark and through a shimmering, transparent background an angel comes floating down, dressed all in white, with magnificent wings made out of hundreds of delicate white feathers? Then the angel steps through the gauze, comes slowly forward, and says, "Hello—I'm an angel." The bachelor, who has just said that he will only marry an angel, whirls around and joins the audience in staring, while the angel takes a few more steps forward. At that point, the audience invariably broke into applause. The role was such that I could do no wrong. I found the part enormous fun. The innocence of the angel asking questions about anything and everything lent itself to a great deal of humor, and the truth-telling at all times was delightful, something we all wish we could do when somebody is rude or pompous.

In a way, it was inspired casting. The jokes which the angel generated often involved situations which I myself had not yet learned about. My command of English was still rudimentary and when the angel, in one of her truth blunders, causes a "run on the bank," I had no idea what this meant. As far as acting was concerned, the "team" left me pretty much alone—they wanted me wide-eyed and amazed, observing the peculiarities of the world I had just entered. Unfortunately, Dennis King, who played the male lead, became so jealous of the applause which greeted my first entrance every night that he began doing one double take after another, while I stood still, calmly looking at this very odd human being. In the end, all that his efforts accomplished was more incredulity on my part—more laughter and more applause. No, there was no way the angel could fail, and it had nothing to do with skill. Everything I did was instinctive, and everyone around me gave me the greatest help. One day at rehearsal there was a conference among Dick, Larry, and Josh: what should the angel be called? Names flew around, and finally Larry said, "Why not call her by her own name, Brigitta?"

I adored Larry—he was tiny, affectionate, with a sad look in his eyes. Though I was probably thirty years younger, I felt protective toward him and sensed a deep vulnerability in his character. Dick was more aloof and *comme il faut*, and I was a bit in awe of him. He did delight me one day: I was running around in my tights and practice clothes when he said, "You are the only dancer I know who smells so good." After that, I put on more eau de cologne and perfume than ever.

I have always loved the rehearsal period of any work I have been connected with. It is fascinating to see all the elements come together—people learning and improving, giving more, becoming confident. During *Angel*, I considered dialogue rehearsals a picnic compared to the rehearsals with Balanchine, though it was rather hard to shuttle from ballet rehearsals to concentrating on my lines with a skillful, veteran group of actors. George planned two ballets, each lasting ten to twelve minutes. In Act I, after the angel has been married, it was to be the *Honeymoon* ballet. George, as always, had wonderful ideas. A group of male dancers became an airplane in which we "flew" off by sitting on top of the shoulders of the tallest dancers, swaying slightly to the right and left, imitating the wings and motions of the plane. George's romantic attachment for me also embraced my Norwegian background. I skied, danced among snowflakes, and at the end of the ballet left the stage in a sled pulled by four real Norwegian huskies!

Things became pretty perilous at times, because George engaged a roller skater. He wanted him to skate with me from the upper wing straight down to the front, and stop at the edge of the stage. I was totally at the mercy of this young man, because George had me standing on his left foot, in a very high arabesque, while he held both my hands for support. We rolled and weaved forward very well, but the boy could never stop when and where he was supposed to. Since everything depended on perfect timing, it became quite a nightmare. Unable to stop at the edge, he would jerk uncomfortably to a halt, let me off, snap his fingers, and say, "Gee, I've got to practice that." George tried to reassure me. "You see, will be okay. Looks fantastic—just like ice skating in St. Moritz."

Then there was the skiing section. I rehearsed with two boys who would lift me high up while I was trying to keep my skis straight, terrified of poking somebody's eyes out. George said, "Looks beautiful! Like gliding through air over snow." The snowflakes were easier to handle, but they presented a big problem the first time we tried them. They were created through lighting effects, which meant that the stage had to be dark while some special spotlights flickered. After a few of the dancers and I had crashed into one another in the darkness, the lighting director found a better way of creating the same illusion. When I remember that all this dancing was crammed into ten minutes, with at least three total costume changes— including getting in and out of toe shoes, tying and untying ribbons —I am not surprised that I considered the dialogue scenes a relative breeze.

Our ballet in Act II was based on surrealism and was very strange indeed. My partner, Charles Laskey, had on little else than snakes coiling around his body. He stood on a platform holding a bicycle aloft, and suddenly the bicycle disappeared into the flies! I did a great deal of acrobatics. What Anton Dolin had forbidden, George loved and used whenever he could. "Body looks like insect" was his comment. During our tryout period in New Haven, dissatisfied with my costume, he went to a drugstore and bought twenty tooth-brushes in different colors, strung them on an ordinary string, and put the "necklace" around my throat—a perfect surrealistic addition.

The rehearsal period was very hard, as I was involved in almost every scene, either acting or dancing—which is the price you pay when you star in a musical. But it was also very rewarding. We began to sense the possibility of success, and it was wonderful to work in a company which was moving forward with high hopes. I may have been dead tired at times, but I was always ready the next day to practice more, try out something new—whether dialogue, steps, or costumes. It meant constant running around—upstairs for dialogue rehearsals, downstairs for ballet, rushing off to the costumer for a fitting and working at least twelve hours a day.

After five weeks, we were approaching our opening night in New Haven. At that time shows opened there at the Shubert Theater and then went to Boston for a more extended run. It was almost a tradition. The whole company would travel together on the train, stay at the Taft Hotel, eat at the restaurant across the street, and work together in the theater until they dropped. This was the time when romances began to blossom and bloom. The tension became so unrelenting that perhaps romance acted as a distraction and an emotional outlet. Anyway, road romances flourished and nobody took them very seriously. There is a delicious story about a properly married producer and a luscious blond showgirl. He borrowed a pal's room for his emotional outlet, and his beautiful blonde was fascinated by the array of medicine and pills lined up in the bathroom cabinet. One night, when everybody was having dinner together, the pal took out a bottle of pills, and she blurted out, "Oh, *you* are the one who has all those pills in the bathroom!"

For the New Haven opening, a great many people connected with the theater and Broadway would motor up from New York— managers, agents, ticket brokers, and, of course, friends and cronies. This was both good and bad, since they spread the news of success or failure like wildfire the following day in New York. Someone's pair of "new eyes" or "new ears" could cause a lot of trouble or spread joy, as everyone gathered after the show across the street for a postmortem. I have a photograph taken during the final dress rehearsal in New Haven. Chuck Walters, Audrey Christie, and I are sitting on a couch laughing hysterically at three o'clock in the morning, the time of night when you become utterly silly from fatigue. Little did we know that we were facing the kind of opening night when Murphy's Law, "If something can go wrong, it will," went into full operation.

Jo Mielziner's scenery was ingenious. We had two treadmills across the stage, one along the front, the second slightly farther upstage. They were like wide bands of moving wooden slats and were operated offstage by a machine. The concept was that furniture and props would be placed on them on the left side of the stage, move to the center, and after the scene was over, the treadmill would move the furniture off on the right side. This required a great deal of fast work by the stagehands and on opening night became a kind of Chaplinesque farce. The commotion in the wings was indescribable, as the stagehands staggered about with furniture while the stage manager hollered, "No! Not *that* chair, the other one!" Also, the treadmills didn't stop at the right spot, so half of the "old" furniture was still on stage while not enough of the "new" had been put on. The treadmills lurched a lot, so that actors who were sitting very nearly fell over. However, nothing surpassed a well-meant but wrong cue given to me. As I stood backstage with my magnificent wings on, ready for an entrance, someone whispered urgently in my ear, "Miss Zorina, don't forget to take off your wings." I whispered back, "Yes, thank you," and promptly removed them. Seconds later, when I made my entrance and looked into the horrified eyes of Dennis King, I realized I had taken them off one scene too early. The whole point was that I would "lose" my wings on my wedding night—a scene we had not yet played. Well, we went ahead just the same, though none of the dialogue made any sense; but in the following scene, when the angel wakes up in bed with her husband and wails, "My wings! My wings are gone!" the laugh was just as big.

The evening was still young and more was to come. The ballet had hilarious moments of mishaps, including my very fast changes, some of them only sixty seconds long. My dresser and I had gone over them carefully: "While you unzip me, I'll take off my head-dress—then you hand me the costume," etc. We decided that I would have to make my changes in the wings, but we forgot that the treadmill would be moving. This forced me, half naked, to walk backward, while every piece I dropped on the floor, from shoes to panties, sailed out on the stage and remained there in sad little heaps.

Finally, my skis, which had been specially constructed in New York with attached boots, arrived twenty minutes before the curtain went up, so I had no time to practice with them. During the ballet, I tore off my toe shoes, got into the ski boots, and pushed myself out of the wings. Instead of gliding silently, I heard something like the rumbling of a truck on cobblestones as I rolled over the two treadmills. It seemed they had put on heavy iron wheels instead of rubber ones. The noise was so loud that it drowned out the orchestra and, mercifully, convinced George to take out the whole ski dance before the next performance. Luckily the roller-skater boy chose the *second* night to fall on top of me instead of landing in the orchestra pit, so George eliminated that too.

In spite of all these minor catastrophes, we were a success and the New York crowd conducted a "postvivam"—if there is such a thing—after the show. That night I received two telegrams from Orson: THE FIRST ACT MUST HAVE BEEN MARVELOUS and YOUR OVATION AUDIBLE ON FORTY-FIRST STREET.

A few days later we opened in Boston and were a resounding success. The critic Elliot Norton gave us a rave review, and we knew we were on the way to becoming a big hit in New York. Actually, the plan had been to tour the show during June, July, and August, and then open in New York in September. It was still the time of no air conditioning in theaters and it was considered very risky to open a show at the end of the season (May) and run it through the heat of a New York summer.

Before that decision was made, I remembered a Boston fortune-teller I had gone to in 1936 with some of the other girls of the Ballet Russe who had predicted, quite correctly, that I would soon leave the company and do something quite different—something with words, which I interpreted as meaning acting. Just for fun, I visited her again—I remember exactly where she was—on the second floor of a dusty building facing the Common. This time she said, "Your plans will change—you will not travel but go back to New York and have a big personal success." Shortly afterward, Dwight Wiman made the announcement that we would go directly to New York and open on May 11.

It was an exciting and wonderful time. April in Boston, the emerald-green Common, flowering trees, and daffodils bursting into bloom. Mama and I stayed at the Ritz-Carlton Hotel. I have always considered the Ritz one of the great hotels, where nothing changes except for the better. Even the elevators smell good. We had adjoining rooms, high up, facing the wide expanse of the park, with the golden dome of the State House in the distance. Room service went on all night, and we could ring for the waiter and order the best rice pudding I've ever eaten. I finally wormed the recipe out of the chef. It was made with thick, heavy cream, with raspberry sauce poured over it, and served ice cold.

Balanchine gave a big party one Saturday night after the performance. He had found a Russian restaurant and arranged with the owner to take it over after eleven o'clock. No one gives better parties than the Russians—and no one gives a better party than a Russian in a Russian restaurant. Vodka and champagne alternated with caviar and blinis, and exuberance ran high. My mother and Lina Abarbanell watched with disapproval as George handed me one vodka after another, insisting that it was good for me, and I downed them with enthusiasm. We all had a marvelous time eating, drinking, dancing, and singing. I remember being blissfully happy as I skipped, twirled, and danced all the way home between the double row of trees on Commonwealth Avenue in the small hours. Lina insisted that I drink a large glass of milk before I went to sleep. It must have done the trick, because I had no ill effects.

I soon noticed that at every performance the left front row aisle seat was occupied by the same person—a striking-looking woman with almost white hair put up in the manner of a Gibson Girl. She was always dressed in black and never missed a single evening during our entire run of three weeks in Boston. Dwight Wiman knew her and one night brought her backstage to meet me. He introduced her as Miss Eleonora Sears, Eleo to her friends. She was then in her early fifties, and I thought marvelous-looking. She had the bluest blue eyes I had ever seen, a wonderful smile revealing exceptionally white teeth, and, one guessed, a trim athletic body hidden under those inevitable black dresses. I think she must have decided to remain within one fashion period and never changed. The length of her skirts, the cut of her dresses, the small black hats with upturned brim on one side were straight out of the twenties. Years later, when I stayed at Prides Crossing in her beautiful house on the sea, her "uniform" was a white flannel skirt hanging low on the hips, slightly flared, a blouse with a kerchief tucked into the neck, to which she added a cardigan on cool days—but a man's cardigan, which reached well down below the waist and closed with three bone buttons. In the evening, she always appeared in Chinese silk pants and beautiful embroidered kimonos, of which she seemed to have an endless supply. Looking for her, I strayed into her dressing room one day. All the cabinet doors were open and there they were: twenty identical skirts, thirty blouses, ranging from white to beige to navy blue—an awesome sight. Even identical bathing costumes hung in perfect precision—sleeveless camisoles which reached to just above the knees, each with its own belt made out of the same material. Matching knickers were discreetly attached.

Eleo was an extremely rich and eccentric Bostonian. If a letter arrived addressed to Eleanora Sears instead of Eleonora Sears, she would not open it but scribble on top "Person unknown" and send it back. If someone sat within a foot of what she considered her private beach, she would chase them away; if they parked in front of her house, she called the police. When you drove with her in Boston, every policeman saluted her respectfully and called out, "Good morning, Miss Sears," and sometimes very mildly chided her for making outrageous driving maneuvers. She once bellowed at a young man: "Do I know you?" He stared at her, petrified, and could say nothing. "Well, who are you?" shouted Eleo. He stuttered out his name, and she bellowed back, "Never heard of you," and turned her back.

Eleo had only maroon-colored cars—one an old 1912 Rolls-Royce and the rest Lincolns, all in that color. They had her initials on the door and were as immaculately kept and polished as her riding boots.

When I met her she no longer lived in the large parental house on Beacon Street where she was born but in her *ga*rage (accent on *ga*), a mews with the romantic name of Byron Street. It housed all her cars, but there any resemblance to a garage ended. Upstairs was a magnificent three-story room where she gave memorable parties.

It had tall windows on one side, a huge fireplace, a large concert piano, some comfortable furniture, and in one corner an enormous vase with autumn leaves which were kept there all year till the next autumn. She said the trick of keeping those branches and leaves so glistening was that glycerine had been added. There was an invisible and extremely well-trained group of servants who never spoke except when addressed. I saw Eleo take a domestic action only once, involving a quart bottle of heavy cream. It appeared incongruously on the finely set luncheon table, to be used with strawberries. After we had rather awkwardly helped ourselves, she marked the level of cream with a heavy pencil on the outside of the bottle so that no one in the kitchen would use it.

These things might seem unsympathetic, but they were not. Nobody resented any of her actions. They knew she was brought up in a certain way and recognized her as an eccentric in a city where there were many. In fact, her "retainers" were proud to work for her, and both sides strictly obeyed the rules. She might be tough, but she was fair, and nothing else was expected. After all, she came from a generation in which the steel magnate Henry Clay Frick employed twenty-four gardeners to cut his lawns by hand with scissors! Eleo told me that when Mr. Frick first bought land in Prides Crossing and wanted to build his summer house there, he was decidedly unwelcome. He was considered a vulgar millionaire who had made his fortune in coal, so the residents banded together and refused him water rights. That did not stop Mr. Frick. He proceeded to lay his own pipes all the way to Salem, twenty miles away, and pumped his water from there. This was considered such an ingenious action by the prudent Bostonians that they accepted him.

Eleo was not only a great horsewoman but had been a champion tennis player in her youth. She was twice U.S. Doubles Champion, but strangely, she was best known as a champion walker—to me a very odd sport. She was the only woman to have walked from

Versailles to Paris; the Parisians had given her a big ovation when she reached the Arc de Triomphe and strode down the Champs-Elysées. She would begin training in March for her walk to Prides Crossing, daily increasing her distances until sometime in May, when she walked from Boston to Prides, had half a cup of tea, and walked right back to Boston.

We were not allowed to be friends that spring of 1938. Dwight Wiman had a serious talk with my mother after Eleo followed us to New York. She had chartered a magnificent yacht and was at anchor in the Hudson. She invited us on board, but I was pressured to refuse, as it was not considered a suitable friendship. I considered this a ridiculous attitude, but I obeyed. Two years later I disobeyed, and we became devoted friends.

On opening night of *I Married an Angel*, shortly before 7:00 p.m., a tremendous storm broke over Manhattan. Those of us who were in the theater early, riddled with nerves before the opening, now shifted our worries to how the audience would get to the theater in the torrential rain. Would the curtain be delayed? Would it make a difference with the critics and their deadlines? All these concerns added to our already high-strung condition. But good luck prevailed, and in spite of the wet pandemonium outside, the first-night audience arrived on time, stepping from their limousines in full evening regalia, while the New York mounted police directed the traffic on Forty-fourth Street in the narrow space between Sardi's restaurant and the rounded corners of the Shubert Theater. The ladies went slithering down the aisles in evening gowns, bedecked with ermines and dripping in diamonds, making strategic stops to greet friends and giving the straining gawkers a chance to admire them.

My contemporaries who are forever reminiscing that things were better, bigger, more romantic, more exquisite, more tasty, more delicious, more exciting than they are now forget that we had no air conditioning in those days, and that it was hell in summer months. However, I will agree that those Broadway openings in the autumn and early winter were full of electric expectations. A new Van Druten comedy, a new play with the Lunts, new musicals by Cole Porter, Irving Berlin, or Rodgers and Hart were very special occasions. Yes, it was exciting.

Ever since that evening in 1938, I have connected rain with success. No one could have asked for more. The show played without a hitch, and as usual, even before I had said one word I was greeted by thunderous applause. And so it went all night for all of us. When the curtain came down at the end, we knew we were a smash hit. There followed an indescribable crush as people came streaming backstage. I was hugged, kissed, and congratulated by friends and total strangers. The lyrics of a very popular German hit song went through my head: *"Das gibts nur einmal, das kommt nicht wieder, das ist zu schön um wahr zu sein."**

Professionally speaking, the day before the opening very few people had heard of me. The day after, I had become a star soon to become the Toast of the Town. It wasn't easy—it nearly knocked me out. The day of the opening night I experienced a peculiar combination of fright and anticipation. The will to win was stronger than fear; the danger of an opening night excited me. In contrast, becoming a hit was totally unnerving. The next day, instead of rejoicing, I could hardly bear listening to my mother reading the glowing reviews aloud. She could not understand, and I could not explain, that I felt as if a heavy burden had descended on me. I sat across the room from her, autographing photos like a robot: "Sincerely, Vera Zorina," "Sincerely, Vera Zorina." Even today when I read of young athletes or rock singers suddenly catapulted into great success and becoming troubled, I understand them completely. In success you'd better be strong.

On the second night I suffered from "bad" nerves, not the kind

* *"This only happens once, it will never happen again, it's too beautiful to be true."*

of nerves which shoot adrenaline into your system and make you perform better. Orson, who had sent me a telegram—HAVE MEMORIZED NOTICES. HAPPIER, PROUDER THAN I CAN SAY—was trying to calm me by saying, "Before the curtain goes up, say to yourself, 'I don't give a damn.' Tell them to go to hell." I looked at him in amazement and said, "But it's just the opposite, I want to please them—and how can I when they expect so much?"

I had been thriving on the struggle to achieve, but achievement itself gave me no pleasure. Always foremost in my mind was the evening performance, and before matinee days I fretted if I couldn't go to sleep early. I disliked all the publicity I had to do—most of it silly—and equally disliked photo sessions, posing, trying to look soulful or sexy while the photographer begged: "One more, please."

The only relaxation I felt was after the performance, having supper and simmering down. As soon as I entered the Stork Club, the band would play the theme song of our show, "Have you heard I married an angel?" That was fun. But it began all over again the next day, and the full force of a hot, humid, New York summer contributed. I had never experienced anything like it before. The heat on the stage and in my dressing room was unbelievable, but worse was the unabated heat during the night. At home, I often took cold showers and went to bed wet, trying to sleep. It is sad to think that I could not enjoy all the outward success more. It was a pity, because that kind of success happens only once or twice in a career.

Throughout all this hoopla, George was steadfast and wonderful, patient and undemanding. He probably understood that one day the fireworks would fizzle out and calm would return—at least comparative calm. As a surprise, he had painted my dressing room at the Shubert Theater himself and made that little hole-in-the-wall as pretty as possible. He also brought me beautiful crystal bottles with tall stoppers from a trip to Cuba and gave me a special mirror. That dressing room was to be my second home for nearly a year.

My other "home" was Sardi's, where I ate dinner at 5:30 p.m. almost every night and then returned after the show for supper. I was very fond of Mr. Sardi and felt he was my cozy Italian grandfather.

George was trying to create a small permanent ballet company and often traveled with them when they had an engagement out of town or abroad. He was also running the School of American Ballet, then located at Madison Avenue and Fifty-ninth Street. The school was only two blocks from the Ritz Tower, so I valiantly tried to get up in the morning to go to class, but often was too tired. I may have been a star on Broadway, but in the school I was just another dancer. Although I religiously did a barre and other warm-up exercises before the performance, the two ballets I danced each night were not enough to further my development as a dancer. Doing eight shows a week, with only Sundays off, was just about all I could handle.

Sunday freedom was very special. We always tried to drive out somewhere to have dinner: Long Island, Connecticut, or across the George Washington Bridge. Sometimes Mama, George, and I went to Radio City Music Hall. All three of us loved the show preceded by the solo organ playing, the kitsch, the huge orchestra which rose out of the depths, the marvelous Rockettes who never made a mistake and whose precision I admired. George knew Leon Leonidoff, the director of the Music Hall show, so we always had good seats. Or we would go to Lüchow's, the German restaurant on Fourteenth Street. When George or my mother was away, things were worse. They were singly or together my emotional anchor, and I became like a willful, rebellious child, staying out too late at night and getting more and more tired. Sometimes during that summer I became so totally exhausted that I "checked in" at Doctors Hospital for a week and just stayed there—eating a very simple diet, sleeping, resting, and leaving only for the show at night, returning directly afterward to my hospital bed.

The return of cool weather restored me. I felt better and learned to cope with my schedule. My mother returned from a trip to Norway and George from a tour with his company. The balance was restored. George and I talked of marriage again, and this time it didn't throw me into a panic. I think success had taught me what did and what did not matter. Everywhere I went, people smiled and couldn't do enough for me. Taxi drivers were thrilled to have me in their cabs. Walter Winchell was my biggest fan and mentioned me almost daily in his column. Whatever went with success, New York gave to me—but there was a time to go home, and when I entered my apartment and there was no one there, I became aware of the loneliness of my life and what was missing. There were really only two people I cared about deeply, two people I could trust absolutely, two people who loved me in spite of my many faults, two people with whom I could share my soul as with no one else. I needed to belong not only to my mother but to my husband. It was time to marry George.

The question now was, How, when, and where? The idea of a publicized wedding was abhorrent to both of us. In our search for total privacy, my dancing partner, Charles Laskey, came to the rescue. He lived with his wife on Staten Island, and with the utmost discretion arranged everything. No one paid any attention when a justice of the peace married George Balanchine and Eva Brigitta Hartwig on the morning of December 24, 1938. Afterward we had a "wedding lunch" of corned beef and cabbage at the Laskey house and then took the Staten Island ferry back to Manhattan. We were very happy and stood at the rail imagining that we were on an ocean liner slowly steaming toward New York Harbor. We promised each other that our honeymoon trip would be to Europe on the S.S. *Normandie*. (We kept our promise and booked a special cabin in the autumn of 1939, but before we could board that beautiful ship, she was sabotaged at her pier in the Hudson River and keeled over like a huge injured whale.) When we arrived back in New York, I had to rush to the theater for a matinee. Everything there was the same, no one suspected anything. Only when Dennis King sang "Have you heard I married an angel?" did the familiar words take on a special meaning. I felt a secret elation that it really had happened and that George and I really were married. George and I thought how wonderful it was that we had chosen *that* day, Christmas Eve, a day of joy and giving, for our wedding. He wrapped me in his present—a snowy-white ermine coat of dazzling beauty—and I felt happier than I had ever been in my life. Someone belonged to me and I belonged to him.

George was a very masculine man in every sense of the word. He was a perfect example of the definition of *virile* in the *Oxford English Dictionary*: having procreative power of mind and character (in addition to the usual connotation). I refer to this in contrast to the present macho image, which is nothing more than swagger signifying nothing. Whatever he touched or was engaged in became creative, as if his perceptions were seen through a different prism. I imagine that it is so with all great artists. It is fashionable at present to insist that he is in the same orbit as Mozart, Picasso, and Stravinsky. Although it is meant as the highest accolade, I don't think he would necessarily consider it a compliment. Great artists know their worth long before the world gives its imprimatur. But Balanchine also knew that he was part of the artistic progression in the biblical sense of having been "begotten" by those who preceded him. If the public or critics did not understand him, that was their problem; he knew that they would one day. People said he was aloof or indifferent. He was not; he simply hid his disappointment better than anyone I know. Also, when you are miles ahead you cannot waste time waiting for people to catch up with you.

George was unique in his thinking, being, and manner of expressing himself. Fame meant nothing to him, money meant nothing to him either—at least not enough for a compromise. I remember how he confused a salesman who attempted to sell him a life insurance policy, pointing out, "When you are old, Mr. Balanchine, you will get all this income and—" George interrupted him and said, "Why don't you give me the money *now* to make beautiful ballets? When I'm old, all I will want is a cup of coffee." His pleasure lay in the realization of his labors. If his dancers executed his ballets the way he wanted them, he was happy.

He loved women and everything about them. He spoke of "wonderful blond hair," "beautiful blue eyes," "marvelous waist and hips," as lovingly as he talked about "wonderful feet," "beautiful legs," "high jumps," "moving very fast." Expressions like these sprinkled his conversation and were emphasized by gestures with his hands and a beautiful look of happiness on his face, tinged with a sly touch of wickedness. He loved perfume, jewelry, cars, dogs (especially German shepherds), and, of course, good food, vodka, and wine. In short, he was a sensuous man. He wanted his dancers to look beautiful—sometimes with their hair streaming loose, other times with sleek little heads topped by diamonds or delicate flowers at the nape of their necks. Above all, he wanted to show their bodies, unhampered by tricky costumes.

When we were married, he always supervised my costume fittings and insisted on the smallest details, and he did the same with my private clothes. He took me to the great Russian designer Valentina, who dressed me for years both on and off the stage. Though he loved that feminine world, he disliked feminine men. He admired "beautiful man" the way he would Michelangelo's David, but he wanted his male dancers to be cavaliers—courtly gentlemen gallantly escorting a lady or presenting a ballerina.

He admired physical beauty in an abstract form the way one might admire a painting by Seurat in terms of pointillism. He would discuss the particular tilt of the neck, those slender, fragile-looking stems actually having the strength of steel, as the "Marinsky look"—after the famous school of ballet in St. Petersburg. This look, together with the upturned wrist like a fly-away bird, marked the dancer as an unmistakable Balanchine ballerina.

He would speak of the "suffering faces" of dancers, comparing them to saints, which reminded me of the angels in Rainer Maria Rilke's poem:

Sie haben alle müde münde
Und helle seelen ohne saum
Und eine sehnsucht wie nach sünde
Geht ihnen manchmal durch den traum.

Fast gleichen sie einander alle;
In Gottes gärten schweigen sie,
Wie viele, viele intervalle
In seiner macht und melodie.

Nur wenn sie ihre flügel breiten,
Sind sie die wecker eines winds:
Als ginge Gott mit seinen weiten
Bildhauerhänden durch die seiten
Im dunklen buch des anbeginns.

All of them have weary mouths
and bright souls without seam
and a yearning (as toward sin)
goes sometimes through their dream.

Almost they are all alike;
in God's gardens they keep silent
like many, many intervals
in his might and melody.

Only when they spread their wings
are they the wakers of a wind:
As though God went with his wide
sculptor hands through the pages
in the dark book of first beginnings.*

* *Translation by M. D. Herter Norton.*

One would have to understand that in his mind "suffering faces" were not to be taken literally, or connected with a dancer's pain and bleeding toes, but meant spiritual suffering. To George dancers were saints because they worked harder and longer, were obedient, and never talked back, were always paid the least, and then went onstage and danced like angels.

George had rented a duplex apartment from his friend Lucia Davidova, who owned a building at 11 East Seventy-seventh Street. It was perfect for us, like a miniature house, with a private entrance and an interior staircase connecting the two floors. The kitchen and dining room were on the ground floor, and a living room and bedroom on the floor above. My mother had prepared it for us and helped with the moving. George usually had only one special concern—his piano. He decided to put it in the dining room, which led to musical evenings when we had friends for dinner.

Since we were both busy, we did not contribute very much to decorating the apartment, except that we had been "inspired" by the startling colors of a Persian painting reproduced in a magazine and so chose a dark-green carpet for our living room and upholstered our couch in a brilliantly quilted red. Otherwise I was delighted to leave the rest of the running around to antique shops searching for beautiful furniture, coupled with the sport of bargaining, to my mother, who adored it.

My mother also found a "jewel" to take care of us and our household. Clara Wachter was German and the sister of the Ritz Tower manager. She was thin, bony, and prematurely gray, and I have rarely seen anyone who worked so selflessly and meticulously. She cleaned, scrubbed, washed, ironed, cooked, and served. Her devotion was unlimited, but she was convinced that no one else did a job properly, so she also washed curtains, waxed floors, and cleaned windows until she collapsed in a flood of tears. However, no amount of pleading with her to get extra help did any good; she insisted on doing everything herself. I loved her wonderful mish-mash of German and English, such as *Pennvansalia* Station, or discussing the usefulness of a card table: *"Na ja,* then you klapp it together and put it in die closet." In her zeal for cleanliness she broke many dishes, but there never was an apology, only a happy comment: *"Scherben bringen Glück"* ["Broken glass brings luck"]. When we had dinner parties, she entered into the spirit, seeing to it that people ate enough. One of our first guests was the composer Paul Hindemith. Clara gave him a lecture as to why he had to have a second helping, and firmly pointed out which piece of meat he should take. I was very fond of her.

George had to go to Florida for a few days, so we decided to postpone making an announcement of our marriage until after his return. But to my acute embarrassment Walter Winchell got hold of the news and covered the entire front page of the *Daily Mirror* with a screaming headline, as if war had been declared:

ZORINA ELOPES—

JILTS FAIRBANKS JR.

Underneath there was a photo of Douglas and me who, the press insisted, were a "romantic duo." A movie star was obviously more newsworthy than a Russian choreographer whose artistic stature was as yet known only to a select group of ballet cognoscenti. After all our efforts for privacy, I was sorry that both my husband and Doug should be subjected to this kind of publicity, but they under-stood that it was beyond my control and that the press is not con-cerned with the delicacy of the heart.

We settled into our marriage like two children playing a game. None of the weightier aspects of marriage troubled us. No financial problems, no in-law problems, no household problems, no concern over babies. All was serene and unclouded. We had our work, we were interested in the same things, and we loved each other—in short, we were very happy. We acquired a beautiful aristocratic dog, Wingolf, from Busecker Schloss. He was a German-born shepherd, pearl-gray and black. He had been rejected for police work because he had failed his last test. No wonder. It consisted of being tied to a tree and whipped. If the dog tries to defend himself, he is accepted; if not, he is put up for sale. He was very shy at first, which was not surprising after his ordeal, but we gave him a great deal of love and he developed into the most wonderfully gentle and intelligent dog. I took him everywhere; he traveled on the train in his own huge doghouse when I went on tour. In Chicago, we often walked to the theater and back for his exercise. He would lie quietly in the corner of my dressing room, very close to the stage, and never budge; but when I began to put on my street clothes, his ears went up, he smiled, and he pranced around the room like a happy creature who knows that the long wait is over. I always remember his great patience with my mother's Pekinese, who was clearly enamored of him. Wingolf bore the adoration with great dignity, even when Buji insisted on putting his head into Wingolf's open mouth. The only time I saw Wingolf severely tested was when we had newborn kittens in our country house. He slowly stalked one of them, but a low "NO, WINGOLF" from me stopped him in his tracks, and he never tried again.

One morning, when George had left for rehearsal, I noticed smoke seeping through the tiles of the bathroom. When I opened the living-room door, thick smoke poured out. I quickly closed the door and yelled, "Clara! Fire! Quick!" She ran out into the street and continued my yell: "Fire! Fire!" and then broke open the nearest fire-alarm box. In three minutes flat fire engines roared up and spilled out firemen, who began to smash everything in sight with pickaxes, drowning the room in water. It seemed that the logs in the fireplace had smoldered through the night and finally caused a fire to break out in the chimney. The firemen did a fast, efficient job, but also made a huge hole right above and into Clara's kitchen, with debris raining down on her stove. *Ach du lieber Gott!* Fortunately, our bedroom and clothes were spared and George's piano was unharmed.

I Married an Angel closed in February 1939, and the company went on tour to Pittsburgh, Chicago, Detroit, Washington, and Philadelphia. George joined me in Chicago, where we played for six weeks. We had a very nice suite in the Ambassador East Hotel, so high up that we could see Lake Michigan. Ernie Byfield, the general manager, ran the hotel to perfection. The Pump Room of the Ambassador was *the* place to dine in Chicago, and it was there that George introduced me to two of his Russian friends whom he considered to be the best musicians in the world, in their respective fields—Vladimir Horowitz and Nathan Milstein.

I don't know how George managed it in the tiny kitchenette of our suite, but he made the most incredible Russian Easter feast for us. He cooked and baked (or, as he liked to say, "prepared" things) for three days, showing me how he "squeezed" cream cheese through cheesecloth, draining it of unwanted liquid, to produce an absolute masterpiece of the famous *paskha*. It was cone-shaped, had a subtle taste, and melted in your mouth. We also had a delicious *kulich*, a sort of dry cake reminiscent of a German *Stolle*. I was as awed by his culinary talents (working in so cramped a space) as I was by his ability to choreograph under trying circumstances.

We had only one disturbing and sad experience in Chicago. Both of us wanted to follow our civil marriage with a religious ceremony, and George agreed to marry me in the Catholic Church. We made an appointment and went to the chancery of the archdiocese, where we expressed our wish to a priest, who treated us with decidedly cool civility. I stated that I was a Catholic, not yet an American citizen, and was told I needed to furnish further proof. George was subjected to a grilling, and one could almost see the rising distaste of the priest when George told him that his religion was Greek Orthodox and that he had been married in the Soviet Union and did not have proof of his divorce. The priest dismissed us without making any attempt to consider the problems of a refugee or without giving us the slightest hope. He stated flatly that, under these deplorable conditions, he could see no way we could ever be married in the Church. We felt so dejected after our experience that we did not make another attempt in New York. As George had never obtained a divorce in the Soviet Union, it was highly unlikely that he could obtain one in the political climate of 1939. He was also concerned that his first wife, Tamara Geva, who had remarried, might be faced with needless problems. As for me, I was deeply offended by the priest's lack of charity and sympathy. I felt that, if this representative of the Church would not bless us, God already had. My sense of humor got the best of me when, years later, I began to wonder whether I or George's subsequent wives were ever really married to him. This vision of George as a blue-bearded bigamist was too silly, as we were all properly married and divorced according to the laws of the United States of America.

EIGHT

Samuel Goldwyn had loaned me to Warner Brothers for the movie version of *On Your Toes*. George was engaged to re-create all the dance sequences, including of course *Slaughter on Tenth Avenue*. In late May we set out for Hollywood on the Superchief, in as carefree a mood as if we were going on a summer holiday. "We" consisted of George and myself, my mother, and Lina Abarbanell, who had been engaged by the studio as my private "coach." We rented a beautiful house in Bel Air which belonged to Tyrone Power. It was built like a Spanish hacienda, with a large inner patio surrounded by bright red geraniums in Mexican pots. All the bedrooms opened out onto a balcony the length of the house, with a staircase down to the patio—very cheerful and comfortable.

We both knew *On Your Toes* very well, and the work at the studio presented no particular problems, except one point which George solved brilliantly. The leading male role, which had been danced so marvelously by Ray Bolger in the Broadway production, was cast with Eddie Albert, a young actor with considerable charm but no particular dance experience. It was typical of Hollywood to disregard totally what was crucial for a part and think only of what might draw well at the box office. George was faced with staging *Slaughter on Tenth Avenue,* which required a first-rate hoofer, with a non-dancer! What he did was ingenious. He found a superb black tap dancer and cut back and forth from Eddie Albert's face and torso to the tap dancer's legs and feet. It worked perfectly. I'm afraid the dancer's name was kept secret, so I can't even now give him credit. Eddie did the rest of the dancing very well, including a sexy *pas de deux* in *Slaughter,* and since he was a fine actor, all turned out for the best.

As with most of the films I made (at least those in which George was involved), I remember very little except the ballets. It was what I was mainly interested in, and our combined energies were concentrated primarily on making them as perfect as we possibly could. George insisted on carte blanche in his contract, making us virtually autonomous, so that some of the ballets are like separate artistic units in otherwise undistinguished pictures. I think this is true of *Slaughter on Tenth Avenue* and the classical *pas de deux* in *On Your Toes.* I like to think that I contributed something toward the popularization of ballet through these films, but of course the lion's share belongs to Balanchine.

As in *The Goldwyn Follies,* we were lucky to have a top cameraman in James Wong Howe, but it was George's inventiveness and choice of unusual camera angles that made these ballets different, like little jewels. He would ask Wong Howe for special light effects, and again (as in *The Goldwyn Follies*) place the camera low in the pit, which gives the classical *pas de deux* its elongated look. George also changed the choreography for the movie version. On the stage it had been a hilarious spoof, but he decided to have all the satirical fun earlier with the ensemble and have us dance it straight, without any attempt at comedy. He dimmed the light, creating a black background, with only a spotlight following Charles Laskey (my partner) and me. As our costumes were white, the whole *pas de deux* is in stark black and white. When one looks at it today, one can see both the past and the future choreography of Balanchine. There are moments in it of *Apollon Musagète* and the choreography yet to come in his ballets. Wong Howe understood and respected George and gave him everything he asked for. One shot in *Slaughter* is upside down to show what *I* would see being totally bent over backward. Another sequence shows me approaching in a slinky manner; it was shot from between the legs of a dancer, making it look very sexy. One isn't always pleased with what appears on the screen, but I was surprised when I saw the results of our labors. It made the whole tedious part of filmmaking worthwhile.

One day Wong Howe said to me, "Never let anyone photograph you from your left, but always your right profile," and he had the director redirect his moves and all the furniture rearranged so that his camera could approach from the right. He never gave any reason for it except some technical camera jargon. The secret of the right profile remained between him and me. He was a very nice man.

In Hollywood I met Gaylord Hauser, the glamorous forerunner of all the nutritionists. I think part of his fame came from his devoted friendship with Greta Garbo, who became his early disciple. I was invited for lunch and expected a severe meal of healthy food, and thus was totally unprepared for one of the most delicious cakes I have ever eaten. I was told it, too, was healthy, consisting of fruit, honey, and nuts. Ah, but what about the whipped cream? "Very good for you" was the answer. I soon tried to follow his regime and bought a juicemaker. We had beet juice, carrot juice, celery, cabbage, and other less palatable concoctions. I was told to make a witches' brew called Potassium Broth, which I was to drink for three days to clean out my system, with *nothing else*. I was not exactly mad about it, but I did it and felt fine. I thereupon became an apostle and insisted that my mother and Lina take "the cure." After one sip, my mother absolutely refused, but Lina started. After her first day, she was violently sick and had to stop the car on Sunset Boulevard.

Before I could return to the stage for another musical, Goldwyn lent me out to Twentieth Century-Fox, then headed by Darryl Zanuck. The film I was to "star" in was *I Was an Adventuress*, to be directed by Gregory Ratoff, the tempestuous Russian-born ex-actor. The cast included Erich von Stroheim and Peter Lorre, two legendary names, and Richard Greene for the romantic lead. George was engaged to create a ballet, which meant we could work together and need not be separated. George and I had planned to go to Europe, but the political situation was so dangerous that we canceled our reservation on the ill-fated *Normandie*. One month later, war was declared when Hitler invaded Poland. I was terribly upset when the war started in Europe. All my childhood fears seemed to have been resurrected. I wept at the horror of impending death, destruction, and separation. But America was not yet at war, and life here went on pretty much as before.

The studio now announced that films were to be made more rapidly (part of an austerity program), working hours would be longer, and we were expected to work hard and finish on schedule. George and I rented a duplex apartment on a quiet street in back of the Wilshire Hotel. I was not very happy there and felt cramped after our lovely summer in Bel Air, but while one is working on a film most of one's time is spent at the studio anyway. The atmosphere on the set was not as relaxed as that of *On Your Toes*. Gregory Ratoff, a large, burly, volatile man, was forever yelling "*Quiet!* !" He made more noise than anyone else, bellowing like a bull: "SILENCE! !"

I was fascinated to meet and work with von Stroheim and Lorre. Von Stroheim had had a distinguished early career as a director, and Ratoff was totally in awe of him, treating him at all times with kid gloves. Peter Lorre was famous in his own right from the German film *M*, in which he had played a pathological child murderer. We three were supposed to be a "team" of jewel thieves on the Riviera, with von Stroheim as the mastermind who used me as bait to snare potential victims, and Lorre of course as von Stroheim's dominated creature, who carried out all his plans.

Von Stroheim knew every imaginable trick of filmmaking. His technique made it virtually impossible to cut him out of a scene (should that necessity arise during editing), since he always knew which camera position would be the most advantageous to him. Ratoff was aware of how von Stroheim applied that knowledge but either didn't dare confront him or was simply deferential, even when it interfered with the way he wanted to direct a scene. Lorre was equally wise; I was the only true innocent. But both von Stroheim and Lorre liked me, so we *did* become an inadvertent team as they maneuvered me around. I was fascinated by von Stroheim's use of "props." He had his famous monocle, which he used with superb skill, putting it in his eye or dropping it for an effect. He invariably had a cigarette which he puffed on and tapped ashes off, or he took out a cigarette case, selected a cigarette, then used a match or a lighter, which meant *more* business. He also carried a newspaper, which he shifted from one arm to the other, alternating that bit of business with an elegant walking stick! The poor script girl, whose job it was to write down all the business that actors perform with their lines, nearly went mad keeping track as von Stroheim shifted his newspaper to his right hand, while puffing on his cigarette, and seconds later put his monocle in his eye, etc. Arguments would ensue: "No, Mr. von Stroheim dropped his monocle on 'Do you really think so?' instead of tapping *off* the ashes while saying, 'I see.'" Meanwhile, Peter Lorre would slink around, looking for other mischief.

One morning von Stroheim and Lorre had a short scene to film. They had rehearsed it, the camera was ready to roll, and I decided to watch. Both men were dressed in white linen suits, having breakfast. Von Stroheim was buried behind his newspaper while

Lorre, in his strange, abstracted way, began to put sugar in his coffee. Each time he slowly stretched his hand out to the sugar bowl, took out one lump, and dropped it in his cup, then slowly reached for another lump: "One—two—three—four—five—six—seven—" He then took an eighth lump, broke it, dropped one half in the cup, and returned the other half to the sugar bowl. Around the fourth lump, von Stroheim slowly lowered his paper and observed Lorre with vitriolic hatred. When Lorre broke the last lump in half, von Stroheim crashed his fist down on the table. Cups flew in the air and coffee soaked the front of both white linen suits while he spoke his lines to Lorre in a controlled rage. When the scene was over, there was a mortified silence on the set as everyone looked at Ratoff. Von Stroheim had improvised the action of crashing his fist down, spraying everything with coffee, which meant several hours' delay while the suits were cleaned. Ratoff behaved admirably. "*Very* good! *Very* good! But now we must try once more without the hand and the crash and the coffee." Everything came to a standstill while the suits were washed and ironed, and the whole setup was readied again. Ratoff spoke soothingly to von Stroheim, who promised not to hit the table. The camera rolled, Lorre broke the last half lump of sugar, and down came von Stroheim's fist, drenching the suits all over again. I think Ratoff burst into tears. The scene stayed in and the reaction in movie houses was terrific. Since by that time we had sugar rationing, the audience thought the scene hilarious, and howled with laughter.

Von Stroheim could be very inventive and always provided a bizarre touch when needed. He and I had a scene together in a railway carriage. He was instructing me on how to ensnare my next victim. I was immaculately dressed, but as he lifted my hand to kiss it, he suddenly stopped short, brought my hand closer to his eyes, and began to scrutinize my nails. He made some disapproving noises and then pulled a small bottle of red nail polish out of his pocket. He rapidly unscrewed the top and applied the polish, while giving me a lecture that I should pay closer attention in the future to chipped nail polish. All of this was totally unrehearsed and entirely his own contribution, but since it was so right for his character, it too stayed in.

As Zanuck pressed to have the picture completed, our schedule became harder, starting at 8 a.m. and on many days shooting past 6 p.m. One Saturday we broke for a brief dinner and resumed afterward. By 9 p.m. I was totally exhausted and asked Peter Lorre for a sip from his coffee cup, which he had been wandering around with all evening. He handed it to me and I took a good gulp, swallowed, and gasped. It was pure brandy, with only a dash of coffee to make it look respectable. It soon became apparent that both von Stroheim and Lorre found the English language more and more difficult to pronounce, so blessedly we were all sent home, and that was the end of *that* day's shooting.

George had decided to base the ballet for the *Adventuress* on the second act of *Swan Lake,* using Tchaikovsky's music. I was the Black Swan, with my faithful partner Charles Laskey dancing the villain. Lew Christensen, who was unusually tall for a dancer, looked even more resplendent as a knight in armor. The set was beautiful, with intertwining trees forming a kind of arch in the background, a black floor shiny as a mirror (but hell to dance on), and a real moat, water and all, with a miniature castle at the end which was to appear in the distance shrouded in mist. George became very busy with camerawork and was using a "boom" for the first time, going up and down on the crane trying out all kinds of new shots. It may have looked interesting, but it was twice as hard for us dancers, because the camerawork was so tricky and the timing so difficult. We had to practice routines over and over again, until the crew got it right. By the time all the technical aspects synchronized, we were worn out.

George also created some very difficult choreography for us, which Lew, Charles, and I rehearsed obsessively. We finally were ready to film it, but it took many, many takes. Either the crew made mistakes or we did, but finally it went perfectly for everybody. As we were all rejoicing, a script girl came up and said, "I'm sorry, but a feather flew off Miss Zorina's costume." I did not swear in those days, but my meaning was clear—*no retake*—and the floating feather remained. In the end I don't think the ballet came off very well. Some thought that Balanchine intended it as a satire on *Swan Lake*, but that is not so. His rich fantasy and marvelous imagination simply did not materialize—that can happen. Also, Zanuck came on the set one day in full riding outfit, beating his crop against his shiny boots, and made it clear that no unnecessary time be wasted for "experiments"—hardly the right climate in which to do something different. Toward the end of the ballet, there was a trick shot where Lew Christensen holds me in his arms and watches me disappear in front of his eyes. He slowly turns, enters the moat, and, in full armor, wades in two inches of water toward the "distant" castle. Cinematically it was totally out of proportion and made Lew look like Frankenstein. This was hardly what George intended. Yes, things can go wrong. George did realize one ambition which he had always wanted to do. Under the improbable name of "Fortunio Bonanova," he is seen conducting an orchestra in the film.

In early 1940 Igor Stravinsky arrived in Hollywood with Vera Soudekina, his devoted friend of twenty years and wife-to-be. We four had dinner together. I remember how excited I was to meet the great composer of *Firebird, Petrouchka,* and *Les Noces*—ballets in which I had danced (even though in lowly roles). I admired all his music beyond compare. In the car I asked him an idiotic question about the "counts" in *Sacre du Printemps,* and he said, "Very simple, my dear. Look at windshield wiper." (We were driving in pouring rain.) "Very easy to watch: one—two—one—two—three-four—one—two—three-four—*one*—is very easy." I leaned deeply into the back seat and never said another word.

Stravinsky was a small, precise, rather severe man to whom one might apply the word "dapper." Vera Stravinsky was a beautiful, imposing woman, tall, voluptuous, and always dressed in unidentifiable dresses with imaginative jewelry, hats, rings, beautiful scarves and fur pieces. Even her hair had a white streak in it which was totally original. But, above all, she had a beautiful warm smile and a cozy manner, and she was flirtatious in a teasing way. This was entirely unobjectionable to another woman; rather it left you with the feeling that here was a *real* woman who would give pleasure, warmth, sympathy, food, caresses, and *no* problems, *no* arguments, *no* self-inflated ego. Stravinsky clearly adored her. One could well understand why he never wanted her out of his sight, why he fretted when she was late, why he loved her as he did. George said that Vera was like a mother hen and Stravinsky (he never called him Igor) like a little bird who wanted to be under her wings, which was right, because she warmed and nested him.

We became close friends only twenty years later, when I performed Stravinsky's *Perséphone*, first in a staged version and then, more and more frequently, in concerts. In those early years I remained as mute as possible, quasi-terrified of Stravinsky, but I observed Vera with ever growing affection and admiration. She remained beautiful until the day she died: her mind was elsewhere —waiting, as she told me, "to pass through a door"—but she said it with a smile as warm and brilliant as ever.

———

My agent, Louis Shurr, had begun negotiations in New York for an exciting project: a new Irving Berlin musical called *Louisiana Purchase*. The book was to be by Morrie Ryskind, one of the best writers in the theater. George was to do the choreography, so the most important things were settled—or so I thought. For weeks Louis had wrangled with the producer, Buddy De Sylva, about my billing and salary. What else? It appeared that the management was rather stingy, and the other stars, William Gaxton and Victor Moore (usually billed as Gaxton and Moore), could not be persuaded to split their names in order to let me have second-star billing after Gaxton. It sounds trivial, but I was sternly instructed that once you achieve star billing above the title you must not allow yourself, come hell or high water, to slip into a less exalted place. I finally solved the problem with infuriating feminine logic: I proposed that it would look very ungallant to have two male names and then a female name on the marquee and proposed something more "harmonious," like GAXTON ZORINA MOORE, with my name in the middle. The real clincher (to the dismay of my agent) was that *if* Gaxton and Moore agreed, I in turn would accept less money (unheard of) until the show was paid off—after which they were to increase my salary. This seemed a delightful compromise to all concerned, but I suspect that Victor Moore was the true peacemaker and yielded his place.

I had not yet finished shooting *Adventuress*, and George had to leave Hollywood because he had agreed to do a musical revue, *Keep Off the Grass*. When we completed the film, I needed a few days of rest before starting rehearsals in New York. I had heard about the wonderful ski resort Averell Harriman had developed in Sun Valley, Idaho. Gregory Ratoff enthusiastically urged me to join him and the Zanucks, who were going there to ski. I had missed the winter in Hollywood and longed for snow and mountain air. Sun Valley was everything I had dreamed of: spectacular beauty outside and great comfort inside the chalet hotel. There even was a heated swimming pool, completely encased by a high glass wall, where one could sun and swim in the open air. I think this impressed me more than anything. Although I did not dare to ski so close to the beginning of rehearsals, I took the ski lift every morning to the last stop. To me, it was one of the greatest delights to ascend slowly in perfect silence, while swinging gently over a wintry landscape, away from the earth and into the sky. At the top there was a lodge where the serious skiers (like Harriman) met and where we all lunched sitting outside in the hot sun. I thought it was paradise.

Averell Harriman was soon to change from a very rich man with many successful projects to a world figure in politics, especially in his diplomatic negotiations with Russia. He became an expert in Russian affairs and remains so to this day. He was a charming man, very good-looking, and a crack skier. He gave wonderful parties at night, and I was introduced to square dancing, which, from my lofty position as a trained dancer, I had to concede was a lot of energetic fun. During the day, the comic relief was provided by my ebullient friend Ratoff. Expertly outfitted in ski uniform, from his Alpine-visored cap with goggles to his ski boots, he was nevertheless the most appalling sight on the slopes. He was intrepid—I will say that for him—but he resembled an overstuffed bear who, incongruously, had managed to stand upright on skis. But he was seldom upright and rolled around in the snow most of the time, trying to get up. After five wonderful days, I left for New York.

Starting a new show was always exciting. I was thrilled to meet Irving Berlin, one of the titans of American popular music. He had the blackest hair I'd ever seen—in fact, blue-black. He was friendly, shrewd, and very businesslike. Since I was not a singer, we did not have a great deal of close work together. I had only one song, called "You're Lonely and I'm Lonely," which I sang to Victor Moore, who then joined me in a duet. Even though Berlin made the vocal range as easy as possible, I dreaded singing it and always felt enormous relief when it was over.

I immediately liked my co-stars, Billy Gaxton and Victor Moore. Billy was an extrovert and a great tease, and at once made me his straight man. I was a perfect foil for him, and he used me in his jokes both on and off the stage. I was playing a newly arrived émigrée, and he had particular fun in a scene in which he questioned my background. His ad libs, especially on matinee days, would throw me completely, until I finally caught on. So one day, when the first question came: "Where are you from?" I answered: "Buxtehude." He was so taken aback that the audience laughed. He then said: "How did you get here?" "In a canoe." Of course it was very unprofessional on both our parts, but after that Billy left me alone for a while.

One of Gaxton's most elaborate pranks was inspired by my "monologue" ballet—old man's darling or young man's slave. We were on tour in Pittsburgh and had just finished a matinee when Billy's dresser asked me to stop by his dressing room. When I entered, I was introduced to an inspector who had come from Washington, D.C., where we were to open the following week. He began by saying, "Well, Miss Zorina, I've seen the show and I'm very concerned about your ballet. Now, Miss Zorina, you're making fun of a United States Senator there—calling him 'old man,' and questioning whether you should marry him. Now, Miss Zorina, we can't have that kind of thing in the capital of the United States of America!" I interrupted, "But that is not my intention. You must understand that I don't write the dialogue." "Ah," he interrupted, "but you have *lent* yourself to it; you're saying it up there on the stage. Now, Miss Zorina, I can't allow that." I interrupted, "But it's not my fault. Why don't you speak to Mr. Ryskind, who wrote it." "That doesn't make no difference—*you're* the one who agreed to do it." By that time, I was near tears from fright that I might be deported, and looked desperately at Billy for help. He moved forward and said soothingly to the man, "Now, isn't there anything we can do? I've got this beautiful case of Scotch here." At this point, I became enraged, thinking, So now we have corruption, he is trying to bribe him—when my eye suddenly caught sight of Billy's dresser shaking with suppressed laughter. I whirled around and stared at him, at Billy, and then at my tormentor, who broke into laughter. I was so relieved that I embraced the fellow and babbled, "That was a great performance!" It turned out that he was a professional jokester and Billy, of course, had the perfect tool for him—*me*.

Victor Moore was the antithesis of Billy Gaxton, which may have been the reason why they were such a great team. He was so quiet and reticent that it came as a bombshell when he married a pretty young woman whose own grandmother was younger than Victor. In *Purchase*, he played the part of an unsophisticated Senator who comes to New Orleans to investigate corruption instigated by Gaxton, who then frames him through me. He seemed to be a befuddled innocent, but there was nothing befuddled about his acting. I used to stay in the wings night after night to watch a scene between Victor and Irene Bordoni, because his comedy timing was so extraordinary. The infallible delivery of his lines, the tiny signals he gave to the audience—a pause, a raised eyebrow—followed by the explosion of laughter out front, laughter which never lessened, altered, or was lost. Not once. He was an absolute master.

Victor was also a kind friend. Opening night in New York I was a nervous wreck, and he said to me, "Think about it this way—it will *all* pass. In a few hours, it will all be over." I have never ceased to remind myself of those words, which were so obvious and simple, but they sank in and made sense. *Yes*, soon it will be over, and you might as well make the most of it.

In *Louisiana Purchase*, George created a ballet for me which later developed into another phase of my career—reciting poetry while dancing. It involved the previously described monologue in which I debate whether to become an "old man's darling or a young man's slave"—Moore or Gaxton? I spoke the lines while dancing a *pas de deux* with Charles Laskey. It was a new challenge for me and I enjoyed performing it. I danced it barefoot, which lends itself better to moving with silent fluidity. The first act had a *pas de deux* on point which had a few typical Balanchinean touches: Laskey throwing me into the air for a turn and catching me on the way down, and an extended arabesque on toe while he walked around in a circle holding my hands. Laskey was a marvel. In all the years he was my partner (three shows and three movies), I don't remember him ever being late for a pre-performance practice session or missing a performance. He was untemperamental and secure, someone who never failed me—a perfect partner. The classical *pas de deux* was followed by "Tonight at the Mardi Gras," a wild showstopper to Latin rhythms. I loved dancing it and really let off steam. Minutes after that number, I had to play a scene in a costume with a bare midriff. I mesmerized the audience with my stomach muscles still contracting after the exertion—an unintentional scene-stealer.

Louisiana Purchase was a big hit, and I settled down into a long run. My life revolved around eight performances a week and trying to stay healthy in order to do them. George embarked on a new show which he loved, *Cabin in the Sky*, with music by Vernon Duke and lyrics by John LaTouche. He staged the entire production, which starred Ethel Waters and the marvelous dancer Katherine Dunham, who also co-choreographed the dances with George. Besides his friend Vernon Duke, he had other Russian artists working with him whom he admired—Boris Aronson, scenery and costumes, and Karinska, who executed the costumes and played such a pivotal part when the New York City Ballet finally came into its own in the late forties. While I was steaming through the summer of 1940, George worked on *Cabin*, which opened in New York to great success in late October.

———

George had slowly prepared one of those generous surprises, or I should say, such largesse, that I associate only with Russians. He had bought twenty-six acres of land in Fort Salonga, near Northport, Long Island, and built a house. I was not allowed to know about it except in hints and whispers—or visit the land or see the construction of the house, or have anything to do with the furnishing. While it was being built in the summer of 1939, a tremendous hurricane hit Long Island. Luckily the force of the storm did no damage, because the outer walls were not yet up and the wind roared right through the structure. Finally, sometime during the winter, we had a "grand opening" weekend. Kopeikine, Volodya, George, my mother, and I all drove out for the "surprise," and I was at last allowed to see it.

A long curving road through woods turned up a gentle hill and revealed a low, rambling house painted pink! We all trooped in through the kitchen (the front entrance wasn't ready) and inspected every room. It was very well planned. A big central living room, with a huge fireplace at one end and opening onto a terrace at the other. It had doors leading to various bedrooms on opposite sides, which made them seem almost like separate apartments. A real American breakfast nook completed the house. Not one of us on that day was American, but the house certainly was—from the wallpaper to the early-American furniture. George had a passion for it and had bought out the entire stock of maple furniture at Macy's. Everything was in place, from beds to night tables, dressers, lamps, mirrors, a rocking chair, even a writing desk with a glass-enclosed bookcase. He had also found a long, hand-painted, Swedish dining table with matching benches, and put it in the living room.

Our wing was especially pretty. George had hung some lovely prints on the wall of nineteenth-century dancers—Taglioni, Fanny Elssler, and Grahn—and had a separate door built which led straight out onto the lawn. Everything reflected his care and thoughtfulness, which I found very touching. The house was properly sanctioned with salt and bread—a Russian tradition when you enter a new house—and someone, after many vodkas no doubt, suggested we call it Balarina, combining both our names. Though it was a natural, we found the name too corny and never used it.

The house saved me when I had to play through the heat of another New York summer. I bought myself a specially designed convertible sports car, called a Darrin. It had a powerful motor and was the nearest thing to what I really wanted: a Mercedes-Benz racing car. As soon as the curtain went down, I raced to take off my makeup and went roaring from Times Square over the Queensboro Bridge, and onto Northern Boulevard, where I was invariably stopped by a policeman. He was my friend, and said, "Now, now, Miss Zorina—you were driving seventy miles an hour, going on eighty. Please don't do that or I'll have to give you a ticket." He never did, but he watched over me.

I loved being home in Long Island. It was cool even when the weather was hot, and I could open the extra door and hear the crickets' nocturnal *cha-cha-cha*, like an energetic lullaby. In the daytime I swam at a private beach or lolled in a hammock under a huge tree outside my bedroom. Even though I had to leave again at 4 p.m. and never got home until 1 a.m., it was worth it. After a day like that, I had so much stored-up energy that it made performing a pleasure rather than an ordeal.

There was a benefit that summer for British War Relief in which I danced with Anton Dolin. George choreographed it to music by Vernon Duke and called it *Pas de Deux Blues*. Although I remember very little about it, two very distinguished pianists played the music: Vernon Duke and George Balanchine.

George now began playing a recording over and over again, usually the signal that he was planning a new ballet. It was Stravinsky's Concerto in D for Violin and Orchestra, played by Samuel Dushkin. At first I found it very hard to listen to—it sounded harsh, scratchy, and dissonant, and was not helped by Dushkin's playing. He was a distinguished violinist and had commissioned the work from Stravinsky, but he lacked the silken dexterity of Heifetz, Milstein, and Kreisler. Because I was continually exposed to the concerto, I soon became familiar with the music and began to share George's enthusiasm. Although I grew up with music, George guided me in a new direction, and helped me to understand modern music. Thank God, I was still receptive, because George was a wonderful teacher of music, which was his abiding love. He was happiest with musicians, talking about music or playing the piano, which he did very well. He often told me that he had really wanted to be a musician—specifically, a conductor. It was his dream to stand in front of an orchestra. I am certain he would have been an excellent conductor, knowledgeable, sensitive, and inventive. But his frustrated love played a major part in his becoming one of the greatest choreographers of all time. Knowledge of music is not automatically a component of choreographic talent, and lack of technical knowledge can be a hindrance in the development of a choreographer. George not only loved music but had taste and technical knowledge. That is why he could approach such an awesome piece as Bach's Double Violin Concerto and create a masterpiece like *Concerto Barocco,* or tackle the most fiendishly difficult pieces by Stravinsky.

His passion for Stravinsky never changed, and it was fully reciprocated by Stravinsky; one could see how much attuned they were to each other and how much they enjoyed working together. I often went to watch George rehearse the Violin Concerto which had been commissioned as a ballet by the orginial Ballets Russes. The leading dancers were Tamara Toumanova, Marina Svetlova, Roman Jasinsky, and Paul Petroff, most of them my old friends. I had a particular affection for Toumanova, who was exceptionally beautiful, a dear childlike girl and a very hard worker. I was also slightly jealous, because I would have liked to be in her shoes, working on a new ballet with George. Stravinsky often came to rehearsals, and there were lively discussions in Russian between him and George. They were not really discussions but conversations of the utmost politeness, each one agreeing with the other, like two Chinese mandarins. They would discuss tempi and musical nuances, both blissfully happy because a point made by one was instantly understood by the other.

I was fascinated watching George choreograph a Stravinsky ballet, and I marveled at the intricacies and musicality of the steps in relation to the music. I realized how different watching him was from working with him, because when you're involved in learning a new ballet you strain to understand the wishes of the choreographer and to execute the steps It seemed to me that the ballet was coming along marvelously. Toumanova, who had a similar problem to mine—blowing up and slimming down—was at her "thin as a needle" stage and dancing beautifully. The scenery and

Preceding page, George Balanchine and I after our marriage. Above and opposite top, at home in Long Island. Below left, war-bond sale. Bottom right, with Mrs. Roosevelt and a group of film stars at the White House; from left: Joe E. Brown, Eleanor Powell, Mrs. Roosevelt, Fredric March, Maria Gambarelli, Ray Bolger, Janet Gaynor, Don Ameche, Zorina, and two unknown child actors.

Guest appearance with the American Ballet Theatre, 1943. *Above left*, LA BELLE HELÈNE with André Eglevsky, choreography by Balanchine. *Above right*, APOLLON MUSAGÈTE, also with Eglevsky. *Below, rehearsal of same ballet with Nicholas Magalanes. Opposite top,* LA BELLE HELÈNE *with Jerome Robbins (left) and André Eglevsky; below,* ERRANTE, *choreographed by Balanchine.*

Top left, in the same season in
PETROUCHKA; *below, cur-*
tain call with Igor Stravinsky.
Opposite top, as Ariel in THE
TEMPEST; *below, in* THE
TEMPEST *with Arnold Moss*
and Canada Lee.

A letter to the author from George Balanchine. The text, beginning on page 2: "Darling! I would not worry about dancing, because if it is simple, beautiful and soft then that [is] what is good for the screen. You can judge yourself what is good. Maybe you could do something little more elaborate—for instance, to make very wide skirt with little bamboo sticks in side like this [Fig. 1], and to project film of birds or water on the skirt. The film must be made specially for that. And while they shoot, at the same time they could project film on the skirt [Fig. 2]. The birds should fly on

Darling Brigittushka—. I don't know what happened to those two letters (have send you long ago. if you did not received by now. then it is mystery to me.

Now I want to thank you for finding me a leading lady. Boys are very exited about new descovery. Wee already gave up idea to find some body new, and almost sined Nanette Fabrai. I caled every body same night after I talked to you.

Next morning wee met and decidet at once to take her. the Lerner and Loewe told me that Brigittas jugment is good enough for us. Wee are going on rehursals Thursday, and will open 8th of november in new York.

Next day I will be on the train counting minutes to have you—. I am waiting for that moment already now.

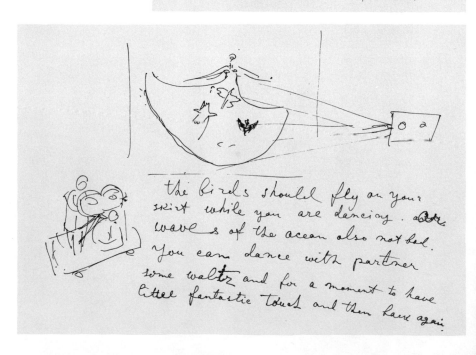

the birds should fly on your skirt while you are dancing. waves of the ocean also not bad. You can dance with partner some waltz and for a moment to have little fantastic touch and then have again

Darling! I would not worry about dancing, because if it is simple, beautiful and soft than that what is good for the screen. You can judge yourself what is good. Maby you could do something little more elaborate for instance to make, very wide skirt with little bamboo sticks inside like this

and to project film of birds or water on the skirt

the film must be made specialy for that. and while tray shoot, at the same time they could project film on the skirt

your skirt while you are dancing, or waves of the ocean also not bad. You can dance with partner some waltz, and for a moment to have little fantastic touch and then back again. God bless you, my love. I miss you very much. Your G. Kiss Mama from me."

On the next two pages, six photos of a rehearsal with Balanchine in 1954, for the revival of ON YOUR TOES. *The male dancer is Bobby Van.*

God bless you my love
I miss you very much.
Your G.

Kiss mama from me.

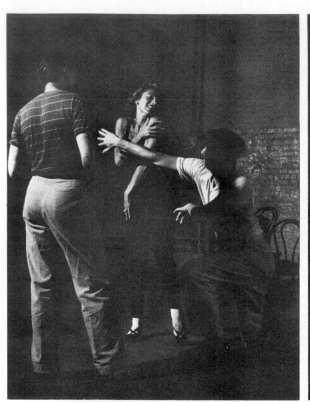

Curtain call for PERSÉPHONE *at the New York City Ballet, 1982.*

costumes were designed by Pavel Tchelitchev and looked extraordinary.

The opening night of *Balustrade*, as the ballet was called, must have been on a Sunday night, because although I was still playing in *Louisiana Purchase*, I was present. I had the highest regard for Tchelitchev, but this time things went very wrong. The background of the set was black velvet, and the male dancers were dressed from head to foot in black tights, except for jeweled skullcaps and wide jeweled belts. The black on black made it impossible to see anything but disembodied pieces of jeweled images floating about, like something out of Radio City Music Hall. Toumanova, who was so slim, had yards of tulle between her legs and large antlers on her head which hampered her movements. The beautiful choreography was practically invisible. I could have wept. The next morning my dismay changed into rage when I read *The New York Times*.

John Martin, then the most powerful dance critic in America, dismissed the entire effort with a short paragraph: "Why can't we have American artists instead of all these foreigners, these Russians, like Stravinsky, Tchelitchev, and Balanchine?" basing the entire review on his misguided patriotism. George would not permit any protest to be made and lectured me that one should never give a critic the satisfaction of showing hurt feelings. On the contrary, if you should meet one, say, "Ah, good evening! Nice to see you. Are you in New York?" That, he argued, would sting more and show how little you cared and how unimportant the whole thing was. George could do that; I couldn't. A few days later I had to attend a big luncheon at the Waldorf and was seated on the dais. I glanced over to see who was going to sit next to me and read JOHN MARTIN. I felt my adrenaline rising and considered my strategy, combining George's advice and my own point of view. I could not have been more charming when Mr. Martin arrived. We chatted animatedly all through the chicken, peas, potatoes, and ice cream, but during coffee I lowered the boom and asked, "Mr. Martin, why did you base your review of *Balustrade* on nationalities? The three artists involved, Stravinsky, Tchelitchev, and Balanchine, are all in the process of becoming American citizens, which they very much hope will be soon. Of course it's your privilege to criticize the music, the costumes, and the choreography—but to make it a political issue for artists who seek refuge in this country is grossly unfair. Surely you didn't mean to do that?" His blue eyes stared at me and a slow blush suffused his face. It can be said that John Martin *was* passionate about American dance and modern American dancers and not yet aware of Balanchine's genius. But he was fair. He never held my remarks against me, and eventually became a strong admirer of Balanchine and the New York City Ballet.

I venture to say that *Balustrade* may have created a new awareness in George of how a choreographic achievement can be ruined by costumes. Tchelitchev had not committed a willful crime, but he taught a painful lesson. I think it was a turning point for George, an explanation of why he stripped his dancers more and more in order to see the "bones of the choreography." I don't believe that the primary reason many of his subsequent ballets were danced in "rehearsal clothes" was lack of funds for costumes. I think George wanted his choreography to be seen, and not have his work spoiled unnecessarily. There is nothing more exquisite than a dancer's feminine grace—a beautiful, lean body seen through transparent material or wearing a properly constructed classical ballet costume with tiny shoulder straps, very tight bodice, cinched waist, with only the most delicate disk of a tutu circling the hips. But I can also appreciate the unbroken line of tights revealing the sinuousness of the body and its incredible agility, and making every twist and turn visible to the audience. George's ballets became leaner and leaner, and more intricate works of art. Sometimes they seemed like scattered pieces from a jigsaw puzzle followed by the sudden perfection of integrated unity. He had different visions from ours.

It was said that George became ruthless in his quest, but all great artists are ruthless. Compromise has no place in that quest. He would no longer use dancers he considered too old; he would find younger dancers capable of being bent like green twigs. He demanded that they be thin—thinner yet—and he used them like instruments, to produce a perfect ensemble. In defense of the charge that he made dancers into faceless machines, he told the truth when he said that he choreographed *on* people or *for* people. He used each dancer's specific gifts and maximum capacity exactly as a composer exploits the full range of technical skills in the cadenza of a concerto. Yes, he used his dancers, but he also showed them off. If that's selfish, then he was selfish.

I saw a good example of this in *Ballet Imperial,* which George choreographed in May 1941 for a tour of South America. Marie Jeanne, a young dancer from the School of American Ballet, was one of the soloists, and George used her amazing gifts of speed and daring to the hilt. She was an exceptionally audacious dancer and seemingly fearless. In the first movement (the Tchaikovsky Piano Concerto No. 2), George created a solo for her which I watched in amazement. I thought no one could go *all out* that way—surely she was bound to slip and fall down—because the combination of steps was too dangerous not to approach with some caution. But she did not fall and produced some of the most brilliant dancing I have ever seen. George, of course, had known all along what she was capable of better than Marie Jeanne herself, and he "pushed" her. Some people can take that push and others can't. Knowing the difference was part of George's mastery in assessing his "instruments."

That late spring of 1941, George produced three ballets for Ballet Caravan, a trio of heartbreakingly beautiful works: *Serenade* (from an earlier version), *Ballet Imperial,* and *Concerto Barocco.* He left with the company in early June for South America and our first long separation began. My contract forced me to travel in the opposite direction—to Hollywood. Once again I had been loaned

out by Goldwyn, this time to Paramount for the film version of
Louisiana Purchase, with Bob Hope. From the sublime to—what
shall we say?

————

Billy Gaxton was very upset because Paramount had assigned
Bob Hope to play his stage part. He was particularly angry with
our producer, Buddy De Sylva, who had recently become the head
of Paramount Studios. He felt he had let him down, and I could
sympathize. However, it was understandable that Paramount
wanted to use one of its biggest stars and moneymakers for the
movie. It was fun working with Hope, but we never became closer
friends than breezy co-workers. Making the film was not very
interesting (after playing the show almost a year on Broadway),
but life was pleasant. This time Mama and I rented a lovely house,
which belonged to Mary Pickford. It was on a quiet dead-end street
and had a beautiful big pool. We felt very grand, even grander
when we engaged a butler and a cook. My funniest memory is
connected with that butler. Mama and I were lying on chaises at
the pool when the butler came out with two large glasses of orange
juice. Offering the tray, he missed his footing and disappeared into
the swimming pool, sinking like a stone but holding the tray aloft.
When he climbed out of the pool, with water pouring down his
uniform, he was so humiliated that no amount of reassurance would
help. He left, taking his wife, the cook, with him.

The time seemed ripe to give a dinner party. A proper snazzy one.
I invited my titular boss, Sam Goldwyn, and Frances; Dolores Del
Rio and her husband, art director Cedric Gibbons; Marlene
Dietrich; and others. The house was pretty, and Ernest and Adele,
our new couple, were excellent. Nevertheless it turned into a first-
class fiasco—at least in my eyes. The first thing I discovered was that
Hollywood protocol demanded that the star's professional name be
written on the place card, *not* her married name. Somehow this was
cause for amusement, since no one knew that Marlene's married
name was Mrs. Rudolf Sieber. Then, after dinner, a bewildering

exodus of females began, known as "going to powder your nose."
Normally this can be accomplished in ten minutes; but when I
went, half an hour later, in search of my lost stars, I found Marlene
sprawled on my bed having a giggly telephone conversation, with
Dolores grabbing the phone and joining in. They didn't seem to
mind my appearance, nor did they seem ready to come downstairs—
which in fact they didn't. I left in a rage and promptly spilled an
entire demitasse of coffee on my evening dress, forcing me to go
upstairs again to change. Marlene and Dolores were still busy on
the phone. Their unselfconscious rudeness seemed to me unbelievable. Never again, I vowed, would I swim in those rough social
waters!

————

George wrote me on July 27, 1941, from Buenos Aires:

Darling, I hope by now you are already citizen. I received your letter
here and I am very happy that you have at last good people to work
with [Ernest and Adele]. The Swan Lake ballet [I Was an
Adventuress] made very big impression here. Everyone tells me that
you are the first ballerina in the world. As far as our ballet is
concern[ed] we are having such a success that I am really asham[ed]
of it. More than Toscanini. Everybody cheers us like Lindberg[h] after
his first flight. Yesterday I spoke on the radio to the students of the
university in Spanish about artistic relations between U.S. and
Argentina . . . From moment I arrived to Rio and until now I am
working like hell. I did two ballets and I am going to do two or three
more* and outside of that I am doing social work meeting the
officials, painters, and musicians . . . Thursday, July 31, we are going
to Montevideo and then we come back to Argentina, to Cordova.
After that we will go to Chile and I hope Peru in spite of war
between Peru and Ecuador. Today is Sunday and I finally have
few hours for myself.

God bless you—

Love G.

* Divertimento, Rossini; Errante, Schubert (revival); Apollon, Stravinsky (revival);
El Murciélago, Johann Strauss; Fantasia Brasileira, Francisco Mignone.

With George thousands of miles away, I suddenly faced an unexpected crisis. My mother became seriously ill and had to have an operation. She was taken to Cedars of Lebanon Hospital, where surgeons removed a large tumor from her uterus and performed a hysterectomy. Thank God, the tumor was benign. I was very frightened and all my terrors engulfed me. I wrote George, but his reply, written from Chile, took weeks to reach me.

> Darling Brigitta
> I receive your second letter on the pier just when I arrived here. It was exactly month since you send it. I was very sorry to hear of mothers operation but I hope she is well by now . . . I am trying to get ticket on Stratoliner from Lima to New York for 17 September and be in New York Sept. 20 . . . I see you soon—
>
> Love G.

George and I struggled through our contractual and geographical separations, because when he finally returned to New York in late September I had to leave for a road tour of *Louisiana Purchase*. Our marriage was not helped by the peculiarly Russian habits of clannishness and intrigue. I don't think Russians like "outsiders" very much and are really happiest with other Russians. They might be nice to you in the beginning, when opposition to a newcomer is useless, but when the slightest crack is visible in a relationship they can hardly be called peacemakers. Russians attract other Russians, no matter where they are. In my many travels with the Stravinskys, it never failed that an old Russian "friend" somehow materialized, ready to devote time and effort to their comfort. Of course, this can hardly be described as "intrigue," but is indicative of the great bond among fellow Russians.

George had his own coterie: Dimitriev, who managed his business dealings; Volodine; Kopeikine; Russian doctors; Russian food; Russian waiters in the Russian Tea Room; the great Russian costume designer, Karinska, who had her own Russian entourage;

Valentina, the great couturier, who had Mme Eugenia, the best fitter who ever existed; and of course the ladies—Lucia Davidova and Natasha Nabokov. Among them were some *intrigantes par excellence,* who have now become authorities on our marriage. Ah well. Perhaps they would be amused by what Stravinsky used to say: "My dear, nobody knows what's going on in bed except when you see the position of the feet sticking out under the cover—and even then"—he smiled triumphantly—"you don't know!"

In Chicago I settled in again at the Ambassador East for a three-month run through Christmas. Ernest and Adele had come with me from Hollywood. They were a fine young couple and taught me a great deal about what it was like to be black in America in 1941. Adele, of whom I was very fond, became my dresser in the theater, and we often talked of athletes and musicians that I admired. I remember her saying, "Black people have to be twice as good as white people in anything they do. That's why you know about Joe Louis or Jesse Owens or Duke Ellington." We were chatting while I was making up my face for a matinee performance when we were both stunned by a bulletin on the radio: Pearl Harbor had been attacked by the Japanese and the United States would declare war. The rest of that day, December 7, we were bombarded with rumors that the Japanese were going to invade the West Coast, and went from one terrifying conjecture to the next. I have no idea how we managed to play two performances or, for that matter, who was interested in watching us. Although San Francisco and Los Angeles were not invaded and the war continued to be fought far away in other parts of the world, millions of Americans were affected by it in a personal way, and I was no exception. A painful change had taken place.

I had not yet become an American citizen, as I had expected to be ever since the previous July, and I now found myself in the position of being an enemy alien. I was promptly fingerprinted and had to report to the local district attorney every time I traveled. It was not the procedure but being labeled an "enemy alien" that hurt most. I often had to reassure embarrassed officials—in the persona of Vera Zorina, Star of a Hit Musical—that I did not really mind reporting, since if they were so careful about me, how much more vigilant must they be with really dangerous people.

NINE

Paramount had bought the film rights to Ernest Hemingway's novel *For Whom the Bell Tolls*, and a hunt was going on for an actress to play the role of Maria. This young Spanish girl was described as having "her blond hair cropped short like a boy," which "moved in the wind like a field of wheat." In the novel Maria falls in love with an American—a role which it was rumored was going to be played by Gary Cooper. It was also rumored that Hemingway wanted Ingrid Bergman to play Maria, an excellent choice, since she was a superb actress and a big box-office star. But she was under contract to David O. Selznick, a very powerful independent producer, who had just loaned her out for *Casablanca*. There was the off-chance that Paramount would want to use one of their own actresses. Since I had just made a film for Paramount, I begged Buddy De Sylva to let me test for the part and he agreed. I was given a two-day leave of absence from the show to fly to Hollywood for the test. I prepared myself as much as I could by reading the book over and over, looking for the minutest clues to Maria's character, and generally trying to absorb the atmosphere of political and emotional passion. I had never played a part like this. Still, I felt I could feel myself *into* Maria.

By the time I went to Hollywood for the test, Sam Wood had been assigned as the director of the film and Gary Cooper announced as its star. I was given a most difficult and emotional scene to do—a scene with Gary Cooper. Sam Wood and Gary Cooper were most pleasant and helpful, and I felt the scene had gone well. I returned immediately to Chicago and fretted until I heard the result of the test. Within a few days, both Sam Wood and Buddy De Sylva called. Each said that the test was excellent (they sounded a little surprised!) and that I had a good chance to get the part. Naturally I was mad with joy, but my joy didn't last long; an interminable period followed as I waited for a definite decision to be made in Hollywood. In fact, as months went by, I finally tried to put the possibility entirely out of my mind.

At last the tour of *Louisiana Purchase* was finished. I had been busy with the show for two years, which was quite enough. When I returned to New York, George and I were reunited. He had a curious new project. John Ringling North, the enterprising owner of the Ringling Brothers Circus, had asked him to make a "ballet" for his troupe of fifty elephants. George, in turn, had the witty idea to ask Stravinsky to write a special piece of music for it. There are many stories about Stravinsky's reaction:

STRAVINSKY: How old are the elephants?
BALANCHINE: Oh, very young!
STRAVINSKY: If they are young elephants, I will do it.

I was not only enchanted with the idea but curious as to how it could be done, so when George had to go to Sarasota, Florida, the winter home of the circus, we decided to make a vacation trip out of it.

When we walked into the large courtyard of a U-shaped building, there were fifty elephants swaying their heads rhythmically from side to side, sometimes touching one another with their trunks. Actually they were in individual stalls, with their trunks hanging out over a low wooden barrier, and seemed to be having collective fun. I was absolutely entranced watching them, and asked their keeper whether there was a particular reason for their behavior. He said, "Nah, they're just amusing themselves—they're happy." To us the sight was unbelievable; after all, one saw that many elephants only in the movies. George soon found that it did not matter *what* choreographic splendor he had in mind for them, because the elephants were going to do the same routine they had done for years. The only thing that ever changed for them was the music and the costumes. So George ordered fifty pale-blue tutus (of delicate sizes!) and jeweled headbands for their foreheads. The "lead" elephant, a very intelligent female called Modoc, did solo routines, her trainer proudly told us. I was dying to ride her, but that was impossible. All the elephants had been oiled for the trip north to protect their hides from the change in climate. I promised myself that somehow or other I would ride her and get in the act when the circus opened in New York.

We continued to wander around the grounds of the winter quarters, where most of the circus people lived. I became absolutely fascinated watching a team of high-wire artists. I don't know whether they were members of the famous Wallenda family, but what astonished me was that the wire they practiced on was no more than three feet off the ground. They walked across it with the same intense concentration as if they were hundreds of feet up at the top of the circus tent. I watched as a little girl practiced under the watchful eye of her father. She couldn't have been more than four years old, and she looked very proud when she managed to reach the other end of the wire without falling off. I spoke to the family and said I was surprised they practiced only a few feet from the ground. The answer was: "Once you know *how*, it doesn't make any difference whether the wire is down here or up there"—pointing to the sky. "What matters is how you walk."

Shortly after our return, I heard that the New York opening of the circus would be a benefit for the army and navy. I volunteered immediately, and my dream came true. I would ride Modoc alone in the middle ring before the Stravinsky *Elephant Ballet*. The first rehearsal of Stravinsky's music by the circus band was unadulterated hilarity. It *sounded* like elephants—their ponderousness, their heaviness of body and slowness of movement, and even the curious dissonance of their trumpeting. I had no rehearsal for my appearance with Modoc. But I did get up on her once backstage, and learned a few things about elephants before the evening performance. I quickly found out that you do not sit astride an elephant like a horse, but quite forward in back of the head, with your knees behind the ears. The ears are very sensitive, and cruel handlers pull at them with metal hooks to make the elephants obey. During my brief lesson, I learned to sway *with* Modoc and almost perform a belly dance in order not to fall off. The rest was blind trust.

When we entered the three-ring circus to roaring applause, it was one of those great moments in life. In that vast arena, we were alone in a blinding spotlight. I felt the incredible grandeur of riding on that noble beast, who knew exactly what to do and needed no directions from me. She walked majestically to the deafening fanfare of the band, past the first ring, and entered the large middle ring. She knelt down and gently let me off. The band then began to play "Invitation to the Dance" by Carl Maria von Weber (ballet lovers know it as *Spectre de la Rose*), and Modoc started her "dance." This consisted of lifting up one front foot (which took eight bars), then slowly lifting the other, then doing a turn, while I danced around her in tempo and improvised a waltz. (I also kept a wary lookout for sudden showers from above, as elephants are notorious for getting nervous in the ring.) At the end, we both knelt toward each other in a deep reverential bow and touched our foreheads in the sawdust. A nice Balanchine touch. We remained in this attitude until she "offered" me her trunk. I lay back on it, holding her jeweled headband with one hand, and felt myself lifted high up as if by a crane. Nestling in her trunk was like lying in a gondola. She carried me out and gently put me down backstage, and my moment of glory was over. I realized afterward that I had never felt fear, because she had taken care of me like a baby.

The only thanks I could give her was something her trainer said she liked—to stroke her eyelid and scratch the sole of her foot. I had to stand on a box to reach her leathery, wrinkled eyelid, but she kept that tiny alert eye shut, so she must have enjoyed my stroking. I poked at her foot and she stood patiently holding it up, while I scratched the sole, which felt to my touch like a suitcase made of crocodile hide. That's all the affection I could give her for one of the biggest thrills of my life. The *Elephant Ballet* went splendidly. The fifty members of the *corps de ballet* entered in their blue tutus, holding one another by the tail, and performed their routine flawlessly, which is more than could be said about the band's playing Stravinsky. Still the music had a robustness that evening that seemed more suited to a sawdust setting than the subsequent perfect orchestral renditions given in symphony halls.

George's and my living arrangement was a bit chaotic. I had been away from New York so long that it seemed impractical to keep the beautiful apartment we now had on East End Avenue. I loved living on the river, but it was too far uptown from the school and theaters where we worked. Then, while I was away, George rented an apartment on Central Park South, which was very convenient but too small. During short trips to New York, we stayed at the Ritz Tower. My mother was the only one who was blissfully happy, living all the year round in our house on Long Island. She had brought her beloved horse Röschen from Los Angeles, built a stable next to our garage, and fenced in some land for him. He was the unwitting cause of one of the little dramas of lost objects my mother was prone to. Feeding Röschen one morning and cleaning out his stall, she noticed that a signet ring to which she attached a great importance had slipped off her finger. A search began, which lasted for days and finally had to be tearfully abandoned. The ring (which is now my own prized possession) has a Viking ship carved on it, with the Latin words *Ego sum mundi* ("I am of the world"—or, as my mother insisted, "I am a world traveler"). It had taken its own curious voyage through Röschen, who had eaten it with his feed; my mother found it outside in the corral after a safe passage.

George and I faced further travels and separations. He had been invited to the Teatro Colón in Buenos Aires to create new ballets and stage some of his existing ones. It was impossible for me to go with him because of my contractural obligations. I was still waiting for a decision about Maria, and as long as no one else had been announced, I assumed I was still in the running. George left in the beginning of June, and once again, I went in the opposite direction —to Hollywood. George wrote me from Buenos Aires:

My darling,
I arrived Sunday night. Flight was almost wonderful. I say almost because was boring. First thing I saw in B.A. was my fotos all over the town pasted on the walls and I was received like if I were Pop[e] of Rome. Everybody askes about you. You have great name here. I hope you will come in B.A. and very soon. Please go to the school as much as you can. I hope you feel good. I miss you very much.
All my love,
G.

I stayed at the Beverly Wilshire, as everything was still so indefinite, and continued my torturous days of uncertainty, which seemed to be coming to an end. The role was almost as coveted as that of Scarlett O'Hara. Of course the studio and the press used each other for the maximum and mutual benefit of suspenseful ballyhoo.

It's hard to explain what the role of Maria meant to me. Of course there were "dreams of glory" involved—a big step up the ladder—but it also meant much more than that. It meant that I would finally have a good acting part. Strangely enough, it was far closer to my temperament than the stereotyped caricatures I had to play in every movie I made. It would be a chance to work with a top director, a top actor—Gary Cooper—and a great cast. It meant a complete change in my career, and I thought I would probably never get another such chance. As it turned out, I didn't know how painful it was going to be.

When I was told officially that I was going to play Maria my reaction was mixed. I was afraid to believe it—afraid that what I had wished for so much could not be true. I was afraid to be happy. Paramount planned a big press release and a public haircutting ceremony. Two photographers were lined up as the first long strands were cut and fell to the floor. My hair was below shoulder-length, but by the time the hairdresser had finished, I had barely two and a half inches left all over my head. Only then did I believe that the part of Maria was really mine. It had seemed like a sacrificial act— the shearing of the lamb—but now it was *public*, no one could take the part away from me. I sent George a telegram. His reaction and advice soon arrived.

Hotel Alvear, Buenos Aires   June 10
Darling!
    Your wire made me very happy. At last you've got Maria. Please write me from Hollywood about everything. I did not understand why you sign Brigitta Hartwig?
    The Colón ballet is not as terrible as I thought. *Louisiana Purchase* opened here last night. I saw it again and I advise you to see it, because you will get some valuable information for your next work. You should speak less fast and with more even sound. And show more your upper teeth.
    God bless you, darling!
    And I am sure that this time you will make great picture. With all my love I think of you all the time.
                                        Tvoi G. Balanchivadze

His name, signed in Russian, was a joke, because I had signed myself Brigitta Hartwig.

June 27

My darling d-Eva-chka* (this is a new "very Evity" name I invented for you). Night before last was "premiere" of *Apollon*. Everybody are very pleased and happy except me. It was not great dancing. This is proof again that if my ballet are not very well danced then nothing is left of it, because there is only a movement and nothing else to do. [Colonel] Basil's company plays at the Politeama and after next two weeks they will stop for a long time.

Basil is trying to come to Colón and become one of the "advisers" there. Nana Gollner married Paul Petroff† and improved tremendously. Basil's ballet stinks, but everybody is crazy about it. Ballet public are snobs and likes boring bad performances.

Now I want to say few words about myself.—First, I miss you very much day and night! and second—I am thinking of you all the time and especially when I hear *Oedipus Rex* [of] Stravinsky.

This is something you should hear next. It will be very difficult at first to understand, but I know you will be crazy about it. You are wonderful in getting hold of some difficult and profound music. *Oedipus* is a great monument, which maybe will be acceptable in 20 years from now. First time I heard that being played in Paris 14 years ago. Now I am preparing dances for Opera (*Masouf*)‡ this is something I did not expected to do and later I am going to start [the] Mozart [ballet]. God bless you my darling and lots of love your G. Balanchine.

July 8

My darling! Your hair arrived safely. It looks dark gold color. I think you are lovely even without your beautiful hair. I know you will be wonderful in that part. I am thinking of you all the time wishing

---

* *George made a pun of my own name Eva and* devuchka, *"girl."*
† *Dancers in the Ballet Russe company.*
‡ *An opera by Henri Rabaud.*

you lots of luck. *Apollon* had a wonderful success. Borovsky danced principal part not badly and Ruanova was enough good. Now I start *Mozart* [ballet set to the Violin Concerto in A Major].

There are some good dancers which never have been used before. Director of the theater and all company are grateful to me for discovering new dancers. Colón want me to come next season for much longer time and they want you to dance.

You must prepare Paramount that you will not be able work next summer. You will have great pleasure to dance here. I want to bring here [Anatole] Oboukhov to give lessons, [Frederick] Franklin and [George] Zoritch. You must continue dancing while you are young. And here you can be presented like never before in your life. Because the theater has all the possibilities. It is like Marinsky Theater in Russia. Huge orchestra, wonderful light. And I have all the liberty to do all I want. And you have a great name here. As far as my everyday life is concerned I am doing nothing but rehearsals all day till very late at night. And when I can I go to opera.

Time is very short, my next ballet will be presented 31 of July. Shabelevsky will dance next time and probably [Tatiana] Leskova. Goodbye now, darling. I want to see you very badly but I can wait with pleasure, because I think you want too.

My love
your Georges

July 15

My darling!

Just received your letter from 6th of July today is 15th. I am preparing *Mozart* like mad. 31st is the first performance. The first and second parts are all finished. It looks rather nice. "I think Mozart will be rather pleased with it." One thing I did not expect is that my tooth, which I had to fix in New York and did not, start to hurt me very much and annoys me. Otherwise everything is all right. Colón ballet likes me and works with great enthusiasm. Your picture is going to be given again starting today and I am going to visit you everyday . . .

You probably started your new picture by now. I am sure you will
be wonderful! (I kiss you long and love you very much and want
you all the time.)

Tvoi

George

After the Paramount haircutting ceremony, I spent several weeks
being tested for makeup and hair—such as it was—and the clothes
I would wear. They consisted mainly of oversized corduroy pants
and rough masculine shirts, as Maria was trying to disguise herself
as a boy. Sam Wood and Gary Cooper were already on location in
northern California. The company was set up in Sonora, in the
Sierra Nevada mountain range, which closely resembles northern
Spain. The Greek actress Katina Paxinou and actor Akim Tamiroff
were already up there, and I was anxious to join them. At last I was
told I would be driven up and advised not to take too much
luggage. Life was going to be very simple and the company camped
out in log cabins. My mother came with me. The drive was beautiful
—more and more so, the higher we climbed. We were housed in
individual cabins but took our meals together in a kind of mess hall.
We settled in and I was raring to go.

But nothing happened. Day in, day out, I looked for my name on
the next day's call sheet, but my name was never on it. Sam Wood
was pleasant but distant, and he and Gary Cooper seemed to spend
most of their free time together, in addition to their daily work. One
day Cooper practiced rifle shooting. I knew he was a famous shot
and I watched him. He had tacked up a target, a cardboard with
circles on it, with the bull's-eye dead center. I asked him what
sort of a gun he used and he told me it was a .22 Hornet with a
mounted gunsight on top. Had I ever shot before? No. Would I like
to? Yes. He showed me how to hold the gun (it was beautiful), and
to look through the gunsight, and then to align the hairline so that
the cross would be on the bull's-eye of the target. I had seen that

done many times in movies. While Cooper leaned over me, I peered through the sight and pulled the trigger. It hit half an inch from the bull's-eye. Cooper reloaded and told me to shoot again. This time it hit even closer to the center. Cooper drawled, "Did you say you never held a gun in your hands before?" We shot a round and my score was 98 out of 100. I thought it was great. Cooper did not. He did not believe that I had never shot before and thought I was making fun of him.

After a week of idleness I was told I would work the next day. The scene had me coming down a narrow pass with a loaf of bread under my arm, seeing Cooper, saying a short greeting—and that was all. It couldn't have lasted more than a minute or two. After that scene was shot I did nothing further. Every night the day's film was rushed to Hollywood and developed in the studio. It was screened for the producer and evaluated. If anything was wrong, it could be reshot while we were still on location.

Two days after my scene I was called in by the production manager and told that I was to return immediately to Hollywood because there was something wrong with my teeth. What? He didn't know, but they wanted to fix something. "It would only take a couple of days," he trailed off. I was mystified. After all, I had made other pictures, and had been extensively tested and scrutinized before I went on location. Why would there be anything wrong with my teeth? I tried to call Buddy De Sylva, but could not reach him. The production manager urged me to leave—a car was waiting; so I left. Although I had no reason to be apprehensive, I felt that something was very wrong.

I tried to push those thoughts out of my mind. After all, Hollywood people were peculiar—one of my teeth had already been capped, moles had been removed, and one producer had even forced me to go to a plastic surgeon because he considered my nose too straight and wanted me to have a "dip" like Marlene Dietrich. The surgeon became so incensed by the request that he wrote a blistering letter to the producer. I tried to think of these foolish things to calm my anxiety. Immediately after my arrival, I was sent to the dentist, who promptly filed down another healthy canine tooth, fitted me for a cap, and declared my smile to be perfect. I was then called in for an appointment with Buddy De Sylva.

There the awful truth came out. Sam Wood and Gary Cooper had given him an ultimatum: First, they would both walk off the picture if I was not replaced with Ingrid Bergman; second, they had three weeks of work on the film which would have to be shelved and add a tremendous cost; third, he would lose his biggest star, Gary Cooper; fourth, Hemingway himself was applying pressure; fifth, Ingrid Bergman had just finished shooting *Casablanca* and was therefore free. De Sylva was as shocked as I was. He felt he had been rendered impotent in his position as studio head of Paramount, forced to give in to a situation and unable to make his own decisions. The "ultimatum" had been ruthlessly engineered behind the scenes by David O. Selznick and acquiesced in by Sam Wood and Gary Cooper.

I could now understand their guarded and at times almost embarrassed behavior toward me in Sonora. It is not without interest how it had all been done. Paramount had borrowed Cooper from another studio at great extra expense and was not willing to do the same with Bergman, under personal contract to Selznick. So a stalemate had developed and by the time *For Whom the Bell Tolls* started shooting, Bergman was filming *Casablanca*.

I believe Sam Wood was sincere months earlier, after directing my test, in saying I would play Maria. Later, under pressure from Selznick, who wanted the role for Bergman, with Hemingway's backing, he had to go along with Paramount's decision and then find a way out. So the machinery rolled on: the news was released, my hair was cut, the die was cast. Sam Wood and Gary Cooper went with the company on location and worked for three weeks piling up a lot of footage and a lot of investment. Wood stalled as long as he could *not* to use me, and then only for a half day's work. The business about my tooth was simply a ruse to return me to Hollywood, where things would have to be settled.

During this period Bergman finished *Casablanca* and first Selznick, then Cooper and Wood, delivered their ultimatums. It put Paramount in an untenable position. Either they had to sacrifice their considerable investment and start all over again or they had to sacrifice me. Buddy De Sylva fought for a few days—as much for his own authority as for me—but in the end he was forced to give in.

I was so stunned by the ruthlessness and cruelty that these people were capable of that I shut off. I believe the mind can take so much and then it becomes incapable of taking any more. I remember lying very still on a couch in my hotel room. Very still, without moving, as if I were in great physical pain. It's strange, but I never thought about the role I was losing. What hurt me most was the awful deception. With my cropped hair, I felt like a walking symbol of defeat. What to do next? I wanted to leave Hollywood at once, but one never can do what one really wants—scream, yell, hurt, sue. One is always talked out of retaliatory behavior—"It's useless, it makes it worse." One winds up doing nothing—at least I did.

I was not a dramatic actress like Bergman, so when I was removed from the picture the automatic reaction was that I couldn't act. Who would believe that I had made an excellent test and had only filmed a short scene? It would have been far easier for me to accept that nasty stigma if I had worked for a week and proved to be hopeless as an actress; at least there would have been a reason. But to be deliberately sacrificed in such a manner, even to the last insult of having my tooth filed down, made me feel ill-used, gullible, naïve, and stupid. Those few who knew what had really happened were too embarrassed to talk to me, except for one wonderful man— Fredric March. We met somewhere, and he thundered his outrage and tried to comfort me. I never forgot.

At least fifteen years later, I sat next to David O. Selznick at a dinner party in New York. Even then, I disliked our enforced proximity and made no attempt to speak to him. At the end of the dinner he turned to me and said, "You know who was responsible?" I looked at him in silence. "*I* was." "I know," I answered.

———

Throughout all this, George was still in Buenos Aires. I longed for him to come back.

July 24

My darling Brigitushka!

Just now I return from British Consulat were I had to get Visa Transit. If everything is all right I will leave on the 9th. My second ballet will go on the 4th of August. Shabelevsky and Borovsky will dance together and Ruanova as ballerina, she is not bad at all. Lincoln [Kirstein] saw some of it and thinks that it is my best ballet. It is very precise musically. Condactor Mr. Castro told me that he could conduct musical score only looking at the ballet.

Everybody are very happy to dance because for five past years they were performing pantomime or something like you imitating Palucca. Lots of funny things like that surrounding me here and I have to laugh alone, but with you in mind. It is useless even to tell anybody why I laugh. My darling! I am counting the days when I'll see you it won't be long now. I love you!

Your George.

P.S. In todays paper was your photo with Louella Parsons column.

———

Paramount wanted me to participate in one of their star-studded films, *Star Spangled Rhythm*. They had asked Johnny Mercer to write a special song which Johnny Johnston was to sing and I would dance in a specially designed production. I did not want to do the picture—in fact, it was the *last* thing I wanted to do. But when George returned and joined me in Hollywood, he persuaded me to agree. Perhaps he thought it would be good for my morale and to get my mind off my lingering wounds. As always, the point of persuasion was that Paramount would engage George to devise the story, choreography, and total production; and I must say he made a little gem out of it. The song, "That Old Black Magic," helped. It was beautiful and became quite famous. We both loved the melody and lyrics, and George made it into a fairy tale. A soldier lies on his bunk and gazes at my photograph, which is inscribed to him. He begins singing, falls asleep, and sees me dancing in a white forest glittering like diamonds. At the end, he wakes up and realizes it was all a dream—a vignette of five minutes which George trans-formed into a visually lovely ballet. Dancing barefoot in falling "snowflakes" among icy, glittering trees, up and down little hills, turning and leaping—"Down and down I go / round and round I go / in a spin / loving the spin I'm in / under that old black magic called love." In reality, the snowflakes were a nuisance. They were made out of untoasted corn flakes, soft as feathers; they stuck in my hair and got in my eyes and nostrils, but looked very pretty on the screen. So did my long, golden curls—a wig. At least outwardly I was getting back to normal.

I was asked to join Laraine Day, Andy Devine, and Jack Oakie on a war-bond tour. We visited mainly in the South, and were flown in military planes from one place to the next. I remember landing at the huge U.S. Naval Air Station in Pensacola, where we entertained, visiting factories which were working for the war effort and making speeches at civic gatherings to raise money for war bonds. When we were touring factories, I was amused to see that almost every woman who worked there wore a snood. I am certain that not one of the millions of women who adopted them during the war were aware that I had been responsible for the idea. It had come about one day when I went for a fitting to Lily Daché, the famous hatmaker. My hair was very long, and I was impatient with it. I said to Mme Daché, "Why don't you make me a kind of coarse hairnet, put an elastic band through it, and then I can stuff all my hair into it and look neat, the way we do on stage or in ballet class? You could put a nice grosgrain bow on top or at the side, and make it for me in different colors." She did, and I wore them non-stop. Soon they were the rage. I wish I had had a patent on them. I hope that at least Daché did.

Our tour was very arduous. Often we made appearances in three different places in one day: civic breakfast at 8 a.m., luncheon in another city, and dinner in a third. We had wonderful and awful experiences. We got so tired in the end that our speeches became mechanical. I remember Laraine being practically in a trance one day. While speaking about the horrors of the wounded, she rambled on and on and forgot what she was saying. I spoke mainly about the bombing in Norway and nearly broke into tears when I mentioned my grandmother and Aunt Fanny having to flee from a burning Kristiansund, when three-quarters of the town had been reduced to ashes. I think Jack Oakie and Andy Devine were a welcome comic relief at those times. Laraine was a nice, forthright girl, and I became very fond of her. She was a *strict* Mormon—no ifs, ands, or buts. She did not smoke or drink, and even tea and coffee were strictly forbidden—but she consumed a prodigious amount of Coca-Cola, blissfully ignorant that it contained caffeine.

One evening some people gave a small party and had a black entertainer sing and dance for us. He was so good and the music so infectious that Laraine spontaneously joined him in a dance and gave him her hand. Immediately a man in our party yanked the dancer away from Laraine, yelling unspeakable things at him. He then threw a dollar on the floor and told him to pick it up and get the hell out of there. It was one of the most shocking things I ever witnessed, treating a human being as if he were a dog. We left sick with shame. The reality of our mission jolted me back from my self-pitying state and gave me a sense of proportion. Seeing and sensing overwhelming suffering in the world made my own troubles seem self-indulgent and rather shameful. We do have to believe in what we are doing, but I was learning the difference between *that* belief and rank egotism.

———

At last I could go home to New York. George was busy doing choreography for the New Opera Company, which gave a season of opera and operetta at the Broadway Theater, starting on October 28 with *Rosalinda*. Adapted from Johann Strauss's *Die Fledermaus*, in a new version by Max Reinhardt, it was charming and a great success. I particularly remember Oscar Karlweis, a consummate German actor, who made the most of Prince Orlofsky as a decadent aristocrat, always mentally five steps behind, who covers up his lapses with a nervous, totally absurd laugh. A few years later he made a big hit in the title role of *Jacobowsky and the Colonel*. The company presented another operetta, Offenbach's *La Vie Parisienne*, and four operas, most of them with choreography by William Dollar under George's supervision.

For the first time in years I had no plans. George had hoped to produce a ballet-play for me based on the nineteenth-century dancer Fanny Elssler. He was enthusiastic about the idea and spent many hours with Alexander King, a writer, feeding him information about Elssler's background and career. Finally, after six months' work, a script appeared, but it was ponderous and overwritten. Between his travels and work, George tried again to work on it, but in the end the project had to be abandoned. Because of his belief in the Elssler project, George had begged me not to accept an offer to play the lead in *One Touch of Venus*. The musical had a score by Kurt Weill, a book by Ogden Nash, and was to be directed by Elia Kazan—a setup which almost guaranteed success. But George was very much against it. He didn't like the music (although he loved Weill), he didn't like the book, but his main objection was: "*Why* do a show like that? You just did a kind of Pygmalion role of an angel who turns into a woman. Always the same stuff. You must do something new." So I said no. It was the only time that George gave me bad advice. However, I had fun one afternoon singing for Kurt Weill and Kazan. I was totally relaxed, because Weill was not the kind of composer who demanded *trained* singing but was famous for the kind of songs which Marlene Dietrich sang so well—not to mention his wife, the great Lotte Lenya. So I sang away my repertoire of German songs, which made Weill want me even more for the show. But it all turned out for the best. Mary Martin did the part and was absolutely wonderful. That's the way it is in show business!

I turned, so to speak, back to the cradle and threw myself into work. I studied hard at the School of American Ballet, taking class every day without fail, and sometimes additional classes in the afternoon. I was twenty-five and kept asking George whether it was too late. Could I still catch up with myself and become a really good dancer? George encouraged me, watched over me, and insisted I work as hard as I could, which I did. We had several teachers: Anatole Oboukhov; Pierre Vladimirov, the husband of Felia Doubrovska; and Muriel Stewart. All three gave special classes in addition to a general class—some for men only, some point classes for girls, and some adagio-partnering classes for both boys and girls. Oboukhov was the toughest, absolutely nothing went by him. He appeared stern and pitiless, but was an excellent teacher. I remember that when I was the toast of Broadway in *I Married an Angel* and still taking class at the school, he stood directly in front of me as I was doing a deep *plié* during an adagio section. I slowly descended along the front of his body, wobbling in the process, while he snorted with displeasure, indicating that he couldn't care less whether I was a star; as far as *he* was concerned, I was doing a pathetic job in his class. Vladimirov was particularly good with men—teaching them partnering, jumps, and pirouettes; and Miss Stewart was very feminine—good for girls. Each one had a little quirk: Vladimirov became bored easily, and Miss Stewart got carried away and forgot the combination of steps she wanted us to do. She would turn around and say, "*Girls!* Now what were we doing here?" George himself taught, and that was very special. He simply asked for unusual things, saw unusual faults, and demanded more.

Vera Nemchinova, the great Diaghilev ballerina, took class every day, and Jerry Robbins came often. I liked Nemchinova. We always got in a little chat, either before or after class, which in her case was Russian telegram-style, mangled words and many pantomimes —"You call me?" accompanied with a gesture of yore when you had to crank up a telephone. She knew I loved cats, but I didn't know that I was also considered an authority on their gender. After class one day, Nemchinova consulted me on the kitten she had just been given. She pleaded, "I don't know whether my pussycat is boy or girl. Please come to my apartment and look." I promised, and a few days later rang the bell on Madison Avenue where she lived with her husband, Oboukhov. When Oboukhov opened the door, we were both taken aback and slightly embarrassed. As I considered him an absolute terror, I felt very much like a pupil who had come on a silly errand to her professor, never having seen him outside of the classroom before. I mumbled something about the kitten, and he promptly produced it. I lifted the tail of the tiny cat and found no clue whatsoever whether it was a boy or a girl. After this embarrassing procedure, I had to admit total defeat. Nemchinova was obviously not at home, and there we were alone. To my relief, Oboukhov revealed himself as gentle, courteous, and extremely shy. He began showing me around the apartment, whose walls were solidly lined with paintings and photographs of Nemchinova's career.

As I was admiring a painting by Zorine, Nemchinova arrived. In front of a particular photograph, Nemchinova asked me, "Brigittushka, you feel something?" "Well, yes," I replied, "it's very beautiful," "No, I mean do you *feel* something in expression?"

Again I produced admiring words—but she interrupted me and said, "I tell you story. One day when I was living with my auntie, she knock on my door and tell me terrible news: 'Veritchka, your mother—she die.' I start to cry and cry, but my auntie she remind me, 'Veritchka, you have to dance *Swan Lake* tonight.' So I have to go. I walk to the theater, crying, crying all the time. I stop on street and there on wall is mirror. I look in mirror and see my expression, and above mirror it says: PHOTOGRAPHER. So I go upstairs to photographer and say, 'Take my picture,' and that"—pointing to the photograph—"is reason for sad expression."

Sol Hurok, the impresario, asked me if I would do guest appearances with Ballet Theatre during their spring season of 1943 at the Metropolitan. They wanted me to do *Helen of Troy*, a ballet by David Lichine which George considered "lousy"—but it was agreed that George would rework it and create new choreography for me. It was also agreed that I would do George's ballets *Errante* and *Apollon Musagète*. In addition, I would dance the doll in *Petrouchka*. Suddenly there was a tremendous amount of work, but I loved it. I was totally happy again, and lived and breathed ballet. I realized how much I had missed dancing, how much it meant to me, and that it was the only thing that could have given me back some self-esteem at this low point in my career.

Igor Stravinsky had been persuaded to conduct his own ballets, *Petrouchka* and *Apollon*, and he began coming to rehearsals. He watched the rehearsals attentively, and I watched him out of the corner of my eye for any signs of displeasure over tempi. He had lively discussions with George in Russian, and sometimes they enjoyed talking to each other so much that they seemed to forget about us. Nicholas Magallanes alternated with André Eglevsky in the role of Apollo. Nicky was a Mexican-born, beautiful young dancer, most polite and very gentle. I think he was the only dancer (at least when I was present) with whom George became exasperated, not because he didn't dance well, but because George wanted him to "present himself—not to creep onto the stage but to make an entrance." Knowing of George's intense dislike of any ego display on the part of a dancer, I now saw George imploring Nicky to "*show* me who you are. Say to me, *Here* I am—look at me!" Nicky's very virtues of kindness and an even temper made him lack some of the necessary inner fire, the sudden burst of energy and the proud bearing that George wanted for *Apollon.*

André Eglevsky had no such problems. He was like a large, well-fed lion. Not fat, but sleek—with the powerful, rippling muscles that enabled him to land silently, even after the highest jump. He was strong and soft at the same time, and a very good partner. *Apollon* was the most interesting, choreographically and musically, of the four ballets I was learning. I felt challenged, and my capacities stretched, and I knew I was improving. It was exhilarating. It was the first time since we met that we had worked on one of George's great ballets. Everything we had done together so far had been geared to effect, as the situation demanded in musicals and films. I learned more and more every day—my body began to behave; I felt my feet becoming flexible, yet stronger; I jumped higher, and my extension, which had always been good, was becoming even more extended (though it was peanuts compared to what girls do now). Nothing hurt, nothing ached, nothing drove me crazy. I became thin, thinner, and even more thin, until even George had enough. "*Eat* something—have nice little vodka—and then you will have appetite. *Eat!*" But I felt well and was glad to feel light as a feather.

Of the four ballets, *Errante* was the most tiring to rehearse. It was less taxing physically, and danced barefoot, but my costume had an enormous train, literally yards long, which George used choreographically. Part of the role was danced with two men, Anton Dolin and Hugh Laing, and we had to rehearse over and over again to learn to manipulate the train properly. *Errante* was exciting to dance, and in many ways it is one of George's most dramatic works.

Dancing *Petrouchka* was the most obvious challenge. When you take on a well-known classical role, you're treading on dangerous ground. Balletomanes know every step, every pitfall, and become expert judges on how to execute this or that sequence. It's the same as when an opera singer does *Carmen* or *Tosca* for the first time.

Because of this, I had practiced every difficult step excessively, especially the eleven *fouettés* (turns on toe in one place) which had to be executed between Petrouchka and the Moor. I had rehearsed with Stravinsky conducting in the studio and on the stage. It was one of the rare times I counted, and I drilled it into my head that there were to be eleven turns. On opening night, all went well until the section when we three were in a line and I started my *fouettés*. To my horror, the tempo was twice as slow and I was forced to adjust to slow motion! I was desperate not to wobble, not to fall off my point, not to lose my place between the Moor and Petrouchka. I looked desperately at Stravinsky, but he was bent deeply over the score and never looked up. Then I suddenly realized that I had forgotten to count and had no idea where I was. But my feet moved automatically at the right moment in the music, and the rest of the ballet went without a hitch.

Apropos *Petrouchka*, I am reminded of a lovely story about Nadia Boulanger, the French musician, which was told to me with wicked glee by composer Francis Poulenc. Apparently Mme Boulanger lectured on Stravinsky at Sarah Lawrence and described the second act of *Petrouchka* in a very heavy French accent. "You see, then we come to the second tableau. The curtain opens and we see the Moor lying on his bed playing with his balls." Of course, the girls broke into giggles. Boulanger wagged her finger and admonished them innocently: "Ah, you naughty girls—you are laughing at my accent!"

A few days later I danced *Apollon* for the first time—again with Stravinsky conducting. This time I was on the alert for any drastic changes in tempi, which indeed came but were less difficult to adjust to. In the solo of the muse Terpsichore, there are a few stops of no more than a split second—but in the performance, I was suddenly suspended in an extended *luftpause*. It seeemed as if I were hanging in the air, but it only seemed like that and soon passed. Twenty years later I often worked with Stravinsky and found him extremely sensitive to the "breathing" of a narrator; but, for a dancer, there were many surprises.

Of *Helen of Troy* there is not much to say. In spite of George's additions, it remained an uninteresting ballet. I danced again with Eglevsky and a very young Jerry Robbins, who was Mercury, and on the edge of his enormous success with *Fancy Free*, the ballet he created to Leonard Bernstein's music. In 1943 Ballet Theatre was at its artistic zenith. It was a vital company with marvelous dancers and choreographers. Antony Tudor produced his greatest ballets during the forties, with *Pillar of Fire, Lilac Garden,* and *Gala Performance*. His choreography was as elusive as his choice of music, such as *Verklärte Nacht* by Schönberg and a piece by Chausson for *Lilac Garden*. I had a particular fondness for *Gala Performance*, in which a Russian, an Italian, and an English *prima ballerina assoluta* dance a solo section to music by Prokofiev each in her own style. The drama and hauteur of the Russian, the lightness of the Cecchetti-trained Italian, and the cool brilliance of the English ballerina were perfectly realized. There were delicious "digs" in the ballet, which the stylistic eye of Tudor caught with affectionate wickedness.

The company itself was a mixture of American and non-American artists. American Ballet Theatre was founded by Lucia Chase, who devoted her life to the company, both financially and artistically, just as her male counterpart, Lincoln Kirstein, has done for New York City Ballet for close to fifty years. Lucia Chase gave American choreographers like Agnes de Mille, Hanya Holm, Jerome Robbins, Michael Kidd, and Eugene Loring their chance to choreograph for the company, but also Antony Tudor, Anton Dolin,

David Lichine, and George Balanchine. Ballet Theatre had *star* dancers like Alicia Markova, Anton Dolin, Alexandra Danilova, Irina Baronova, Hugh Laing, and Freddy Franklin, but also Janet Reed and the first American dramatic ballerina, Nora Kaye.

The company received me in their midst with cordiality but also with some resentment. They were understandably irritated that I was paid a great deal more per performance in contrast to their extremely low salary. That kind of fight is still going on to this day, when superstars (which I was not) make guest appearances with a ballet company. However, I never felt any open hostility; I think they understood that it evolved from a money-making scheme to attract a different and wider audience. I had several old friends among the dancers: Pat Dolin, my former mentor, and Sono Osato, my roommate from the Ballet Russe days. I shared a dressing room with Alicia Markova and Nora Kaye, two of the most contrasting personalities imaginable.

Alicia Markova was the epitome of a nineteenth-century dancer. She had a very special style—an unearthliness, a quality which seemed to come from another century. When one looks at prints of Taglioni and Elssler, one comes a little closer to what I am trying to convey. She was not an athletic dancer and never showed off her formidable technique, but danced with total effortlessness. It is a curious fact that the incredible lightness of Markova was often achieved at the expense of her partners. I was told that she was the heaviest of all dancers to lift, although she weighed the least. This was because she would not help her partners by an extra little jump, thus creating a momentum upward which makes lifting a great deal easier; otherwise, a partner literally lifts a dead weight, even if that weight is only ninety pounds. I am certain that it was not meanness on Markova's part but that she wanted to achieve the effect of total, floating effortlessness, and in that she succeeded magnificently.

Although Alicia was born and trained in the twentieth century and danced many avant-garde roles in the Diaghilev repertory, she was at her best in the nineteenth-century ballet *Giselle*, and was the greatest Giselle I have ever seen. Her thin, ethereal body and incredible lightness made the transition from young girl into spirit perfectly conceivable, in a way that no other dancer has been able to achieve. There was an asexual, disembodied quality about her which made the whole unbelievable story of *Giselle* believable. You could readily imagine that so frail, so neurasthenic a creature could go mad and die, so that her reappearance out of the tomb did not come as a shock but, rather, as a natural consequence of her tragic death. The apparition, swathed in white veils, advancing slowly to the middle of the stage, and then, in a flash, free of her veil, spinning rapidly and disappearing again, was eerie and electrifying.

This very great dancer was born Alice Marks in England, and was given the Russian name Alicia Markova by Diaghilev. She was very British indeed—understated, soft-spoken, disciplined, with a spine of steel and a will of iron. She was also punctual to a second and expected other people to be the same. Our evening performance started at 8:30 p.m. Alicia was dancing the opening ballet, *Les Sylphides*, and was sitting, fully dressed and ready to go on stage, when the assistant stage manager knocked on the door and called, "On stage, Miss Markova; curtain going up." Alicia did not move, just sat there looking at her clock, and quietly said, "It is 8:28. I shall come at 8:30." Two minutes later she got up and left the dressing room, not a second before.

Her dressing table had all its various cosmetics and necessities placed in military precision, including nine large steel hairpins, which were hard to get during the war, lined up like soldiers. When Alicia returned to the dressing room from a triumphant performance, she took one look at the table and said, "Who took my hairpins? There were nine before, and now there are only seven." Nora, who was the antithesis of Alicia and whose dressing table looked like the contents of a Mixmaster, with ballet shoes on the table, ribbons in cold cream, tubes of makeup, Kleenex, and rouge scattered around in happy confusion, confessed her guilt at having taken two hairpins, and promptly had to return them. Since she couldn't find any others to replace them, she lost a piece of false hair on the stage in the middle of *Pillar of Fire*. Being an organized stickler myself, I could well understand Alicia. On the other hand, I loved Nora, who was easygoing and could see a funny point and didn't take things too seriously. On the stage she had tremendous dramatic power and imbued her roles with passion and considerable technical skill.

Being with these two great dancers raised my own temperature and pre-performance nerves. My only concern was to keep them under control and dance well. I was tired of being labeled a star of Broadway and Hollywood as if this was a reason to be ashamed of myself. I felt no stigma attached to my professional life, nor do I think George did. Of course he would rather have had his own company and choreographed serious ballets, but he knew it was just a matter of time before that dream was realized. As for me, I felt I had wasted time as a dancer—perhaps irrevocably—but I also felt that in those years I had helped to popularize ballet. (Actually, the real ballet boom was going to take another twenty years.) Besides, I had never pretended to be something that I wasn't. Not a prima ballerina, not even a ballerina. To earn that title, you really must devote your life to ballet and dance all the great classical parts. No, all I worked for was to be a good dancer, and I *was* dancing very well that season, especially in George's ballets *Apollon* and *Errante*. But *no*, I was whacked by the critics of the day. They seemed to resent my re-entry into the hallowed halls of ballet, forgetting that that was where I originally came from and that my training had been serious and extensive. One of them went so far as to write: "A dancer who calls herself Zorina," which, considering my name in 1943, was lunatic bile. What mattered to me was what George thought, and he was pleased with me. Strangely for a man who had taught me "not to care" about critics, he wrote this sharp rebuttal to *Time* magazine in answer to an article which had referred to me as a "soubrette":

May 14, 1943

To the Editors of Time
Rockefeller Center
New York City
Gentlemen:

Thank you for sending me the article entitled *Danseuse Noble*. As you are kind enough to ask for my comments, I would like to say a few words about it.

Most professionals of the dance have long ago given up wondering at the strange writings of the dance critics in the daily papers because they have finally realized that many of them simply don't know their subject. However, it seems a pity that, when a magazine as important as *Time* devotes an entire page to the ballet, it is unable to come closer to the truth.

The author of your article juggles with magic-sounding words: *ballerina assoluta, danseuse noble, mime dansante* without apparently realizing that the first one denotes an official rank in the theater (such as colonel or general in the army), while the second one describes a quality and the third one a style of dancing. To say that the *danseuse noble* Markova "is well above a *mime dansante* (like Irina Baronova)" is equal to saying that Caruso was less great than Chaliapine because he was just a tenor while Chaliapine was a basso. As to the word *soubrette* this is the first time I have heard it mentioned in connection with dancing and have associated it, until today, with the unfortunate maid in comic plays who brings in the breakfast tray and upsets it upon finding the *ingenue* in bed with the *jeune premier*.

Most professional dancers and choreographers consider Markova as one of a few great contemporary ballerinas, but they refrain from making comparisons between dancers because they know that each is outstanding in her own way and has qualities completely different from the others. It is your right to praise the ballerina you prefer, but I do not think it wise to do so by disparaging other prominent artists who may in their turn become the critics' and the public's favorites.

George Balanchine

Altogether, the guest appearances had been a revitalizing experience, and when Hurok asked me to make additional appearances in San Francisco later in the summer I accepted with joy. But Hollywood would not leave me alone. Again, I had to consider breaking my contract (which, of course, my agent was against) or making another meaningless picture. The question was: If I refused, would I be able to dance with a ballet company or would that also come under breach of contract? I remember staying with Eleonora Sears at Prides Crossing and being bitterly disappointed because neither George nor my mother gave me encouragement to fight. Without rancor, I can say that I did not expect anything else from my mother—she had lived through too much to face uncertainty. But that George did not support me hurt me deeply. If he, whom I worshipped for his courage and disdain for money matters, did not understand how unhappy I felt to face once again the stultifying work of making a movie I wasn't interested in, then he misunderstood me like everyone else. What I could not bear to hear from him was: "Just make the picture, take the $25,000, and be free." I felt abandoned and equated his attitude with a lack of caring—a lack of love—and I feel even now that it marked a turning point in our marriage. Had he said, "The hell with Hollywood! Come and dance with me," our lives might have been very different. I complied, and was ashamed of my compliance. I cannot remember a single thing from the picture (*Follow the Boys*) except that I had to dance with an aging and overweight George Raft. I never saw the end result.

Coming home one day to the Beverly Wilshire hotel, I stopped at the desk for my key. Leaning on the desk, and obviously checking in, was a young man who said hello to me. I recognized him but could not think of his name. Gottfried? Gotthardt? What was it? While we exchanged the usual inane questions—"What are you doing here?" "How long are you staying?"—I suddenly realized where and when we had met. It had been three months earlier in New York at a tea given by Efrem Kurtz, the former Ballet Russe conductor. We had sat apart and had chatted almost exclusively with each other. I had seen him once more at the Russian Tea Room, when George and I had dined there, and I remembered that he had constantly turned around toward us and made funny remarks, which I thought was rather rude to his own dinner companions. As this was ticking through my brain, his name came to me: Goddard. That's it—Goddard Lieberson, director of classical music at Columbia Records. It appeared that he was in Los Angeles on a recording job and would only be staying for a few days. "Could we meet?" I told him I was starting a new picture and had to go downtown tomorrow to Magnin's to see a dress designer. He jumped in and said he too had to go downtown, could he go with me? Our rapid exchange came to an end with the promise of a shared ride the next day.

It is a curious fact about women that when they visit a famous designer or go to a couturier showing they dress to the teeth. I was no different. The following morning suit after suit, dress after dress was put on, looked over by my mother, and discarded. I then hit on the perfect choice: a black silk knitted suit which was elegant, understated, and very East Coast. Since it had been cleaned, I thought I had better try it on, and discovered that the sleeves were hanging over and beyond my hands, with the jacket approaching my knees and the skirt around my ankles. I looked like a long, sad, droopy clown. I fixed my expression accordingly and marched into my mother's room. She took one look at me and became hysterical with laughter. When Goddard, my mother, and I drove downtown together, she was still incoherent, which must have puzzled him, because she could not get the words out to describe what she was laughing about. *That* was the beginning.

Goddard was witty and charming. He was tall, good-looking, and very funny, and when he turned on the full force of his personality, he was fairly irresistible. Even my mother could not make a discouraging remark about his hands, because they were beautiful. When we met at the pool, I noticed that he also had beautiful feet. I was becoming very observant—very alert, the way you do when an extraordinary person has entered your life. Goddard left after a few days, and we did not see each other again until I returned to New York in late autumn. What is one to say about that? We were deeply involved in our marriages and neither of us was ready or willing to jeopardize the lives of those we loved. But moralizing has nothing to do with it. Certainly one is selfish, certainly one hurts another human being, but I think we both had married too young, and neither one was capable of turning resolutely away from the other. I think we tried harder than most young people not to become irrevocably involved.

I have a streak in me of tenaciously clinging to the person I love and, in spite of all upheavals, will try again and again to patch up a rift. I had begged George to try again when we had had a bad time in 1940, and we had been very happy since. Goddard (for whom I cannot speak—even now) had his own problems, which unhappily ended in a bitter way. Our struggle had begun and was to last two years.

———

That summer made me aware of the strange invasion the war had brought to Hollywood. The influx of intellectual German and Austrian refugees was extraordinary. I could understand actors and directors coming to Hollywood, but why it became the mecca for intellectual literati was never quite clear to me. Maybe one writer started it and others followed, or maybe it was the climate—the easygoing exotica of palm trees—or maybe even an emotional need for warmth. But there it was—Thomas Mann, the epitome of the aristocratic Prussian German doing air-raid-warden duty in Beverly Hills; the outspoken Communist writer Bertolt Brecht among the orange groves; and Erich Maria Remarque writing in his fastidious German script while sitting in his suite in the Beverly Wilshire and having to observe the curfew at 8 p.m. sharp. At lunch in the dining room, one could often observe an imposing woman, Alma Mahler Werfel, still beautiful in a slightly blowsy manner, who had been the beloved (sometimes scandalously) of Gustav Mahler, Kokoschka, and Gropius. Her husband, Franz Werfel, was the only writer making money at the time, from his bestseller, *Song of Bernadette*. And strange to think that both Arnold Schönberg and Igor Stravinsky lived in Hollywood, as did Aldous Huxley, Christopher Isherwood, and another remarkable man in his field, the conductor Bruno Walter.

Since we lived at the same hotel, Mama and I saw a good deal of Remarque. I found him very charming and interesting to be with. He was down-to-earth and not as fancy as his name suggested (he had simply turned it around from Kramer). He was cultivated, worldly, and thought I was a straitlaced, pedantic goose (a rather mistaken idea), a prissy person who wouldn't drink with him (which he could do prodigiously). So he often invited the German actor Oscar Homolka to share a bottle or two of red wine, while I sat there receiving good-natured insults from Boni (as he was known to his friends), baiting me to break down and also calling me "*Die eiserne Jungfrau.*" He wrote in beautiful German, as even my inadequate translation from a letter of his dated July 21 shows. It was mailed to me at Sonora in the Sierra Nevada mountains, where I was on location for the filming of *For Whom the Bell Tolls*:

> July blooms into a heavenly summer here, with many shades of
> blue in the late afternoon. I sit in different gardens and at different
> pools, with white vodka cocktails in my hand, and observe the

colorful dresses of the ladies—and breathe and think and feel and
live and praise God. It always seems as if it were the last summer,
the last year of a dying time. So often it *was* the last time—in
Venice, in St. Moritz, in Antibes, in Salzburg, in Budapest, in
Vienna—a painful awareness of feelings, of adieus, and of love.

Sometimes in the waning evening I remember the silhouette of
your young Antinoüs face, when only your large eyes catch the light
bending forward towards a future which as yet has so short a past.
Your face is full of *Will* and *Want* and (since it still wants so much)
is wary of tenderness, so that when you say "I will miss you" it means
more than another with a bucketful of beautiful words.

The days fly like the balloons of children, swift and light, while
you—Amazon in faded men's trousers—fight the days of the Spanish
Civil War once more, and laugh and cry over remembrances and
live a double life.

————

George had two projects that summer and autumn which made
it impossible for him to leave New York. While I did the wretched
movie and then joined Ballet Theatre in San Francisco, George
supervised a production of *The Merry Widow* and then staged and
choreographed a musical by Lerner and Loewe called *What's Up*.
It opened in New York on November 11 and I must confess I
don't remember very much about it.

TEN

That winter I read that the distinguished actress Eva Le
Gallienne was hoping to revive her Repertory Theater.
She and Margaret Webster, the director, were planning
to organize it in the near future. On impulse I went to
the theater at which Le Gallienne was appearing in a
play and asked if I might see her before the performance. She was
kind enough to invite me to her dressing room, where I asked her,
if her Repertory Theater came into being, to consider my joining
the group. She was, I think, a bit astonished to see me simply
coming to the stage door without an appointment, but I've often
found that's the best way. A third person usually bollixes up a
perfectly simple matter. Nothing more was said at this first meeting,
nor in weeks to come did I hear anything further.

In early spring I was offered a new musical, *Dream with Music*.
It was a fairy tale, and sounded nice on paper. It had a lovely
selection of music, in special arrangements, ranging from Borodin,
Grieg, Saint-Saens, Chopin, Schumann, and Tchaikovsky to Beethoven. I know that sounds awful, but it was quite successfully

done. Even George liked it. The book was mild, but as often happens when a show opens out of town and is "in trouble," too many people give well-meaning advice. The show was padded with terrible jokes and turned into a mess. George did some lovely choreography, combining ballet and speech again, but even that couldn't save it. I remember *Dream with Music* for two particular incidents. At the end of the first act, I danced a ballet in which I flew high up on a "flying carpet"—then stepped off and floated down to the stage, thanks to a flying belt. All went well for several performances, until one night: when I stepped into space, the wire slipped out of my belt and I crashed to the floor below. I got up and in a state of shock danced the whole ballet, but when the curtain descended I burst into tears and became hysterical. The doctor was already backstage, and after he had determined that, by some miracle, I had broken no bones, I calmed down and finished the show. The next night I had not one but two wires for safety. Talk about locking the barn door after the horse is stolen! The other incident was our unforgettable opening night in New York. We had worked hard and were putting our absolute best into the show when the main fuse blew and plunged the entire theater, orchestra pit, and stage into pitch darkness. Our stage manager managed to beam a flashlight toward us as we stood frozen in horror on the stage. The weak beam of light at least prevented a panic both on and off the stage, as we bravely made some noises. We had no spare master fuse and someone had to sprint across the street to *Oklahoma!* to borrow one. Even though the runner raced like an Olympian champion, it took an eternity. It was our coup de grâce, and we closed after a few performances.

———

There I was, out of work again with undesirable rapidity, when I received a call from Margaret Webster. She came straight to the point: did I know *The Tempest*? "Of course," I lied. "Well then, how would you like to play Ariel?" "Wonderful," I shot back, having no idea what was involved. She then explained that Cheryl Crawford, the producer, Eva Le Gallienne, and she were planning a production for late autumn. I was very excited by the idea. What a marvelous opportunity—how could I prepare myself properly?— what about my accent? After reading the play thoroughly, I signed a contract and began working with Professor Sommerville of New York University, a distinguished professor of English, who was deeply interested in the theater, and a Shakespearean scholar. We worked five days a week, more or less, for six months. He placed my voice properly, so that I never again strained my vocal cords; he taught me diction and how to read poetry; but best of all, he initiated me into the world of Shakespeare. We worked not only on Ariel but on speeches from all the plays, the marvelous choruses from *Henry IV* and *Henry V*, and of course the sonnets. It was a rich experience that laid the groundwork, not for acting necessarily, but for technical skill. The one thing I dreaded was to have the critics say, How dare she play Shakespeare with that accent! I felt as reverential as if I had attempted to become an abbess. What did the critics eventually say? That I moved like a dancer! Well, I should hope so.

Having grounded myself thoroughly in *The Tempest*, I suggested to Webster and Le Gallienne that the most perfect designer for the production would be Pavel Tchelitchev. Who else could create an island of fantasy and mysterious beauty as magically as he? They thought the idea a good one and asked me to speak to him. Sadly, he said no. He wanted to devote himself to painting and to painting only. I was then asked to speak to Eugene Berman, another wonderful Russian designer. He was a prickly man, easily offended, sometimes even before any offense had taken place. I approached him cautiously and begged him to discuss it with Webster and Le Gallienne. We went together to Crawford's office, and I froze when I saw a model of a stage set sitting on a table. To my dismay, Webster and Le Gallienne moved toward it and began explaining that *this* was what they envisioned—a set which would be on a turntable, with hidden openings for exits and entrances, the whole surrounded by a cyclorama which would make it look like an island. Berman was ominously silent as he listened. Then he said, "Looks like hospital, exactly like New York Hospital. If that is what you want"—he pointed to the set—"you don't need *me*," and he left. I was mortified, but had to admit he was right. It *did* look like New York Hospital.

George and I were no longer living together in 1944, but we had never ceased to care deeply about each other and had again become very close during the rehearsals of *Dream with Music*. He had come to Boston for the dress rehearsal and opening night and seen the mess we were in. He had tried to help, but as the trouble lay in the book and not in the dances, there was nothing he could do. George was also aware of my emotional turmoil and inability to come to any decision concerning our marriage.

People on the sidelines never seem to have any trouble sorting out marriages and assigning the role of the "guilty" partner. Two people may love each other but be wrenched apart by their own temperaments, their individual needs, ambitions, and, most of all, the stages of their development. George was forty years old, a mature man, a great artist approaching the full flowering of his genius, while I, at twenty-seven, was still very immature emotionally. He had his destiny to fulfill, but so did I. When I was a small girl, I had made a vow that I would become a great dancer and then, at thirty, I would marry and have two children. I knew that George and I did not have that kind of marriage, and I had also come to the sobering realization that I would never be a "great" dancer—that it was indeed too late. I could see it at the school. There was a whole class full of young, little bees—thin, ambitious, full of drive and talent, faster, lighter, more flexible, more daring— just as a new young crop will always be. I saw Tanaquil LeClercq as a twelve-year-old, and thought, Aha, a buzzing little bee—*she* will be something.

Rather than being depressed by this, I realized that I was losing interest in ballet—that another world was opening up for me which I wanted to know more about. The relentless pursuit of ballet simply had not allowed me time for intellectual growth. It is a world of physical interiorization, a world in which the body is the dominant factor, a world in which the mind controls the body by radiating *in*, not radiating *out*. The dancer's brain is a giant computer programmed to read not the intricacies of a Proustian sentence but the intricacies of a complicated series of steps. As George so often said, "Don't think, just *do. Dance!*" I had a hunger to learn other things.

As George had begun my musical education, so Goddard began to educate me—period. I read and read and read. I became aware of how little I knew about everything, how narrow my life had been, how much I wanted to know. And so George and I moved away from each other, very gradually at first, like two children who miss each other badly. He wrote me from Los Angeles, where he was staging and choreographing *Song of Norway*: "Why don't you join poor choreographer? I have lousy room but the bed is big enough for two." When George returned from California, he signed up for two years with the Ballet Russe and choreographed *Danses Concertantes* (Stravinsky) and *Bourgeois Gentilhomme* (Richard Strauss) for them. He then did *Waltz Academy* for American Ballet Theatre and a *pas de deux* (Paul Bowles) for Ballet International. He was very productive that autumn, and all the dancers from the different companies, including those of the School of American Ballet, bridged the professional barriers to work with him. Maria Tallchief's name appears for the first time in the programs of 1944 as a rising young star. She married George six months after I married Goddard.

Margaret Webster and Eva Le Gallienne had gathered together an unorthodox cast for *The Tempest*. In addition to the rather offbeat choice of me (Ariel was traditionally played by a man), Canada Lee (a black actor) was cast as Caliban. Two brilliant

Czech actors, George Voskovec and Jan Werich, were cast in the parts of the sailor Trinculo and Stephano, his drunken companion. They had run a politically slanted cabaret in their native Prague which had been famous for its satirical sketches. They were absolutely marvelous in their parts, accents and all. Arnold Moss played Prospero beautifully, and his delivery of "Our revels now are ended," which Webster transposed from the masque in the middle of the play to the end, was one of the most perfect renditions of that jewel of poetry I have ever heard. On the night that President Roosevelt died, when Arnold spoke those lines, ending with:

> We are such stuff
> As dreams are made on, and our little life
> Is rounded with a sleep.

an almost audible sob came from the audience.

At the first reading of *The Tempest*, sitting as usual in a circle on the stage with a pitiless single-bulb work light above us, I did myself proud. After six months of work with Professor Sommerville, I was letter-perfect. I was held up as an example, and felt relieved and elated. It was also the last time I heard any praise. I had drilled so much that I "peaked" on that day, which is a dangerous thing to do, since I had no place left to go. Instead of struggling like the other actors, learning the text, growing *into* the part and gradually improving, I never changed. Finally one day Webster screamed at me, something like: "For Christ's sake, why don't you make a mistake sometimes!" and I fell apart. It was very salutary and really shook me up. But I never could quite find a spontaneity or learn to explore the role—I simply didn't have the confidence. However, I did learn never to *overwork* like that again. One thing that frightened me more than playing Shakespeare was the three songs Ariel had to sing, all of them hauntingly beautiful. My favorite was:

> Full fathom five thy father lies;
>   Of his bones are coral made:
> Those are pearls that were his eyes . . .

David Diamond, who composed the music for *The Tempest*, had written lovely melodies, but they were far too difficult for me, so every night I had my own private little agony until the songs were over. Our "hospital" stage set was very effective from the front, but it lacked the mystery which Caliban speaks of in his beautiful soliloquy. It looked like a craggy rock rising out of the sea and presented problems for the actors. Since it was totally surrounded by a pale-blue cyclorama and revolved according to different scenes, no actor could get on or off the stage once the curtain was up. This meant, for most of us, sitting crouched for twenty minutes while the opening storm, shipwreck, and long exposition scene took place. I sat hidden in something resembling half a telephone booth, trying to control my nerves by practicing the Stanislavsky method. I imagined that I was trapped electricity and that I would shoot out of there like a bolt of lightning when I heard Prospero's command: "Approach, my Ariel; come!" I tried to visualize a dragonfly skimming over a lake, never settling down, so that when I had to stand and listen, I would remain on half-toe, as if momentarily resting, but ready to take off instantly.

There was one scene in which I was seated on a lower step at Prospero's feet. It is the only scene in which Ariel tries to persuade Prospero to forgive those that have wronged him, with the words: ". . . if you now beheld them, your affections would become tender." *Prospero*: "Dost thou think so, spirit?" *Ariel*: "Mine would, sir, were I human." During this scene, ending with Prospero's great speech, "Ye elves of hills and dales," a phenomenon would take place that only I saw and sometimes became part of. Arnold Moss was blessed with an extraordinarily resonant voice, which seemed to be irrigated by an unusual amount of saliva. During those long sentences, in which there was no opportunity to swallow, a spray of tiny droplets would cascade in an arc out of Arnold's mouth and be picked up by a spotlight and illuminated against a dark background. Actually, it was quite beautiful—only, I learned not to look up too often for fear of being hit by a stray drop.

Canada Lee was immensely touching. He was a kind and gentle man with a sad, ugly face. As an actor, he gave a raging power to Caliban, spitting out his venom when he was forced to obey Prospero. But he also had a very moving quality when he recalled how Prospero treated him when he was shipwrecked on the island: "When thou camest first, / Thou strok'dst me, and mad'st much of me . . . and then I lov'd thee . . ." Canada displayed an incredible sangfroid on the first night of *The Tempest* in New York. While I sat shivering with fright in my telephone booth, I heard gentle snoring emanating from somewhere below me. It was Canada having a nice nap before his entrance.

George, as always, had been very good to me. He came to rehearsals and advised me on Ariel's movements. He also came to both our openings, in Philadelphia on December 26 and in New York on January 25. *The Tempest* had a fine critical success but was not a hit, and after a fairly good run we closed in late spring. We went on tour, and what I chiefly remember was our opening in Chicago. Because David Diamond's score for the play was so difficult, we had brought along our own key orchestra players at considerable extra expense. But in the Windy City of James Petrillo, boss of the musicians' union, our players were not allowed to play music but had to content themselves with playing cards in their hotel rooms while the Chicago players struggled through the score and nearly ruined the performance—at least musically.

Throughout the late spring and summer of 1945, George and I gently drifted farther apart. As so often before, we were in different parts of the world. While I toured, in the Midwest, George went for almost two months to Mexico City. He took some of his own dancers with him to work at the Opera Nacional, and no doubt used the opportunity to work with them on choreographic works other than just opera ballets. His connection with the Ballet Russe continued, and he had earlier created a new Grand Adagio for Danilova and Freddy Franklin. On his return from Mexico, he plunged into another musical, *Mr. Strauss Goes to Boston,* which opened in early September.

One afternoon George came to visit me at the Ritz Tower, and I finally said it: "Perhaps we'd better think of getting a divorce." After agreeing almost silently, we behaved like two reluctant children who had to do something that they didn't want to do. We embraced and kissed each other and said goodbye.

It is true that one part of my life came to an end like the iron curtain which descends in the theater after a performance. A radical change was in store for me—far more than I could ever have imagined. I was twenty-eight but still a coddled child, with my emotional needs focused on the classic triangle the child wants from those who give her love and protection. Throughout my marriage, my unusually close relationship with my mother had remained unchanged. It had been a life of continuous work, travel, rented houses, hotels and, as our careers demanded, often long separations from George.

I imagine that George's friends and associates heaved a sigh of relief when we officially separated. During our marriage, Lincoln Kirstein is supposed to have said: *"Balanchine, c'est un homme perdu"*—but then how could he have thought otherwise? George's marriages and girls were probably deeply distasteful to him and, at best, things he had to put up with like a peculiar aberration.

In December of 1945 I went to a place in Nevada with the curious name of Dog Creek Ranch. There I spent six weeks, including Christmas and the New Year of 1946. Some years are more extraordinary than others, like great vintage years. It occurs to us only much later that our entire life changed at a given point; 1946 was such a year for me. After seven years of marriage, George Balanchine and I were divorced in January. On the second of April, Goddard Lieberson and I were married, and on October 25 our first son, Peter, was born. I finally faced adulthood and, with it, the end of my protracted childhood. Someone else needed coddling when I became a mother. Every woman knows how that event changes her life, but few women were less prepared for domesticity and a proper marriage than I. The changes began gradually and then accelerated as my husband's career moved forward. He was then a brilliant, upcoming recording director at Columbia Records, and during the next thirty years he became a legendary figure in the recording industry. I followed him into his world, and as my former professional life receded, the world of music welcomed me.

After our marriage my mother gradually assumed another role. In 1955 she decided to return to Norway, surprisingly choosing to live in a small farming community of great natural beauty but without modern conveniences except for electricity. Her house was on the edge of a fjord with a magnificent view. My dear mother never ceased to amaze me. I visited her for a fortnight two or three times a year and the morning after my arrival she would inevitably sigh and sadly say, "Oh, Brigitta, only thirteen more days left!"

George Balanchine and I remained friends through the years, seeing each other occasionally. Although I was no longer connected with ballet and my professional life was entirely involved with music, I followed his career and rejoiced when at last he was recognized as the greatest choreographer of his generation. One forgets that for him the years between 1933 and 1949 had often been an uphill fight; it was a period when money was scarce and his style was severely criticized. Now he had rapidly approached the stage where he could do no wrong. His company had become stronger, his repertoire larger, his dancers renowned, and his school had developed as he wanted it. During the last years of his life, Balanchine's choreography took on a heartbreaking quality of delicate sentiments, a nostalgia for lost love, and a prescience of approaching death.

To my surprise, in December 1981 Balanchine asked me to participate in the festival he was planning in honor of the centenary of Stravinsky's birth on June 17, 1982. Would I perform the role of Perséphone and stage it? He himself would do the choreography. My reaction was one of incredible joy at being asked to work with him after all these years. It did not occur to me to question his decision. After all, there was no need to remind him of my age and he knew I had not danced on the stage for years. He also knew I had performed the role of Perséphone many times, with Stravinsky himself conducting, and he was also aware that Stravinsky thought highly of my performance. I simply did not question Balanchine's judgment, and the only suggestion I made was that there be *two* Perséphones, one who recited the poetry and one who danced. When he agreed, I felt secure in the concept of only speaking my role and moving in and out of the ballet. We met occasionally to discuss the production, and when we did, time stood still.

Once we met in the studio of Kermit Love, who was designing the scenery. George was brilliant in illustrating the effects he wanted, but at times he also seemed removed in spirit. He took me aside and complained of pain in his ear and extreme dizziness. He was making a supreme effort to function in spite of his debilitating symptoms. I began to realize that George was not himself. It was therefore all the more frightening when he screamed one day in total rage during a production meeting: "Only *I* know what to do— nobody else knows anything!" It was as if he wanted to assert the supremacy of his will even as his body was failing.

With the opening set for June 17, I began to fret because rehearsals had not begun. By the end of May, still no rehearsals. I became anxious and alarmed but everyone said, "It's always like this. Don't worry, everything will be all right." At the beginning of June, the first rehearsal was called for the dancers. It was a poignant moment watching George's effort to choreograph the first entrance of the nymphs. He valiantly tried to organize the groups, but was overwhelmed by his physical problems and handed the reins over to John Taras. He did choreograph two *pas de deux* for Karin von Aroldingen and Mel Tomlinson, which were very good, and a short interlude with the nymphs. Whenever George came to the general rehearsals, he sat silent and distant. I wondered whether I had done something to offend him, because his behavior was so unusual. Occasionally we went for a bite between rehearsals, and he said: "When I go, never will be another Balanchine—that's finished." It was not a grandiloquent statement; he meant it as a simple fact and he was right, for who would now see what only he saw as he stood in the wings every night, absentmindedly picking at his fingers—his head raised like a bird that is intently watching and listening—and when the ballet was over catch the hand of a dancer and make a few rapid suggestions: "Next time do it this way," or "Don't forget, do it that way." Another time at a rehearsal he said: "I'm finished. I can't see anymore, I can't hear, and I walk like drunken man. If I can't do ballet, I'll go to Long Island and cook."

I became part of the silent conspiracy which was inevitably forced on us all. No one spoke openly of his illness except him. At the rehearsals, I was afraid to go near him. At times he looked as if he did not know who I was. The company too behaved strangely to me; perhaps we were all affected by the same bewilderment. Once I stood in the wings to watch a performance, and a tall man stepped directly in front of me. It was Peter Martins. Not a word was uttered. It wasn't even rude—I simply didn't exist. Finally I too stopped smiling and saying "good morning" or "hello" to the dancers. I was in the middle of a most brilliantly disciplined cult, a foreign object who was tolerated only because of Mr. B.

On the opening day of *Perséphone*, we worked until five o'clock and that night somehow we got through. As I came offstage, all George said to me was "Excellent," and outside my immediate family not one person, not a single member of the New York City Ballet, came backstage to see me. I did not see Balanchine again until late September, when he was in the hospital.

As I entered his room, he cheerfully called out: "Oh Brigitta, come in!" He was surrounded by his friends, Jacques d'Amboise and his wife, who had brought him borscht from the Russian Tea Room. He was eating with relish while I sat on the edge of his bed, chatting. He regaled me with a perfect delivery of a speech he had made *in Danish* in Copenhagen. After the d'Amboises left, Helgi Tomasson came for a visit and reminded me of the same chilling indifference I had experienced at the theater. When he and Balanchine began to discuss choreographic problems, I kissed George and left.

Each subsequent visit, spread over the next six months, became more upsetting. On one visit toward the end, I brought him a bottle of champagne. I had been told he liked to take a few sips. He also liked chocolate—very soft chocolate he did not need to chew. He had deteriorated badly and was hardly able to swallow. I fed him tiny bits of melting chocolate in his mouth, which he opened like a hungry bird, still seeming to enjoy the taste. Then he insisted on holding the cup for a few drops of champagne. It must be the helplessness we feel which makes illness unbearable. All one's instincts are to soothe, to love, to rock like a child, to comfort as best one can.

During my last visit, we were alone momentarily. All I could do was hold his hand in mine, which he held tight with the same strength that unseeing newborn babies have. With my other hand, I stroked his head. His left hand clasped a crucifix, hanging from a ribbon around his neck. I was very frightened to feel death so near. When his nurse returned, I kissed him goodbye. The tears came that night, like a violent summer storm. I knew I had seen him for the last time.

George was a deeply religious man to whom God and the angels were a reality. There was nothing intellectual or mystically obscure about it. He expressed his attitude toward death clearly and publicly in 1971, at an earlier festival in honor of Stravinsky. At the

New York State Theater, before a packed house, he raised his glass to give a toast and said: "Let's drink some vodka to Stravinsky. He's not gone—he's very happy flying around the theater." George too joined those immortals whose work defeats death as long as their creations continue to live.